Steve Allen's
Private
Joke File

Books by Steve Allen

Listed in chronological order by publishing date:

Bop Fables	Simon & Schuster	1955
Fourteen for Tonight	Henry Holt & Company	1955
The Funny Men	Simon & Schuster	1956
Wry on the Rocks	Henry Holt & Company	1956
The Girls on the Tenth Floor	Henry Holt & Company	1958
The Question Man	Bellmeadow Press, with Bernard Geis Associates	1959
Mark It and Strike It	Holt, Reinhart & Winston	1960
Not All of Your Laughter, Not All of Your Tears	Bernard Geis & Associates	1962
Dialogues in Americanism (with L. Brent Bozell, William F. Buckley Jr., Robert M. Hutchins, James MacGregor Burns, and Willmoore Kendall)	Henry Regnery Co.	1964
Letter to a Conservative	Doubleday & Company	1965
The Ground Is Our Table	Doubleday & Company	1966
Bigger Than a Breadbox	Doubleday & Company	1967
A Flash of Swallows	Droke House	1969
The Wake	Doubleday & Company	1972
Princess Snip-Snip and The Puppykittens	Platt & Monk	1973
Curses!	J. P. Tarcher	1973
What to Say When It Rains	Price, Stern & Sloan	1974

Schmock!-Schmock!	Doubleday & Company	1975
Meeting of Minds, Vol. I	Crown Publishers, Inc.	1978
Chopped-Up Chinese	Price, Stern & Sloan	1978
Ripoff: The Corruption That Plagues America	Lyle Stuart, Inc.	1956
Meeting of Minds, Vol. II	Crown Publishers	1979
Explaining China	Crown Publishers	1980
Funny People	Stein & Day	1981
The Talk Show Murders	Delacorte Press	1982
Beloved Son: A Story of the Jesus Cults	Bobbs-Merrill	1982
More Funny People	Stein & Day	1982
How to Make a Speech	McGraw-Hill Book Co.	1986
How to Be Funny	McGraw-Hill Book Co.	1987
Murder on the Glitter Box	Zebra Books	1989
Passionate Nonsmokers' Bill of Rights (coauthor, Bill Adler Jr.)	William Morrow Company	1989
Dumbth: And 81 Ways to Make Americans Smarter	Prometheus Books	1989
Meeting of Minds, Vol. III	Prometheus Books	1989
Meeting of Minds, Vol. IV	Prometheus Books	1989
The Public Hating: A Collection of Short Stories	Dembner Books	1990
Murder in Manhattan	Zebra Books	1990
Steve Allen on the Bible, Religion & Morality	Prometheus Books	1990
Murder in Vegas	Zebra Books	1991

Steve Allen's

Private Joke File

Steve Allen

THREE RIVERS PRESS • NEW YORK

Published by Three Rivers Press, New York, New York
Member of the Crown Publishing Group
Random House, Inc. New York, Toronto, Sydney, Auckland
www.randomhouse.com

Three Rivers Press is a registered trademark and the Three Rivers Press colophon is a trademark of Random House, Inc.

Printed in the United States of America

Designed by Susan Maksuta

Library of Congress Cataloging-in-Publication Data
Allen, Steve.
    Steve Allen's private joke file / by Steve Allen.
    1. American wit and humor.   I. Title.
    PN6162.A18 2000
    818'.5402—dc21   00-032596

ISBN 0-609-80672-6

10 9 8 7 6 5 4

To my dear grandchildren—Dan, Julie, Stephanie, Christopher, Michael, Bobby, Bradley, Amanda, Jeff, Maria, Andrew and Ryan—in gratitude for their so greatly adding to my happiness.

Contents

Introduction

Years ago, when the realization dawned upon me that I had rather accidentally become a professional comedian, it occurred to me that it might be a good idea to begin salting away jokes—my own or any in the public domain—in order that I might one day have a nice substantial joke-account to draw on should creatively grim times set in.

For a while I filed gags like a beaver—or more to the point, like Milton Berle, Bob Hope, or Red Skelton—and then came the day when I began having trouble finding particular jokes in the stack. I had created not a gag-file but a gag graveyard. Jokes went in, but they hardly ever came out again.

It has always seemed to me that my old *What's My Line?* friend, the late Bennett Cerf, was involved in precisely the same sort of cemetarial pursuit. Although one of his joke books was titled *The Life of the Party,* the reader will not become the life of most parties by retelling the stories this collection includes for the reason that these are the stories that were told at the preceding year's parties. Bennett did an effective job of gathering and indexing them, and laying them away to rest in straight-faced peace.

The ultimate value of such books, I think, will not accrue to us at all; they will become valuable a century from now as a means of informing our descendants what it was we laughed at way back in the 1980s and '90s.

And, sad to contemplate, they will probably think at least some of our jokes just as unfunny as we think of those of the nineteenth century, for humor is a fragile thing and little of it keeps well over the years. Even Shakespeare's comedies would no longer be performed did they depend solely on their humor content.

Our progeny are apt to be a bit confused, by the way, by the impression some joke books give that our public figures were all great wits, for joke compilers usually go along with the established belief that a good joke will seem better if you credit it to a popular humorist or other prominent person. There is no particular harm in this; it's just that someone should let our grandchildren know that most jokes are created by relatively anonymous professional gag writers. Or even if they are ad-libbed by a comedian or senator, they will shortly be credited to fourteen other people.

Caution: Take the present anthology in small doses. Such books are designed to give you weeks of pleasure, not to be read in one night.

Oh, one last albeit depressing thought.

As the twentieth century drew to a close one of the more troubling social issues was the degree to which the popular media—television, radio, films, and recordings—had become unprecedentedly coarse and vulgar. Consider, in this context, two old sayings: *You are what you eat* and *Tell me what you read and I'll tell you what you are.* Both refer to human appetites and incorporate the common-sense perception that we are influenced, physically and mentally, by what we ingest. Even those who might concede their own depravity were traditionally careful that their children be shielded from the grosser aspects of life. But there was something new about the ugliness of much popular entertainment of the 1980s and '90s, and that was that, far from having a concern for the innocence of children, the modern marketers of sleaze openly resented any and all attempts to inhibit their public expression and obviously, to put the matter as simply as possible, didn't give a damn about the sensitivities of the very young.

Naturally all of this affected the field of comedy itself. Many inexperienced comedians, noting that the easiest laughs come from any reference to drugs, drinking, or sex, became dependent on shock and schlock, and in a surprisingly short period of time were permitted, by broadcasting executives of their own age bracket, to trample on standards of good taste that had prevailed for centuries.

One of the factors contributing to such a state of affairs was simple ignorance, in this case of that branch of history which is cultural. Perhaps many of us today simply do not know that such esteemed wits as Mark Twain, Will Rogers, Fred Allen, Groucho Marx, George S. Kaufman, and Robert Benchley, all of whom were simply naturally funny, never depended on vulgarity to amuse others.

And even the 1930s and '40s generation of nightclub comedians, some of who might work a little rough in clubs, would never have dreamed of doing anything the least bit coarse when they appeared on the Vaudeville stage, on Broadway, in radio, films, or eventually television. It isn't that they wanted to do so but were restrained; the thought literally never crossed their minds.

Well, a quite heated debate is now raging about this and related issues, which is itself all to the good. All across the political and philosophical spectrum thinkers, after nothing more demanding than a casual survey of the wreckage of American society, are beginning to perceive cause-and-effect relationships between the morning, noon, and night barrage of vulgarity and the tragic statistics about teenage promiscuity, illegitimate pregnancy, AIDS and other sexually transmitted diseases, drugs, excessive drinking, and broken homes that are now such common features of our social landscape. They have consequently begun to entertain the once common notion that even in the creative arts there really is such a thing as Going Too Far.

Although some of today's younger readers—who are almost certainly TV viewers and radio listeners as well—may find it hard to believe, American humor was, for a very long time, to deliberately restate the point, overwhelmingly clean and inoffensive. In other words, exposure to it could do no harm to children. What is still rightly referred to as the Golden Age of television comedy—that glorious period when we laughed heartily, every night of the week, at Sid Caesar, Red Skelton, Jackie Gleason, Milton Berle, Lucille Ball, Phil Silvers, and other funny men and women of that time—we asked of our humorists and performers only that they be amusing. We did not have to worry that they might literally disgust us, as is all too often the case at present.

But what about the jokes heard on the street, in our offices and factories, read in magazines or enjoyed at public events? They too were largely innocent enough, and in those instances in which a given joke was frankly vulgar—and sometimes also very funny—at least we waited till our children had left the room to share such stories with other adults.

Concerning the stories in this collection then, I guarantee that they are both funny and inoffensive. As regards over 98 percent of them I naturally make no claim of authorship. It is rarely the case that a popular song or poem is quickly swept up into the public discourse without attribution to its source, but the same cannot be said for jokes. Frequently over the years people tell me an amusing joke or story of which I myself was the original author, but the great flow of those witticisms that one hears daily, and which are now, because of modern technology, transmitted and broadcast more quickly than ever before, are almost never credited to their authors.

Steve Allen's

Private
Joke File

ABSENT-MINDED

I forget what I was talking about. I wasn't listening.

Joe, did you see what I did with that newspaper clipping I had here a minute ago? (fumbling with papers) Honest to gosh, I lose everything. I don't think I could keep track of my head if it wasn't fastened onto my shoulders. In fact, one time, you may not believe this . . . but I actually had to go to Arizona for my lungs.

So absent-minded I played hooky from school on weekends.

ACCIDENT

I know a fellow who died of snakebite . . . He bit a snake.

STOREKEEPER: Dear me, did you fall down the steps?
CUSTOMER: Yes, but it's all right. I was going down anyway.

THE WIFE: Henry, the baby has swallowed the ink. What shall I do?

PROFESSOR: Write with the pencil, my dear.

"When you cross the street, always be calm and collected."

"My uncle crossed the street and he was calm, but he's still being collected."

"My baby brother swallowed ten firecrackers."

"Is he improving?"

"We've heard some good reports."

"I fell through a grating, which was full of garbage. I shouted, 'Fire, fire, fire!'"

"What do you mean 'fire'?"

"Well, if I hollered *garbage,* would anyone come?"

Liza had been in a railroad accident. Said the lawyer: "I've come to assist you in getting damages!"

Liza said, "I got all the damages I want. What I need is repairs!"

"And how could you bite yourself on your forehead?" somebody asked him.

"Well," he replied, "I stood on a chair."

BILL: Tell me, why is your brother in the hospital?
JOE: He bet Mike that he could lean farther out of a window—and he won.

ACTING

The telephone rang in the office of a theatrical agent.

"Hello," said a voice. "I want a job. I can sing, dance, and juggle."

"So can a thousand other people, and they're all out of work," snapped the agent.

"Just a minute. Don't hang up. I can play the piano, walk the tightrope, and recite 'Paradise Lost' backwards."

"So can a lot of others. You're wasting my time. Good-bye."

"Just a minute," pleaded the voice. "There's one other thing. I'm a dog."

I was brought back here to this theater by popular demand.
The last time I played here was in 1947.

You think I have to do this for a living?
You're damned right I do!

Before Howard Thurston became famous, he sometimes did his bewildering tricks of magic for audiences at lodge meetings, and even in private homes. Once, when he was booked to entertain the guests of a woman who had more money than breeding, he called at her home to arrange details of the show, including his fee. Thurston's price for the evening was one hundred dollars, to which the woman agreed.

"However," she said haughtily, "I must make it quite clear to you that when your performance is over you are not to mingle with my guests."

Thurston pretended to be surprised. "Oh, in that case," he said, "my fee will be only fifty dollars."

STRAIGHT MAN: I promised my mother I would never be an actor.
COMIC: Well, you've kept your promise.

Ladies and gentlemen, I won't take much of your time today because I'm double-parked.

Diveena, the girl who does an underwater act, hasn't been around town lately. I think she drowned one night while taking an extra bow.

When she first opened at the Mermaid Room, though, she was great. Did such a great job, she was held under for another two weeks.

An actor is a man who earns as much as $750,000 a year . . . some years.

A certain actor we know is a matinee idol—and he doesn't work much at night either.

Dear Steve: Your new show will be dynamite at the box office, and you know what dynamite would do to a box office.

HE: Did you see *Enchantment?* I was at MGM when they made it. In fact, I stole the picture.
SHE: What part did you play?
HE: No part. I just went into the film library and stole the picture.

ACTOR *(To stagehand):* And what, my good man, is your vocation?

STAGEHAND: I'm a Baptist.

ACTOR: No, no, that's your belief. I want to know your vocation. For example, I am a great actor.

STAGEHAND: That's *your* belief.

You've heard of the play *Flahooley*? Well, they're thinking of making a Mexican version and calling it *Frijole*.

I was booked with Dagmar, Dizzy Gillespie, Art Baker, and Jo-Jo, the Dog-Faced Boy. That show won the Hickock Prize as the wildest bill of the year.

If there's any place in the world I like, it's Chicago. And the people there liked me. They said they wished I would stay forever. When I got ready to leave, the paper printed the following notice about me: "Steve Allen closed his engagement at the Orpheum Theatre last night and leaves for the East today. We would like to have him stay forever."

STEVE: I was thrown out for shouting "Author, author!" after a play.
STRAIGHTMAN: Really? What was the play?
STEVE: *King Lear.*

STEVE: I put on a performance yesterday, and in no time at all, I had the audience eating out the palm of my hand.
STRAIGHTMAN: Where did you appear?
STEVE: At the Los Angeles Dog Show!

"How are the acoustics here?"
"Great, I can hardly hear you."

The audience was large and respectable. One man was large and the other was respectable.

An actor is a man who works in a dinner jacket without the dinner.

He was hit with a tomato last week. He worked so long on the radio he'd lost the art of dodging.

"So you had the audience with you?"
"Yes—for three blocks."

Jack finally found out why he hasn't worked for so long . . . his agent died three years ago.

"Since Charles turned fifty it's impossible for him to find a part he can get his teeth into."
"No luck?"
"No teeth."

SHE: I'd like to do *Romeo and Juliet* with John Travolta.
HE: John Travolta doesn't do Shakespeare.
SHE: I can have fun imagining, can't I?

"I happened to go on the stage because my friends egged me on."
"Then why did you quit the stage?"
"The audience egged me off."

"That's what you always say? Must get pretty monotonous—just saying that all the time."

He's a retired actor from Richmond. A Virginia Ham.

ACTOR: I think it's within my right to ask for real wine in the banquet scene.
DIRECTOR: Right, old man. And perhaps you would like real poison in the death scene.

"Don't butt into my lines like that. Wait for the laugh."
"Okay, but I've got to catch a four o'clock train."

"That was a great reception you got when you arrived."
"Yeah, but I think they got my name wrong. They kept hollering, 'Lynch! Lynch!'"

MAN *(to girl hanging by teeth):* I've been waiting a long time for this chance to tell you what I think of you.

His favorite movie star was Sal Hepatica.

"We're going to build a statue of him all in brass."

"Does the whole statue have to be brazen? Wouldn't the face be enough?"

"There's a letter for you from the electric fan company."

"At last . . . some fan mail."

BOB: I'm Henry the Eighth. Who are you?

ROB: I'm August the twelfth.

DIRECTOR: Where's the man who is to play the part of the Drunkard?

ASSISTANT: He's too drunk to go on.

ADS

WANTED: Man to undertake the manufacture of a new patent medicine. The originator guarantees the venture will be very profitable to the undertaker.

NOTICE: I will no longer be responsible for any debts contracted by my wife. (Signed) Pvt. R.C.B.

Pvt. R.C.B. does not have to be responsible for any debts which I might make. He can't even pay his own. (Signed) L.B.

ACTUAL WANT-AD: Room for Rent—Sleeping room for man $7 a week. Will rent for $5 to man who is sober, conscientious, reliable, and a good Republican, if that combination is possible. Apply at newspaper office.

Man who gets paid on Tuesday and is usually broke by Friday would like to meet woman who is paid on Friday and is usually broke by Tuesday.

Aspirin 200 for 9 cents. At that price you can't afford not to have a headache!

Will trade a rooster that crows at 4 o'clock for one that crows at 5 o'clock.

POSITION WANTED ... Refined girl looking for nightclub work. Has no bad habits. Willing to learn.

Saw an ad in the *Mirror* tonight. AN ADAMS HAT FITS YOUR HEAD LIKE A GLOVE ... And you know how a glove would fit your head.

FOR SALE: Piano by a young lady with mahogany legs.

Man who's alone, wants to meet Woman with Savings ... Object: Savings and Loan.

Bank manager, just released from prison, seeks employment.

LOST: Set of uppers and lowers between Coney Island Avenue and Prospect Park entrance. Sentimental value only—I love to eat.

Young Republican woman would like to marry young Democrat. Object: Third party.

FOR SALE: Mandolin. By a young man in good condition except for a loose peg in the head.

Man, honest, will take anything.

Lady's purse left in my car while parked. Owner can have same by describing property and paying for this ad. If owner can explain satisfactorily to my wife how purse got into car, will pay for ad myself.

Gentleman, 59, who enjoys music, art, and drinking, is looking for woman who can play accordion, draw pictures, and make bathtub gin.

Room for rent, by young lady, freshly plastered.

Young man, 27, with 350 acres of farmland, would like to meet charming, intelligent young lady with tractor. Please send picture of tractor.

Male piano player would like to meet female piano player. Object: Baby grand.

I see where the Owl Drugstores are also selling the Stopette underarm razor for people who like to keep a razor under their arm.

WANTED: Baby-sitter to take care of a forty-year-old boy.

WANTED: Girl to milk cows who can speak German.

LOST: Green fountain pen by a man half full of ink.

WANTED: Man to wash dishes and two waitresses.

WANTED: Man with horse sense to drive a truck.

WANTED: Energetic housekeeper who can milk cows, to keep house for one.

NOTICE: Anyone found near my chicken house at night will be found there the next morning.

I saw an ad the other day that read: "Bathing suits reduced." I've seen several bathing suits lately that wouldn't stand much reduction.

I have two nice airy bedrooms for gentlemen twenty-two feet long and ten feet wide.

St. Bernard dog for sale. Will eat anything. Very fond of children.

1934 Chevrolet. A good running car, completely refinished. This one won't last long. Only $145.

Inserted by man running for job as City Treasurer: "My loyal friends, in twelve years of city employment I have never stolen a dollar. All I want is a chance."

Position wanted about March first. At present I'm employed at City Hall, but will work if I have to.

Advertisement: Woman with secondhand car would like to meet gentleman with four new tires. Object: Schenectady.

Wonderful bargain in shirts for men with sixteen or seventeen necks.

WANTED: A young couple to run a boardinghouse out of town.

LOST: Wristwatch by widow with a cracked face.

LOST: A trunk by a widow with a false bottom.

LOST: Milking stool by a young man with three legs.

AFRICA

Once a Bwana Time . . .

The best way to hunt elephants in Africa is to hide in the jungle and make a noise like a peanut.

"She's very mysterious. I think there's some secret connected with her birth."

"Yeah, it's the date."

"How old is your girl?"

"She's in the neighborhood of eighteen."

"But how old?"

"She moved."

A man is as old as he feels. A woman is as old as she likes.

I don't know how old he is, but he's had the seven-year itch fourteen times.

For a woman of her age, time has touched her very lightly.

It's the retouching she gets that makes her look so young.

HE: How old are you?

SHE: Twenty-five.

HE: Aw, you're more'n that.

SHE: Well, I should have been twenty-seven, but I was sick two years.

"When I was a baby I was given a cup by the president for being the best-looking baby."

"That's the first time I ever heard of Lincoln judging a baby contest."

"Is she very old?"

"Very old? Say, she can remember when Captain Kidd was only a second lieutenant."

A professor, trying to emphasize a point in logic, asked his class: "If the United States is bounded on the east by the Atlantic Ocean, on the west by the Pacific Ocean, on the north by Canada and on the south by Mexico, how old am I?"

The brighter students sat dumbfounded, but the dopiest of them all spoke up: "You'd be forty-four."

Dumbfounded in turn, the professor said, "That's right, young man. But how in the world did you know?"

The student answered: "That's easy. I have a brother who's *half* nuts and he's twenty-two."

An old gentleman of eighty-four, having taken to the altar a young damsel of about fifteen, was told by the clergyman:

"The baptismal font is at the other end of the church."

"What do I want with the font?"

"Oh, I beg your pardon," said the cleric, "I thought you'd brought this child to be christened."

"How old would you say she was?"

"To her face, or behind her back?"

"My grandmother just got her hair bobbed."

"Yes?"

"Yeah, she doesn't look like an old lady anymore."

"No?"

"No, she looks like an old man."

"She's a lot older than she looks."

"She looks it."

AIRLINES

PILOT *(to tower):* What time is it?

TOWER: Who is speaking?

PILOT: What does it matter? I'm just ready to take off, and I want to know what time it is.

TOWER: Well, if you're Pan Am, it's 1400 hours. If you're United, it's two o'clock, and if you're Ozark Airlines, the little hand is on the 2 and the big hand is on the 12.

Popular jokes often do more than amuse, they sometimes relate a social moral as well. Consider, for example, the story of a certain 747 flight across the Atlantic. During the course of the flight, extremely unusual weather, as well as mechanical complications, led the pilot to order drastic measures to lighten the weight of the huge plane. The situation was so extreme that the crew had to ask for volunteers to bail out.

A brave Frenchman rose, shouted, *"Vive La France!"* and jumped out.

An Englishman leapt to his feet, shouted, "Long live the Queen!" and jumped into the blue.

Finally a tall Texan rose, shouted, "Remember the Alamo!" and pushed a Mexican out.

ANIMALS

A young mouse announced his engagement at lunch one day. "Tonight," said an older friend, "we'll decide whether you're a mouse or a man. If you kiss her tonight, you're a man. If you're afraid to assert yourself and put off the happy day, you're just a mouse."

"I guess I must be just a rat," said the young mouse sadly. "I kissed her *last* night."

A parrot had two strings attached to his legs. A pull on one would make him sing "Hail Columbia." A pull on the other, "Stardust." Question: What happens if I pull both strings? Answer: He falls flat on his face!

Junior was getting a pickle out of the pickle jar. His mother said, "Junior, if you get into the pickles again, I'll snatch you bald-headed." The parrot overheard her. A preacher came to dinner, and when he took off his hat he was bald-headed. The parrot saw it and said, "Another dummy's been into the pickles."

Comedian Bill Dana tells the story of Tarzan, who was on his way home one day from a hunting trip. As he swims across the river he is pursued by three angry crocodiles. Upon reaching the shore he is forced to engage in hand-to-hand combat with a ferocious lion, is chased by a tribe of angry natives, and sustains an injury when his vine breaks as he is escaping from a rampaging elephant. Finally he arrives at his tree house and is greeted by his loving mate, Jane.

"What happened, darling?" Jane says, surveying disheveled condition.

"Boy, I'll tell ya," Tarzan says, "it's a jungle out there."

ARGUMENTS

"I'm a self-made man."
"Which just goes to show the horrors of unskilled labor."

I'm so mad I could chew the paper pants off a lamb chop.

My wife and I had words, but I never got to use mine!

HE: You're extremely offensive.
SHE: As a matter of fact we both are. But I'm trying to be, and you can't help it!

CONDUCTOR: Madam, pardon me, but you're standing on my foot.
PASSENGER: Why don't you put your foot where it belongs?
CONDUCTOR: Don't tempt me, lady; don't tempt me.

One of those pushy women came into my butcher shop and started her old habit of always pushing ahead of other customers who had been standing there waiting to be waited on. She said to the butcher, "A half-dollar's worth of cat meat, please!" Then, she turned to the woman in back of her and said, "I hope you don't mind me being served first" and the woman shot back, "Why, of course not, darling, if you're *that* hungry!"

ARMY

PRIVATE *(returning late from a furlough):* Well, Sergeant, I'll bet you can't guess what held me up.
SARGE: I can, but go on with your story.

AWARDS

The people in Dayton have been wonderful to me, particularly the employees of the National Cash Register Company. I was informed this morning that they have just voted me "Mr. No Sale" of 1952.

BARTENDER

I'm not sure why so many jokes are told about bartenders, but here's another:

A guy walks into a saloon with a duck under his arm. The bartender says, "What are you doing with that pig?"

The guy says, "What are you talking about? This is not a pig. This is a duck."

The bartender says, "I was talking to the duck."

A martini lover asked Shippy the Bartender at Toots Shor's for a "very dry" martini—"about 35 to 1." As the amazed Shippy put in one drop of vermouth, he said, "Would you like a twist of lemon peel?" The customer shouted, "Listen, if I wanted a lemonade, I'd have asked for it!"

Man dashes into bar, orders double shot of Scotch, gulps it down, places a $5 bill on the bar and rushes out. Bartender walks over, picks up the money, folds it neatly, puts it in his pocket, turns around to the boss and says, "Can you beat a guy like that? Orders a double shot of Scotch, leaves me a five-buck tip and beats it out of here without paying for it!"

SHE: What do you call the person who brings you in contact with the spirit?
HE: A bartender.

BASEBALL

One thing I'm surprised at in looking over the new songs, no one seems to be writing sport songs anymore. Take baseball . . . there's just one baseball song: "Take Me Out to the Ballgame." Think of the possibilities for baseball songs . . .

"I Knew He Was a Baseball Catcher. He Tipped His Mitt Right Away."

"You'd Be So Nice to Slide Home To."

One of the best Babe Ruth stories relates an incident that took place in 1932 when the Babe had a heated argument about his

$80,000-a-year salary with the New York Yankees owner, Col. Jake Ruppert. When the beer baron reminded the high-living Ruth that there was a Depression on, Babe couldn't see what that had to do with him. Ruppert proceeded to argue that even with the proposed salary cut, Ruth would be receiving more than Herbert Hoover, the President of the United States. The Babe retorted:

"What the hell has Hoover got to do with it? Besides, I had a better year."

Crime is everywhere these days. When an umpire walked out of the stadium, went to his parked car, and stuck his key in the door, a man stepped up, put a gun in his back and said, "Give me your money."

"Don't shoot," the official said, "I'm just a poor umpire."

The guy said, "You're tellin' me; I saw the game."

A good story invariably is repeated in ever-changing form over the years so that ultimately it is difficult to trace it to its origin. One of the baseball classics concerns pioneer Honus Wagner who, at the height of his career with the Pittsburgh Pirates, was a terror to all pitchers. "Crazy" Smith, a National League hurler of the day, was noted for keeping voluminous handwritten notes on opposing bats-men. One day a teammate asked Smith what he considered Wagner's weakness as a hitter. Smith turned the pages of his notebook to the W's and held up the notation under "Wagner" for his teammate to read. It said, "Honus Wagner. Hitting weakness: a base on balls."

BASKETBALL

Howard Cann, old-time coach of NYU, though able, occasionally had fits of absentmindedness. One night a UCLA team was giving the New York University Violets a hard time. At a crucial moment in the last quarter Cann suddenly sprang to his feet.

"Plutz," he shouted. "Where's Plutz? I want him to go in there right away."

"But, coach," yelled one of the second-stringers, "Plutz has been playing all through the game. He's in there now."

"Well, then," Cann snapped, "get him out of there. He needs a rest."

BIGOTRY

"Do you know how to save a bigot from drowning?"
"No."
"Good!"

BILLIARDS

Mark Twain, one of the best amateur billiard players of his day, enjoyed telling stories about his talent with the cue, even if the laugh was on him.

"I was traveling in Nevada," Twain claimed, "and I dropped into a billiard parlor one day to pass a little time. Now I kind of fancied my skill with the cue in those days, and when a stranger came up to me offering to play me a game for a modest side bet, I figured I could take him on. I was choosing myself a nicely balanced stick when the stranger turned to me and said, with a trace of pity in his voice that I did not like, 'Pardner, I'll tell you what I'll do for you. I'm afraid your skill may not match mine so I'll just play you left-handed.'

"That made me mad," Twain said, "and I thought I had better give the churl a lesson. To begin with, we increased the bet to make it more interesting. Then we banked for first shot, this fellow shooting left-handed as he promised, and he won. He started playing, still left-handed, of course, and I stood alongside the table chalking my cue and waiting for him to miss so I could take over and show him where he got off.

"Well, he played on and on and I just chalked and chalked. As a matter of fact, he ran out the game without even the hint of a miss. I paid the fellow but I couldn't help being somewhat astonished. 'Gracious!' I exclaimed. 'If you're that good with your left hand, how well would you do shooting right-handed?'

"'Wa-al,' replied the stranger to me as he tucked away his ill-gotten gains, 'mebbe not so good. I've never played right-handed.'"

BOOK TITLE

Dissertation on Roast Lamb by Charles Pigg.

BOWLING

Then there is the one about the ardent bowler—he wouldn't dream of missing his regular bowling session on Tuesday nights—who suffered amnesia after a bad fall. He didn't know who he was for three years. One Tuesday night three years later, he showed up at his home again, suddenly recovered. His wife, overjoyed, began telephoning friends.

"What are you doing that for?" the man asked.

"I'm having a homecoming party for you," explained the happy wife.

"Oh, no, you're not," he objected, "not on my bowling night!"

BRITISH

A Briton, reporting on American manners, exclaimed that they were terrible, brutal, and uncouth. He said, "I've never seen such people. At parties, a fellow takes a drink of water, puts some ice into it to make it cold, puts some alcohol in it to make it hot, puts some lemon in it to make it sour, puts some sugar in it to make it sweet. Then he stirs it, raises the glass and says, 'Here's to *you*,' and then the blighter drinks it himself."

Two Britishers were sitting in their living room.
FIRST: The parade is going by. Where's Mary?
SECOND: She's upstairs waving her hair.
FIRST: Can't we afford a flag?

An enduring form of collegiate humor involves puns on the names of Greek fraternities. What freshman has not, in his time, referred to that honored society *Tappa Kegga Beer*? I have traced one of the commonest of these jokes back as far as the time of that celebrated English wit, William Hogarth. In a charming book called *Tavern Anecdotes and Sayings,* by Charles Hindley, my late edition of which was published in London by Chatto and Windus, in 1881, the following story is related:

"Having invited a party to dine with him at the Mitre Tavern [Hogarth] engraved a card on which was represented, within a circle, a *pi,* with a *mitre* at the top, and the supporters—dexter and sinister—a *knife* and *fork;* and underneath, in Greek characters, the motto '*Eta Bita Pi.*'"

BUSINESS

A vice president of a Madison Avenue advertising agency died after a short illness. His friends in the business were understandably shocked.

"What did he have?" asked one executive.

"I think it was Lever Brothers, General Foods, and Revlon," replied his companion.

Fred Allen once said: "Business is so bad in some cafés that waiters have to go out in the streets to insult people."

A reporter was interviewing a businessman who was noted as much for his wealth of current information as for his financial success.

"Tell me," the reporter asked, "how do you manage to do all the work you do and still find time to read every book that's printed?"

"It's quite simple," the wizard answered. "I keep a good book open on my desk, and start reading it whenever someone has said to me over the telephone, 'Just a moment, please.'"

CARS

In a busy parking lot outside an office building a car leaving the premises, backing up too fast, smashed into the side of a parked vehicle.

A moment later the driver emerged, surveyed the damage he had caused, and began to write a note, which he stuck under the windshield of the vehicle he had hit:

Dear Owner,

A moment ago, I'm sorry to say, I caused some pretty bad damage to your car. There are a number of people watching me at the moment, some from windows in the adjacent building. Quite understandably they think that I am leaving my name, phone number, address, and license number so that you can get in touch with me.

   I'm sorry to tell you that that's not what I'm doing.

                                                    Cordially,

A typewriter repairman was called in to fix an old Smith-Corona, but couldn't find a parking place. He put the automobile in a no-parking space and put a note on his windshield that said:

STANLEY WINEBUSH, WORKING INSIDE BUILDING.

When he came out from his job, he found a parking ticket on his car, with a note clipped to it. This one said:

J.M. FLAGELMEYER, POLICE OFFICER, WORKING OUTSIDE BUILDING.

BEULAH: What an automobile that is! It ain't got no motor and it ain't got no wheels.
HARRY VON ZELL: Wait a minute. If the car hasn't any motor and it hasn't any wheels, how does it go?
BEULAH: It can't go. But brother, can it park!

Think you're fat? A matron phoned a reducing salon to lament that her husband had just given her a lovely present and she couldn't get into it. The operator made an appointment for her and then added, "Don't worry, madam, we'll have you wearing that dress in no time."

"Who said anything about a dress? It's a Volkswagen."

CHEAP

The story is told that Scottish poet Robert Burns one day happened upon the quay at Greenock just in time to see a wealthy merchant being rescued from drowning in the waters of the harbor. After the merchant had been brought ashore he thanked the sailor who had rescued him and presented him with a shilling. Bystanders protested—some of them vociferously—at such stinginess, but Burns admonished them saying, "There is no need to criticize, my friends. The gentleman is the best judge of the value of his life."

He isn't cheap; he just has low pockets and short arms.

A: Nice fellow, but have you noticed how he always lets his friends pick up the dinner bill?
B: Yes. He has a terrible impediment in his reach.

He gave till it hurt, but he never could stand pain.

An old joke of Jack Benny's:
He's so stingy he sharpens his pencils over the fireplace, so he won't waste the wood!

CHINESE

The Chinese, too, have their jokes about stupidity. Old American joke books of the 1920s often present the unintelligent person as a dumb Irish cop or laborer, sometimes also intoxicated. In the late 1930s Dumb Jokes were told about "The Little Moron." The "Po-lack" joke craze of the early 1970s was merely a continuation of the theme. Here is precisely such a story from Chinese folk-lore.

There was once a fool whose wife had taken a lover. The husband happened to return home one evening unexpectedly and the lover had to run for his life. But as he was climbing out a window he lost one of his shoes. Close on the intruder's heels, the husband picked up the shoe and put it under his pillow, planning on the following day to use it as evidence against his wife in court. His wife, however, had observed the proceedings and during his sleep exchanged the shoe for one of her husband's own. When he woke up in the morning the husband looked carefully at the shoe and, recognizing that it was his own, offered an apology to his wife. "I'm sorry about last night," he said, "I hadn't realized that it was me who jumped out of the window."

At a circus, a talent scout is looking for Midgy the Midget. The manager says, "I'm sorry, but he's home today, he doesn't work on Monday." The talent scout goes to Midgy's home, the door is opened by a man, six feet tall.

SCOUT: I'd like to speak to Midgy.

MAN: I'm Midgy.

SCOUT: But you're six feet tall.

MAN: I know, but today is my day off.

Young circus man with two heads would like to meet young lady with two heads; interested in sharing a case of four-way cold tablets.

CLOTHING

JUNE: But I'm glad you like this little number, Steve. It's the latest thing. Low around the shoulders, with a gathering at the side.
STEVE: If it were any lower, that gathering would be a mob.

She has a veil of tulle in her hope chest.
She calls it her tulle chest.

COSTUME

I went to a masquerade party the other night and I won the prize for the best costume. I pulled a pair of bathing trunks over my raccoon coat and I went as a French poodle!

COUNTRY

A man is driving on a country road and notices that a chicken is running beside his car. He speeds up and the chicken speeds up, until finally both are doing about eighty miles an hour.

The chicken then turns up a side street toward her farm. The man notices that the chicken has four legs instead of two. Surprised by this, he follows the chicken home and asks the farmer about the amazing four-legged chicken.

"It's a new breed," the farmer says. "And I'm going to get rich selling drumsticks!"

"Well, how do they taste?" asks the man.

"Heck, I don't know," says the farmer. "Haven't been able to catch one of them yet."

Because of his health, the Eastern city dweller went looking for a place to live in the Southwest. In a small town in Arizona, he approached a man sitting in front of the general store.

"Say, what's the death rate around here?"

"Same as it is back East," the man said. "One to a person."

Another man, also traveling for his health's sake, went to the same small town. He asked the same fellow if the place was healthy.

"Why, this is the goldarndest healthiest place you'll ever come into. Shucks, nobody ever dies in this neck of the desert."

"Strange that you should say that," the visitor said. "On the way in, I passed a funeral procession."

"Oh, that. That was only the local undertaker. He starved to death."

A city dweller was spending his first week on a dude ranch. He left the ranch one morning to view the countryside but returned shortly, battered and bruised, and with his clothes torn.

"What happened to you?" demanded a ranch hand.

"A little black snake chased me."

"That little snake isn't poisonous," answered the cowboy.

"Listen," said the dude, "if he can make you jump off a 50-foot cliff, he doesn't have to be!"

The old Atchison, Topeka and Santa Fe steamer came to a grinding halt. "What's wrong, conductor?" an elderly woman cried.

"Nothing much," the conductor replied, "we hit a cow."

"Oh," said the relieved passenger, "was it on the tracks?"

"No," the conductor said, dryly. "We chased her into the barn."

A veterinary surgeon was instructing a farmer as to a suitable method for administering medicine to a horse.

"Simply place this powder in a pipe about two feet long, put one end of the pipe well back in the horse's mouth, and blow the powder down the throat."

Shortly thereafter the farmer came running into the veterinarian's office in a very distressed condition.

"What's the matter?" asked the vet.

"I'm dying!" cried the farmer hoarsely. "The horse blew first."

Bennett Cerf once told the story of a driver of a small sedan in a rural district of England braking hastily as the tweedy mistress of a large estate came hurtling around a sharp bend in the narrow road in her large Rolls. Before he could say a word, she shouted "Pig!" and drove on.

"Cow!" he cried after her in retaliation.

Then he drove around the bend himself—and crashed head-on into the biggest pig he had ever seen.

I've never been sure why, but jokes in which one or more characters are animals with the gift of speech have been popular for untold centuries, going at least as far back as the period in which the Bible was written.

An urban vacationer driving along a country road suddenly had trouble with the engine of his car. He got out, raised the hood, and was staring intently at the motor when he heard a clear voice behind him say, "Your trouble is in the fuel pump, Mac."

Looking around the man could see nothing but an old swaybacked horse, leaning against a nearby fence. The visitor was so astonished that he turned and raced down the road, not stopping until he came to a small, dusty gas station. Gasping for breath he explained the situation to the attendant, who did not seem particularly impressed. "You say you couldn't see anyone but the horse?" the attendant asked.

"That's right," said the tourist.

"Tell me, was it an old gray, sway-backed horse, with one eye closed?"

"Yes, it was."

"Well, don't pay him no mind at all," the attendant drawled, "he doesn't know a damned thing about fuel pumps."

A man was taking his family for a ride in the country when their auto became stuck in a muddy hole in the road. Luckily, a farmer on a tractor came by and the man paid him $50 to pull the car from the mud. Once on dry ground, the man remarked to the farmer, "At fifty dollars a crack, I'd think you'd be busy pulling people out of the mud night and day."

"Wish I could," replied the farmer, "but at night I have to haul water for the hole."

Then there's the tale of the young female tourist from New York, dressed in her summer best, who approached a Maine lobsterman on the wharf one day while he was mending his traps. Her attempts at conversation were greeted with an occasional noncommittal grunt. Finally, she shook her head and said, "Maine is sure full of lots of peculiar people."

The old man looked up from his work and said, "Yes, ma'am, but they all leave by Labor Day."

CRIME

Two gentlemen on the Lower East Side were talking. "Vito," said Gino, "I hear you had a fire sale."

"Shhshssh," said Vito, glancing up and down the street. "It's tomorrow."

Some time ago I was trying to employ what is technically known as "help" for our modest domestic ménage.

One of the applicants remarked, in the course of an interview, that she had worked for the Bing Crosbys. Since I had learned from previous experience that such claims are not always to be accepted at face value, I asked if she could prove her boast.

"Well, sir," said the prospect, "I can show you some spoons and things with their initial on them."

They gave a "Coming Out" party for my sister. She was paroled.

He was also in the Steeplechase—one night the cops chased him all over town. Finally they chased him up a steeple.

DANCING

"Do you remember the Varsity drag?"

"My dear, I *was* the Varsity drag."

I learned to rhumba very early in life . . . I had a tricycle with a loose seat.

Of a hula dancer who appeared on *You Bet Your Life,* quizmaster Groucho Marx asked: "Just what is a hula?"

"It tells a story of dancing," said the lady.

"And all this time," Groucho said, "I've been wasting my time reading books!"

He rushed to her. "This is my dance, you know," he said breathlessly.

She gave him a haughty stare. "Oh, really? I thought it was the Junior Prom."

STRAIGHT MAN: where did you learn to dance?

COMIC: Arthur Murray's!

STRAIGHT MAN: Arthur Murray's? Say, they've sure got a lot of beautiful gals over there, haven't they?

COMIC: How should I know?

STRAIGHT MAN: You don't know. Who did you dance with?

COMIC: Arthur Murray!

DEAFNESS

I've just invented a new hearing aid. It's practically invisible because it's shaped exactly like a human ear—the only trouble is that you have to wear it over your nose.

I called a piano tuner and he worked on my piano for six hours. I was getting anxious about how much it was going to cost but when he finished and asked for only four dollars I said, "How come you can spend that much time on the piano and only charge me four dollars?"

He said, "What?"

The president of a certain Southern college is deaf, a condition which certain wily students, arriving late for classes, have learned to employ to their advantage.

Raising his voice on certain words and lowering it on others, a student will proclaim: "I am sorry I was late this morning, I wish I could say that THE BUS BROKE DOWN—but I can't."

"Well, since the bus broke down," the president replies, "you're excused."

DEATH

A man who retired to Florida was about eighty and looked it, but he didn't feel eighty. So he decided to do something about it. He dyed his hair black, put silicone shots in his cheeks, went to a gym, got new clothes and looked thirty years younger. Then he bought himself a sports car, put down the top, drove along Collins Avenue and picked up a girl. There he was, riding on the avenue, looking at this beautiful woman and a bolt of lightning kills him. He goes to heaven and stands in front of God, exclaiming: "God, why me?" And God says: "I'm sorry, Sol, I didn't recognize you."

"Nobody has any sympathy for a hen because she is not beautiful, while everyone gets sentimental over the oriole and says how shocking to kill the lovely thing."

—Don Marquis

When Goodman Ace, one of the great comedy writers of the century died in 1982, he asked that the epitaph on his tombstone read "No flowers, please. I'm allergic."

The hit musical *Miss Saigon* was very hard to get tickets for. So there's a fellow watching the show who waited six months for tickets, and there's an empty seat next to him. Halfway through the show, he leans across to a woman sitting there and says, "I'm going crazy, would you mind telling me why there's an empty seat here?" And she said, "Well, we bought the tickets many months ago, and my husband passed away." He said, "I'm really sorry to hear that, but couldn't you have gotten someone else to come and fill the seat, perhaps a friend?" And she said, "No chance, they're all at the funeral."

The dying man gasped pitifully.

"Grant me one last request, June," he pleaded.

"Of course, Herb," she said softly.

"Six months after I die," he went on, "I want you to marry Joe."

"Joe," she cried, "I thought you hated that man."

"I do," he said, and passed away.

"I got rid of my chauffeur, he almost killed me four times."

"Ah, give him another chance."

"I was out to the cemetery."

"Anybody dead?"

"Yes, all of them."

Lives of great men all remind us,

As their pages o'er we turn,

That we're apt to leave behind us,

Letters that we ought to burn.

"I'd like you to paint a picture of my late uncle."

"Okay, bring him in."

"I said my late uncle."

"Well, bring him in when he *gets* here."

Sam Russell, justice of the peace in Crawfordsville, Iowa, was a reticent man. One day a saleslady breezed into his residence and inquired if his wife was at home.

"No, she ain't home," the justice said.

"Do you mind if I wait?" the visitor asked.

"Nope, have a chair."

After a full hour of waiting, the woman asked, "Where is your wife?"

"She went out to the cemetery."

"How long do you think she'll be gone?"

"Well, I don't know," said the justice deliberately, "but she's been out there eleven years so far."

DEBT

"Who," asks an ardent Southern orator, "would countenance the idea of robbing Peter to pay Paul?"

"Well, dunno, unless it might be Paul."

WIFE: The man from the furniture store is here.
HUSBAND: Ask him to take a chair.
WIFE: I did, but he wants the piano too.

DECORATING

The landlord was generous. He gave me wall-to-wall floors.

DENTISTS

PATIENT: Twenty-five dollars is an awful lot of money for pulling a tooth—just two seconds' work.
DENTIST: Well, if you wish, I could pull it very slowly.

DENTIST—a man who lives from hand to mouth.

She was so dumb, she went to her dentist and he put dunce caps on her teeth.

Speaking of teeth always reminds me of the two fellows I overheard arguing in a diner one night. One said to the other: "Wise guy, huh? How many teeth have you got?"

"Thirty-two."

"Wanna try for thirty?"

I had my teeth checked the other day. The dentist said, "Your teeth are okay . . . but your gums have to come out."

I knew a guy who had so many cavities he talked with an echo.

Dentists, like all other professionals, face one constant danger—they lose their perspective. A friend of mine who was in the Marines told me about going to the movies with the battalion dentist one night at a base way out in the Pacific. Gene Tierney was starring in the picture and all the men—who hadn't seen a woman in at least a year—whistled and sighed and ahhed and oohed. But not the dentist. He, too, had been overseas for a long time. But all he could say was: "Malocclusion—bad bite."

Song sent into "Songs for Sale" by Dentist: "Hand Me Down My Novocain."

The dentist song: "I Saw You Last Night and Got That Gold Filling."

Epitaph on dentist's tombstone:
"Here lies Dr. Krelman, filling his last cavity."

"Are there any cavities in my teeth, doctor?"
"Are there any cavities in my teeth, doctor?"
Dentist: "Where do you think that echo is coming from?"

Do you swear to fill the tooth . . . the whole tooth, and nothing but the tooth?

HE: I travel in pretty influential circles. Tonight I'm having dinner with the upper set!
SHE: The steak might be tough. You'd better take along the lower set, too!

She had teeth like pearls.
She and Pearl bought them from the same dentist.

A blacksmith in Biddenden, England, made a set of false teeth for himself out of pieces of scrap aluminum.

There's only one trouble with this: he has to brush his teeth with steel wool . . . not only that, but every time he needs a filling he has to go to Lockheed.

Wouldn't it be crazy if this got to be a popular thing? The ads would read: "Goodbye to old-fashioned white teeth . . . today . . . go gray . . . the aluminum way." "Be right with a light bite." "The Aluminum Company presents choppers that are whoppers . . . for that flash-in-the-pan look. (Also available in stainless steel.)"

A: Hey! Whatcha lookin' for?

B: I'm lookin' for a piece of candy.

A: A piece of candy? During my act? Why go to all that trouble for a lousy piece of candy?

B: It isn't the candy so much . . . my *teeth* are in it.

I kissed her on the bridge at midnight—and the bridge fell out of her mouth.

PATIENT: A-A-A-AH.

DENTIST *(inserting rubber gag, towel, pliers, and sponge):* Now, how's your family?

"I'm sorry," said the dentist, "but you cannot have an appointment with me this afternoon. I have eighteen cavities to fill." And he picked up his golf bag and went out.

DETECTIVES

HOLMES: Looking at your hand, I would say you were economical.
SUSPECT: About what?
HOLMES: Soap and water.

"Charlie's wife is a brunette, isn't she?"
"How'd you know that? You've never seen her."
"I just noticed a blonde hair on his lapel."

HOLMES: The man was shot by his wife at close range.
WATSON: Then there must be powder marks on him.
HOLMES: Yes . . . That's why she shot him.

DIME STORE

She was a rather nice girl, but dumb, so dumb that she was fired from a five-and-ten-cent store because she couldn't remember the prices.

I'll never forget the first time I met her, we were at Woolworth's. I was in Pots and Pans, she was in Men's Underwear.

DIVORCE

PHIL: Well, Bill, the rapidly increasing divorce rate certainly shows that America is indeed becoming the land of the free!
BILL: Yeah, but the marriage rate still makes it look like the home of the brave.

An 86-year-old couple went to a lawyer for a divorce. When they were asked why they waited so long, the old man said, "We wanted to wait until all the kids had died."

People wouldn't get divorced for such trivial reasons if they didn't get married for such trivial reasons.

The judge had just awarded a divorce to a wife who had charged nonsupport.

"And," he said to the husband, "I have decided to give your wife fifty dollars a month toward her support."

"That's fine, Judge," said the husband cordially, "and once in a while I'll try to slip her a few bucks myself."

A: "Did you say that Elizabeth Taylor is writing a book?"
B: "Yes . . . It goes Chap one, Chap two, Chap three . . ."

FLASH: Boise, Idaho: Mrs. Brown was granted a divorce today when she told the judge that since her marriage her husband had spoken to her only three times. She was awarded the custody of their three children.

The high cost of leaving . . . alimony!

A: By the way, do you realize that today was our twelfth wedding anniversary?
B: Our twelfth anniversary? Are you sure?
A: Yes—today's the fourth anniversary of our third marriage.

An English nobleman who lived in a castle near Hereford took off his wife's diamond rings and threw them in her face. He was condemned by the courts on the grounds that people who live in stone houses shouldn't throw glass.

"Why is it so easy to get married and so hard to get a divorce?"
"You've got to have a reason for a divorce."

DOGS

Truman Capote has told of the young man who accepted a dinner invitation at a friend's apartment on the nineteenth floor of a New York apartment house. While his hostess was in the kitchen, he played with her German shepherd. He threw the rubber bone several times and the dog fetched it. Then, throwing harder than he meant to, he threw the bone out the terrace door and over the railing.

Incredibly, the dog followed it and bounded over the railing to the street nineteen floors below.

Horrified, the young man began wondering what to say. When finally they sat down to dinner, he looked at the hostess and said, "Perhaps it's my imagination, but your dog seemed rather depressed tonight . . ."

Some dogs get regular haircuts. The first word they're trained to understand is "Next!"

I've always wanted a dog called General . . . so when I throw a stick I can say, "Brigadier, General!"

"I think he'd make a good watchdog . . . but he looks a little run down."

"Have you wound him lately?"

"I've got a new white dog."

"Spitz?"

"No. He just dribbles a little."

STUDENT: My dog slobbers at the mouth. What shall I do for him?

VETERINARIAN: Teach him how to spit.

DRINKING

Columnist Robert Sylvester used to tell of the man who came into a bar and ordered a martini. Before he drank it he removed the olive and carefully placed it into a small glass jar. He then ordered another martini and did the same thing. After an hour, when he was full of martinis and the jar was full of olives, he reeled out.

A customer said, "Well, I never saw anything quite as peculiar as that!"

"What's so peculiar about it?" asked the bartender. "His wife sent him out for a jar of olives."

Father John Lee tells a joke I'm particularly fond of.

Mike Murphy had a serious drinking problem. One day his wife, Bridget, was out looking for him and found him in a neighborhood saloon drinking with his buddies. Being basically polite chaps the men stood up and asked her to have a drink with them. Bridget, who had never tasted whiskey in her life, took a large gulp, gagged and said, "Ugh! What did you give me? This stuff tastes horrible."

"Now you see, sweetheart?" Mike says, "and all this time you thought I was having fun."

W. C. Fields was in the habit of taking martinis to work at the studios in a fine silver cocktail shaker. Because there was a rule against liquor on all lots, and the players faced suspension if they were caught using it, Fields called his booze "pineapple juice." One day a man sneaked the shaker out of Fields's dressing room, poured out the martini mixture, and substituted real pineapple juice.

Fields, right off a scene, went straight to his changing place and picked up his shaker. A second later he came charging out, roaring, "Some son of a bitch has been putting pineapple juice in my pineapple juice!"

A drunk went up to a telephone pole and felt his way all around it. "Good Lord!" he cried, "walled in!"

The jazz drummer Zutty Singleton, who hardly ever drank, had a few one night, and got up the next day with a terrible hangover.

"Whiskey won't kill you," he said, "but it'll sure leave you sittin' there wishin' it had."

A chap goes every day to a cocktail bar and asks for two glasses of Scotch. He drinks first one, then the other. He repeats the order. Then he orders two more. The bartender asks him to explain. "You see," says the customer, "I lost my best buddy in Vietnam. We always had three Scotches each. I swore I would keep to the tradition. One glass represents my buddy, the other me."

However, some time afterward he comes in and only asks for one glass. Then a second. Then a third. The bartender asks why. "Doctor's orders," says the customer. "I'm off the booze."

A Thoroughbred racehorse walks into a cocktail bar, orders a dry martini, drains it with his tongue and asks for a second. He then reaches into his saddlebag with his hoof and asks for the bill. "That will be four dollars," said the bartender, marveling. "You know, this is the first time I've seen a horse in this bar."

"I'm not surprised," says the horse. "And judging by your prices, it'll be the last."

COLONEL *(inspecting quarters):* Could you explain how all those empty bottles came into your tent?
PRIVATE: I don't know, sir. I never brought any empty bottles into my tent yet.

MAN *(with gun):* Stick 'em up!
DRUNK: What is this . . . a holdup?
MAN: No. Take a drink out of my bottle.
DRUNK: No, thanks. I don't drink this early in the morning.
MAN: See this gun? Take a *drink,* I said!
DRUNK *(after drinking, coughing, and choking):* Gee, this stuff is awful!
MAN: Yeah, I know. Now you hold the gun on me, while *I* have one.

Comedian Alan Gale: "The crowd in the club was so drunk that I couldn't even see them."

A: My doctor advised me to quite drinking.

B: Did you?

A: No, I changed doctors.

Mark Twain still ranks as the greatest American humorist, but even the master was not above borrowing a good joke and altering it slightly so as to disguise its origin. Everyone is presumably familiar with Twain's famous observation about swearing off cigarettes. Contrary to those who say that it's very difficult to stop smoking, Twain argued that it was the easiest thing in the world, explaining that he personally had done it dozens of times. The same story is found in an ancient volume called *Tavern Anecdotes and Sayings,* concerning a man who had repeatedly promised his friends that he would stop drinking. One day a friend who called was entertained briefly by a manservant. "Tell me," said the visitor, "has your master left off drinking yet?"

"Oh, indeed," said the servant. "He has left off two or three times today alone."

"I won't offer you a cocktail, Mr. Thompson," said the lady of the house, "since you are the head of the Temperance League."

"No, no. I am president of the Anti-*Vice* League," Mr. Brown said.

"Oh. Well, I knew there was something I shouldn't offer you," the hostess replied.

TEACHER: You saw that the worm thrived in water, but when put in alcohol it wiggled a few times and died. What does that prove?
JUNIOR: If you drink alcohol you'll never have worms.

The *New York Post* reports a sign in a cocktail lounge: PLEASE DON'T STAND UP WHILE ROOM IS IN MOTION.

He is a very light drinker. He only weighs a hundred and ten.

The wife of a well-to-do industrialist was in the act of instructing the new maid in her duties.

"Sometimes," said the mistress, "it will be necessary for you to help the butler upstairs."

"I understand, madam," replied the girl, "I drink a bit myself."

Some taverns don't serve women at the bar. You have to bring your own.

A: Do you hear something right now?
B: No, not a thing.
A: That's funny. I'm talkin' to you.

A drunk wakes up, tries to put on slippers, puts on one slipper and one empty Kleenex box, which is on the floor beside the bed.

He never had a hangover in his life. He never got sober.

To keep from getting up with a hangover, don't get up.

So your name is Taylor?
I knew your father, "Old Taylor."
And your mother-in-law, "Old Crow."

She was an old-fashioned singer. After downing about five of them she'd start to sing.

A man was out on a drunk for a week. To square himself with his wife he called her up and said, "Don't pay those kidnappers a dime, honey, I escaped."

Consider: A woman's great love for dry goods and a man's love for wet goods.

"Young man," the judge demanded, "what were you doing boarding a bus last Monday dressed only in your underwear?"

"Sorry, Your Honor," the man apologized, "I thought it was Tuesday!'

He quit drinking. He now dips his bread in it.

HE: I don't know why I was so drunk last night, I only had one glass.

SHE: Yes, but they kept filling it up.

"How do I avoid getting stiff in the joints?"

"Stay out of them."

A guy I know, having collected the fruits of a judicious wager, was walking down the street in a cloud of good spirits when he was approached by a panhandler who begged for two bits.

"I suppose you want to buy yourself a drink?" my friend demanded.

"That's right," the bum admitted.

"Since you're honest about it," my friend said, "I'll go you one better." And he guided the bum into a nearby bar. "Two double bourbons," he said to the bartender.

The bum said, "Make mine the same."

She is going to be stiff competition. Even if she wasn't stiff she'd be competition.

A: Hopscotch? That's no fun.
B: It is if you use real scotch.

"We are now passing the most famous brewery in Milwaukee," explained the guide.

"The hell we are," said the visiting fireman as he hopped off the sightseeing bus.

She came home tight as a drum, so the old man beat her.

"I don't object to a guy drinking. As a matter of fact my grandfather drank all his life and when he died he still had all his hair and teeth."

"How old was he?"

"Thirty-seven."

Watching an inebriated man try without success to unlock the door to his house, a policeman asked if he could handle the key for him.

"No, thanks," the man replied. "I can hold the key—you hold the house."

He was evidently suffering from one of those morning-after-the-night-before headaches. He came up to me and says, "Say, buddy, can you show me the way to Alcoholics Anonymous?" I said, "Yes, why? Do you want to join?" He says, "Heck, no—I wanna resign."

How much rum would a rum-runner run if a rum-runner could run rum?

The man who enters a bar very optimistically often comes out very misty optically.

Let there be no moaning at the bar when I pick up the check.

"I'm sorry, Roger can't come to the phone. You can't reach him at all. He's incommunicado."
"He's what?"
"Incommunicado."
"How do you spell that?"
"D-R-U-N-K."

I don't know whether this place serves the smallest drinks in town, but it's the only joint I know where they serve the martini in the olive.

Removing his shoes, the husband climbed the stairs, opened the door of the bedroom, entered, and closed it after him without being detected. Just as he was about to get into bed, his wife, roused from slumber, turned and sleepily said, "Is that you, Fido?"

The husband, relating the story later, said, "For once in my life I had real presence of mind. I licked her hand."

HE: I found fifty cents today.

SHE: I know, I can smell it on your breath.

STRAIGHT MAN: What's the difference between a Scotchman and a coconut?

COMIC: I don't know, what is the difference?

STRAIGHT MAN: Well, you can get a drink from a coconut.

COMIC: Ha ha ha. Aw, that's a dirty trick. But, I'm a good fella. How would you like to have a drink?

STRAIGHT MAN: A drink? I'd *love* one.

COMIC: Well, go get yourself a coconut!

"One of our members lost his reason last night."

"How did it happen?"

"He had one when he left the saloon, but he forgot it before he reached home."

Some of the joints in town have developed a new gimmick to save wine-cellar bills. When you order a shot, they flash an amber spotlight on your table. It makes the liquor look stronger.

FIRST DRUNK: Say, know what time it is?
SECOND DRUNK: Yeah.
FIRST DRUNK: Thanks.

Steeplejack James Swootan was in the hospital today with injuries suffered when he fell off a bar stool. Don't laugh. You can get pretty high in those bars.

DRIVE-IN

One motorist had his car stolen from a drive-in—he had to identify it.

"It's a green sedan, with whitewall tires, and brown gravy dripping from the door."

I used to be head of the car-hops at a drive-in. "Hop-head Allen" they called me.

DRIVING

A guy has just invented a device to cut down on unnecessary noise inside an automobile. It fits right over her mouth.

Last year gas killed four thousand, nine hundred and fifty-two people. Thirty inhaled it, nine hundred and twenty-two lit matches over it, and four thousand stepped on it.

Signboard reads:

TUCSON: 36

PHOENIX: 92

"Sounds like a pretty good game."

JUDGE: How long did it take your wife to learn to drive?
MAN: It will be ten years in September, Your Honor.

I had to buy a car this morning. I found a parking space.

WOMAN: What are all those holes in the lumber for?

LUMBERMAN: They're knot-holes.

WOMAN: If they're not holes, what are they?

"Say, I don't think you knew who I was when we met the other day."

"No, who were you?"

(To nurse): Tell me quick, am I a mother or a father?

The young lover was obviously reeling out a heavy line trying to impress the beautiful young girl at his side. "Those soft, lovely hands," he whispered. "Your warm lips. And those beautiful eyes! Where did you get those eyes?"

The girl answered, "They came with my head."

(Snaps fingers, remembering something): Oh, nuts . . . today is Lincoln's birthday and I forgot to send him a card.

OFFICER: Have you a zither?

PRIVATE: No, Lieutenant, but I got a couple of brothers.

My aunt is the dumbest woman you ever saw.

Yesterday a tramp came to her door and said, "Lady, I haven't eaten for three days." And she said, "That's no good. You should force yourself."

"What do you mean, I'm stupid? Apologize, say you're sorry."

"All right, I'm sorry you're stupid."

QUESTION: Would it be right for me to marry a girl more stupid than myself?

ANSWER: It would be impossible.

A: Of course I look like Jones! I *am* Jones!

B: Ah, that accounts for the resemblance.

Him have gone—Him have went—Him have left

I all alone—Us cannot went to He—ah, cruel world, how can it was?

Him won't come to I, Me won't go to her, it can't never was—
Don't it awful?

"Hello, Sydely?"
"My name is Sydney."
"I said Sydely, diddle I?"

A passenger was sitting in a subway car, clicking and shaking his head from side to side like a metronome. Finally the Pullman asked him what he was doing that for.

"So I can tell the time," he replied.

"Well, what time is it?"

"Four-thirty," said the man.

"You're wrong. It's quarter of five."

"Oh, then, I must be slow," he answered, speeding up.

"I'm sure glad I wasn't born in Spain."
"Why?"
"I can't speak Spanish."

SLOB: Me and my father know everything.
BOB: Where is Asia?
SLOB: That's one of the things my father knows.

"My uncle is in the hospital again."

"What's the matter with him?"

"He was sleeping in an upper berth and somebody played 'The Star Spangled Banner.'"

Boy, is he dumb. He followed a sprinkling wagon for a mile to tell the man it was leaking.

A: We have scads of children.

B: How many are there in a scad?

EDUCATION

Students enrolled in a Russian language course at Eckerd College approached their first class with some apprehension about its difficulty. The professor entered the room, followed by his dog. Before saying a word to the students, he commanded the dog to sit, beg, lie down, roll over—all in Russian. The dog obeyed each command perfectly.

"See how easy Russian is," the professor said. "Why, even a dog can learn it!"

Sister Eileen Rice, Assistant Professor of Education at Siena Heights College in Adrian, Michigan, told me the story of one of her young students who had never seen nuns in their traditional garb. One day he came running to her and said, "Sister! Sister! I just saw a nun!"

A history teacher was trying to pound a few facts into the resistant skulls of an assemblage of ten-year-olds.

"Tell me, children," he said. "In what battle did General Wolfe, knowing his forces were victorious, cry 'I die happy'?"

"His last," said the brightest boy in the class.

Richard Popkin and Avrum Stroll, in *Philosophy Made Simple,* relate the story of the American philosopher Morris Raphael Cohen, who in teaching Descartes to his class had carefully explained Descartes' reasons for doubting his very existence. He then sent his students home to read the philosopher's *Meditations.*

The next day a worried young man, looking much the worse for wear, reported to Professor Cohen. He had been up all night studying and worrying about the assignment.

"Professor Cohen," he said anxiously, "please tell me, do I exist?"

Professor Cohen considered the question and then answered, "And who wants to know?"

Two college kids were plagued by a hard examination.

"What did you think of those questions?" one asked.

"They weren't so bad," the other said. "It wasn't the questions that were so tough—it was the answers to them."

Monroe Sloyer, a teacher, used to amuse his classes by this test:

A teacher inquired of his class, "How do you say 'Macbeth'?"

"Mac—Beth," they said.

The teacher said, "Very good. What about 'MacIlherny'?"

They chorused: "MacIlherny! MacIlherny!"

"What about 'M-A-C-K-Earney'?"

"McKearny! McKearny!"

"'M-a-c-h-i-n-e-r-y'?"

"Mack-Hinery."

"Funny," Sloyer would say. "Most people pronounce that word 'machinery.'"

Teachers not only perform vitally important functions in our society; they are also great straight men.

"Are your mother and father in?" asked one instructor when a small boy opened the door.

"Well," said the boy, "they was in but they is out now."

"They was in? They is out?" said the shocked teacher. "Where is your grammar?"

"Oh," said the boy, "she's upstairs takin' a bath."

There's no question that our early social experiences dictate our interpretation of important social questions and events. A teacher asked her class, "In ancient times some people believed that a certain heroic figure supported the earth on his shoulders. What was the name of this personage?"

"Atlas," said a little girl.

"That is correct," said the teacher, "but if Atlas carried the earth on his shoulders, how was Atlas supported."

"Maybe," the little girl said, "his old lady took in washing."

The same history teacher asked, "Where was the Declaration of Independence signed?"

A bright youngster replied, "At the bottom."

"I've added these numbers up ten times," said Knucklehead to his hard-working instructor.

"Good for you," the teacher answered.

"And here are the ten answers," said Knucklehead.

A teacher said to her primary class the other day: "If your father gave your mother $7 today and $8 tomorrow, what would she have?"

And a small boy over in the corner replied: "She'd have a fit."

A first-grader down in Birmingham, Alabama, came home from school one day and announced excitedly, "They've got a magic record player at our school."

"A magic record player?" said his aunt, puzzled.

"Yes," the boy explained. "You don't have to plug it into electricity—you don't even need electricity to make it play. All you need to do is wind up a crank!"

FAN MAIL

Dear Mr. Allen:
I have always paid for theater tickets in the past. But now I understand that CBS Television gives out tickets for nothing. Is this true?

Yes. They give them out for this show . . . and if it isn't nothing, I don't know what is.

I'm practically a fugitive from a chain letter; got another one yesterday: Dear Sir: This chain letter was started in Reno in the hope of bringing happiness to tired businessmen. Unlike most chains this does not cost money. Simply bundle up your wife or girlfriend and send her to the fellow who heads the list. Then cross his name off, add your own and send copies to at least five male friends. When your name works to the top you will receive in return 15,168 gorgeous girls. Have faith. Do not break this chain. One man broke the chain and got his wife back.

Dear Mr. Allen:
I love the way you introduce guests on your show, but let me ask you . . . when you're introduced to someone you think you've met before, is it correct to say, "Haven't we met before" or what?

Clara Thorndike
Teterboro, New Jersey

No, Clara·. . . "Haven't we met before or what" is wrong. Unless you *haven't* met before . . . or what. In which case you say, "We've met before, or what, haven't we?" However . . . if you *have* met before and are being introduced again, you say, "Nice to meet you again again." On the other hand, if you have never met before and nobody is introducing you now, you approach the person to whom you are not being introduced and say, "Let's not meet . . . shall we?" If this is not clear . . . send for my free etiquette booklet explaining why you should never ask questions of strangers.

Here's a card from a gentleman who is evidently in hot water . . . All he writes is: OW!

Dear Mr. Allen:
For several weeks now you've been making a big fuss about
the flies that land on your breakfast table. You've even gone
so far as to have your cameraman take close-ups of them.
This, Mr. Allen, is ridiculous. Who in the world cares about
a stupid, old fly.

Signed,
A Bumble Bee

Dear Mr. Allen:
I don't like you. I don't like your program. I don't like television. I didn't like radio, either. Also, I hate movies, the
circus, records, and ball games of all kinds.

Very truly yours,
The Good Humor Man

Received your letter and was pleased as punch to hear from
you. At least everyone says I've been acting a lot punchier since
you wrote me.

Dear Allen . . . Sure enjoy your show . . . Think you're much funnier now that you're no longer with George Burns.

Dear Mr. Allen:
Please send me thirty tickets for July the 4th . . . or if not available, how about four tickets for July the 30th?

Dick DeSantis

Dear Steve:
Regarding the Automobile Hooper Rating you took by having listeners in cars blow their horns . . . I was having my car worked on in a garage at the time and there was a mechanic under the hood. Without thinking I blew the horn . . . the last we heard of him, he was circling Gallup, New Mexico, at five thousand feet.

As per request I blew my horn at the specified instant . . . it just so happened that there was a girl walking in front of my car at the time. My case comes up Friday.

Dear Mr. Allen:
You probably don't remember me, but I am the small girl who stopped you on the corner of Madison Ave. and 55th Street and asked for your autograph for my autograph book. My mother thinks I should write and thank you for the autograph.

Thank you,
Jan

P.S. She also thinks I should ask you for my fountain pen back.

Dear Mr. Allen:
You are a godsend. For months, I have had trouble getting my three-year-old son, Billy, to take his nap. But now, since your show has changed from 11:30 to 12:00 I have no problem. We eat an early lunch, then when you come on, I put Billy in front of the television. In no time at all, he is fast asleep.

Incidentally, Mr. Allen, please don't be insulted that a child should fall asleep on your show. I have done the same thing myself.

Thanks again,
Mrs. Ruth Stone

Dear Mr. Allen:
I have been listening to you off and on for the past five years . . . and I like you much better off than I do on.

Here's a letter I just got. It says "Dear Steve Allen: Enclosed please find $2, please send me the 15 recipes."

Must have the wrong program. *I'm* not Mary Margaret McBride.

Oh, here's a P.S. *(Reads):* "Then why don't you send back the 2?"

FAT

"You turn my stomach."

"Yeah, well, turn it back the other way. It's coming out your pants."

FITNESS

I took a bodybuilding course by mail. Every week the school would send a special exercise weight to add to my bodybuilding. I didn't improve much—but you should see my mailman!

Famous Strong Men: Atlas, Samson, Hercules, the man in Vaudeville who tears phone books with his bare hands and the man who can open a child-proof aspirin bottle.

"I could kill that man for selling me a corset three sizes too small!"

"Now now, pull yourself together."

FOOD

Isaac Bashevis Singer, seventy-nine, Nobel Laureate, speaking of his diet:

"I did not become a vegetarian for my health. I did it for the health of the chickens."

The modern girl is dressed to kill; and cooks the same way.

TRAMP: What business are you in?
BUM: The food business.
TRAMP: What part?
BUM: The eating part.

"Give me one of those animal crackers."
"If you guess what's in my hand, I'll give you one."
"It's a lion."
"Wrong."
"It's a bear."
"Wrong."
"An elephant?"
"Wrong. What does your mother call your father?"
"Don't tell me it's a louse!"

"I told you to get a domestic turkey."
"I did."
"But there's a bullet in it!"
"I 'spect that was meant for me."

Triumphantly the new bride placed the dessert on the table. It was a rectangular piece of covered pastry about 18 inches long and 4 inches wide. "What is it?" her husband inquired.

"Why darling, can't you see? It's a pie."

"Rather long for a pie, isn't it?"

"Of course not, silly, it's rhubarb."

"This steak is burned. Who said a woman's work is never done?"

Get your hot dogs right here, folks. They're skinless, boneless, harmless, and homeless.

SHE: How do you like the omelet, dear?

HE: If it had a handle on it, it would make a nice tennis racket.

SHE: Would you like something before lunch?

HE: Yeah . . . my breakfast.

It was late in the day and the butcher had already sold all but his last roast from the refrigerator, when a woman came in and ordered a roast. He lifted it onto the scale and told her, "That will be $6.95."

"That's too small, don't you have anything larger?" The woman asked.

The canny butcher returned the roast to the refrigerator, paused a moment, then took it out again. "This one," he announced, "will be $7.50."

"Fine," said the customer, "I'll take both of them."

FOOTBALL

According to *Sports Illustrated,* a journalist visiting the Oakland Raiders' training camp in Santa Rosa, California, had just come from the nearby Jack London Home State Historic Monument. He read the following sample of London's prose to quarterback Ken Stabler:

"'I would rather be ashes than dust! I would rather that my spark should burn out in a brilliant blaze than it should be stifled by dry rot.

"'I would rather be a superb meteor, every atom of me in magnificent glow, than a sleepy and permanent planet. The proper function of man is to live, not to exist. I shall not waste my days in trying to prolong them. I shall use my time.'"

"What does that mean to you?" the newspaperman asked.

"Throw deep," said Stabler.

Now they even talk back to the officials. The ref called off-sides, took the ball and walked off five yards. One of the players said, "You stink."

The ref kept walking another ten yards, put down the ball, and said, "How do I smell from here?"

COACH: And remember—football develops individuality, initiative, and leadership! Now get in there and do as I say.

FRENCH

Dr. John D. Garwood, in *Back to the Basics,* recalls the story of the French taxi driver who once played a joke on Sir Arthur Conan Doyle.

Sir Arthur had been driven from the railroad station to his hotel. When the driver received his fare he said, "Merci, Sir Arthur Conan Doyle."

"How did you know my name?" asked Sir Arthur.

"Sir, I saw in the papers that you were leaving the South of France for Paris. Your hair has been cut by a barber of southern France."

"This is indeed remarkable. Did you have any other evidence?"

"The underside of the right sleeve of your coat appears to be shiny and worn as though it had been moved in writing, while the elbow of the left sleeve appears to be worn as though from leaning on it."

"Go on," urged Sir Arthur, delighted at a man so perceptive. "What else did you see?"

"Well," said the driver, "there was also the fact that your name was on the luggage."

An American tourist in Paris was struggling to use some of his high-school French in a restaurant.

"Garsong," he said, *"je desire consoome royal, et un piece of pang et burr*—no hang it—*une piece of burr*—"

"I'm sorry, sir," said the tactful waiter, "I don't speak French."

"Well," snapped the tourist, "for God's sake, send me someone who can."

GAMBLING

An American tourist, home from China, told of how one night he decided to kill a little time playing poker with three wealthy Chinese. As he spoke no Chinese, and the almond-eyed brothers spoke no English, they decided to get an interpreter. All went quietly for a while, but in due course, the American was dealt a four-card flush and bet a hundred dollars. At this, the Chinese gentleman next to him exclaimed, "Ah moy," which the interpreter explained meant he raised a hundred.

The next Chinese man announced, "Ah foy," and the interpreter said, "He raised you two hundred more."

The third Chinese man grunted, "Ah goy," which the interpreter explained as another hundred raise.

In spite of the competition, the American decided to stay with the pot and drew his one card. Noting that he failed to fill his flush, he cried, "Ah, phooey," at which all the Chinese threw down their hands.

"Nice going, mister," cried the interpreter, slapping him on the back. "Your million-dollar bluff won the pot."

Comedian Joe Frisco used to tell that while playing at the Miami Beach 5 O' Clock Club, he went to the racetrack. As he stood at the $100 window, a guy asked where the $2 window was. Joe barked that he didn't know. The guy snapped, "You will if you stay at that $100 window long enough."

GERMAN

The late Ray Marshall used to like to make up jokes for his friends. One he told often was about the celebrated German detective, Herr Herr. A woman had been killed in a house in Munich. Herr Herr received an anonymous telephone call, informing him of the murder and giving him the address. He and his assistant, Herr Heinz, immediately got on their motorbikes and sped there. Using one of a collection of skeleton keys, made from old skeletons, Herr Herr got into the house. There was blood all over, but no body. Obviously, the corpse had been dismembered and carried away. The great sleuth was baffled. No body in the living room, the dining room, the kitchen, the basement, or any of the seven bedrooms. But presently Herr Heinz found something behind a radiator in the dining room. He held it up.

He said, in triumph, "Here, Herr Herr—her hair!"

GOLF

Tim Conway tells the story of the golfer who was preparing to tee off when the caddy master noticed that his ball was six inches past the tee-off line.

"You've got to move it back," he said.

The man ignored him.

"I said, you've got to move it back," insisted the man. Again the golfer ignored him.

Once more the caddy master spoke. "Please, sir, you've simply got to move your ball back to the starting point."

At which the golfer turned to his partner and said, "Will you tell this guy that this is my second shot."

An avid golfer was at the 18th hole, quietly lining up a putt that would win him an important match, when a funeral procession passed on the road alongside the course. The golfer paused, took off his cap and placed it over his chest until the procession passed from sight. A second golfer who saw him do this said, "That was a wonderful, respectful thing you did."

The first golfer responded, "Well, it would have been our twenty-fifth anniversary today."

Another golfer Conway claims to know had been having a terrible time. First he sliced his ball into some bushes, then into a trap, then across a highway, then finally deep into the woods.

The man went hunting for the ball, but could not seem to find it.

"Why not forget it?" said his friend.

"No, it's my lucky ball," said the golfer.

GOOD NEWS/BAD NEWS

I've got some good news . . . and I've got some bad news . . . First the good news—Your ex-wife is getting married again and you no longer have to send her alimony. Now for the bad news—She's marrying your boss and you're fired.

Art Expert to Collector: Bad news—I regret to tell you that your Van Gogh was not painted by Van Gogh. Now for the good news—It was painted by Picasso.

Airline Pilot to Passengers: Bad news—We have a hijacker aboard the plane. Good news—He wants to go to the French Riviera.

South American Dictator to his People: Bad news—The crops have failed and we have nothing to eat but lizards. Now for the good news: There aren't enough to go around.

Thomas Alva Edison to Mrs. Edison: Good news—I just invented the lightbulb. Bad news—I can't get it to ring.

HISTORY

Not all puns are good news: George S. Kaufman, the revered jester, once claimed—this was during the Spanish Revolution—that he knew a way to get the people of northern Spain out to freedom. He knew a secret mountain trail, he said. "I'm putting all my Basques in one exit."

The line has been attributed to Dorothy Parker, but she did not, in fact, say it. It was uttered by the late Wilson Mizner. While playing cards, he and some friends were interrupted by a man who rushed in, shouting, "Coolidge is dead! Coolidge is dead!"

Mizner looked up at him and asked, "How can they tell?"

HONEYMOON

They had just been married that afternoon and had journeyed to the city to spend their honeymoon. Night had fallen and the bride had already put on the beautiful silken nightie reserved for the occasion and was lounging voluptuously upon the bed. For an hour now, the groom, still fully dressed, had been gazing out the window into the darkness. Impatiently his bride addressed him. "Why don't you undress, John, and come to bed?"

"Never mind me," he replied. "Go ahead and go to sleep. My mother told me this would be the most wonderful night I'd ever see and I don't want to miss a single minute of it."

HORSES

A farmer asked his veterinarian what to do about his horse, which sometimes walked normally and sometimes limped as if seriously lame.

"Next time he's walking normally," the vet advised, "put him up for sale."

"Is your horse balky?"

"No, he's so afraid I'll say 'whoa' and he won't hear me, that he stops once in a while to listen."

"That horse you sold me dropped dead."

"That's funny; he never did that before."

MAN: Do you go horseback riding?
WOMAN: Yes.
MAN: Do you go riding alone?
WOMAN: Yes.
MAN: That's odd; I always take the horse with me.

"Do you ride horseback?"

"On and off."

"Horses neck!"

"Oh, do they?"

A city child in the country for the first time, rushed to his mother and said: "I've seen a man who makes horses. He had one nearly finished when I saw him. He was just nailing on its back feet."

STEVE: Do you have a Racing Form?
WEN: No. I'm just built that way.

My horse was white until I started to chew tobacco.

"I'm taking riding lessons."
"How much a lesson?"
"Two dollars a throw."

"You better take my tip and bet on my horse. In the last race I gave a guy a horse that was sixty to one."
"Did he win?"
"Don't change the subject!!"

"Why do you wear only one spur, cowboy?"
"If one side goes, the other will follow."

I bet on Petticoat to show.

This horse is so slow, instead of timing him with a clock, they used a calendar.

"I ride horseback every day."
"How much time do you spend in the saddle?"
"About half."

HOTELS

I had a lovely room and bath. I don't like to complain but the room was in the Miami Hotel . . . and the bath was at the Biltmore.

It was a nice room with adjoining . . . I couldn't tell what it was because I couldn't get the door open.

Man staggers into the hotel:

MAN: I'm Mr. Smith of Room 22.

CLERK: Impossible, I just took Mr. Smith up.

MAN: You're right. I fell out the window.

HUNTING

"Out of the way, wretch. I'm riding to the hounds."

"Give us a lift; I'm going to the dogs myself."

"Quick! Quick! I just caught three skunks!"

"Eureka!"

"You're telling me!"

"What made you suspect me of shooting ducks?"

"Well, firstly you're on my land with a gun. Secondly, I heard a gun go off and I saw some ducks fall. Thirdly, you've got four ducks in the bag here, and I don't think the ducks flew into the bag and committed suicide."

I had a strange experience while out hunting the other morning. It was thirty below zero, and the lake was frozen. On the lake there were five thousand ducks, with their feet frozen into the ice. I took a shot at one and the whole lot flew up into the air in a body, and took the lake with them!

IGNORANCE

If ignorance is bliss, he ought to die of joy.

You were born in ignorance and you've had a relapse.

IMPERTINENCE

Orson Welles told of a busboy he knew in Ireland who won £5,000 in the Irish Sweepstakes. "Are you going to quit your job now that you're rich?" the busboy was asked. "No," he answered, "but I'm going to be awfully impertinent."

INDIANS

"That Indian was a lawyer."

"Yeah?"

"Yeah, he belonged to the Sue Tribe."

He wears feathers to keep his wigwam.

WHITE MAN: How do you like our city?

INDIAN: Fine! How do you like our country?

We bought New York from the Indians for twenty-four dollars and thirty-two cents—the thirty-two cents was for Bensonhurst.

IN-LAW

He came for the weekend and stayed till the ripe old age of eighty-four.

"They built a swimming pool with diving board at the insane asylum."

"How do they like it?"

"They love it. They are diving all the time. They can't wait till Saturday comes."

"What's going to happen Saturday?"

"They're going to fill it with water."

A madman chased me for three miles and when he caught me he tapped me on the shoulder and said: "Now you chase me."

A man from the asylum calls on the governor to convince him of his sanity. Having received a promise of help in being released, he prepares to leave, saying to the governor, "Say, would you happen to have a piece of toast in your pocket?"

"No, I don't," replied the governor.

"Why do you ask?"

"You see, I'm a poached egg and I want to lie down."

INSULT

"She has an air of culture about her."

"Yeah. Agriculture."

"You belong in a home for idiots."

"Okay, speak to your landlord for me."

An indignant lady barged up to the host of a formal dinner party and said, "I will never enter your house again, sir. Your wife has just grossly insulted me."

"I'm sure there must be some mistake," soothed the host. "What did she say?"

"She called me a whore."

"That's just her way," the husband replied. "I have been out of the Army for thirty years and she still calls me colonel."

INSURANCE

AGENT: You want all your office furniture insured against theft?
BOSS: Yes. All except the clock. Everybody watches that!

"Mr. Jones, how would you like your wife and child to get fifty dollars a week after your death?"

"Very much. Do you supply the wife and child?"

"You say he carried life insurance."
"No, fire insurance."
"Maybe he knew where he was going."

"What is life insurance?"
"It's keeping a man poor all his life so he can die rich."

INTELLIGENCE

HE: It's to be a battle of wits.
SHE: How brave of you to go unarmed.

INTERRUPTION

After being released from a Japanese prison camp in Manila, NBC correspondent Bert Silen began his first broadcast: "As I was saying when I was so rudely interrupted three years and a month ago . . ." —*Time*

INTERVIEW

"Now, I suppose you want to know when I was born?"
"No, just why."

INTRODUCTION

BROWN: "Allow me to present my wife to you."
WHITE: "Many thanks, old man, but I have one."

IRISH

Although much humor has a universal quality and would elicit laughter anywhere on the planet, certain jokes and stories, on the other hand, can be properly interpreted only in their ethnic or geographical contexts. Consider, for example, the story related by Thomas J. O'Hanlon in his brilliant book *The Irish* about the dreadfully congested traffic of Dublin:

A foreign visitor, attempting to find a parking place near the city center, asked a policeman what a single solid yellow line represented.

"It means you can't park there at all."

"Well, what about a solid double yellow line?"

"That means you can't park there at all, at all."

Irish comedian Hal Roach submits the story of Father Hennessey, who went to the hospital to see a fellow named Murphy, who had been struck with a bottle in a public brawl. The priest said, "I'll say a prayer for you." Murphy said, "Don't bother, Father, I'm all right now. I'm getting out of here tomorrow, so say a prayer for the fellow who hit me with the bottle."

O'Brien let his friend Casey borrow his new car to drive to a village dance. He got back about four in the morning. Flannigan said, "How did it go?"

"Fine," Casey said, "we had a great time, but I'm sorry to tell you that I got some water in the carburetor."

"Oh, really?" Flannigan said. "Well, where's the car?"

"In the river," Casey said.

At a certain foreign embassy in Dublin, which has a reputation for being involved more in undercover work than in diplomacy, they sent an agent to a County Kerry town with instructions to make contact with the local secret agent, whose name was Brosnan. On meeting him, he was to whisper the secret passwords: "The grass is green and the cows are brown," before getting down to business.

The agent hurried to the Kerry town in the guise of a tourist, and met a local resident on the street.

"I'm looking for a man called Brosnan," he said.

"Which Brosnan would that be?" asked the local. "You see our town is full of Brosnans. There's Brosnan the grocer and Brosnan the publican and Brosnan the butcher and Brosnan the draper. Sure, me own name is Brosnan."

The visitor was confused but decided he would have to start somewhere if he were to complete his mission. So, in a low voice, he said, "The grass is green and the cows are brown."

"Oh," said the local, "'tis Brosnan the spy you want."

KIDS

A child, who supposedly had gone to bed, began calling downstairs as though in mortal fear.

"There's a spider on the ceiling of my room!"

He yelled it again and again.

His mother called back: "Now, Billy, you're not scared of that spider! You know you're not scared by a spider!"

Silence, for about four beats.

"Then," Billy asked, "what am I doing out here in the hall?"

A mother and father were worrying about their troublesome son. "You aren't a good father," she said. "If you were a good father, you'd take him to the zoo!"

"Oh, no," the father said. "If they want him, they'll have to come and get him."

There were two twin brothers, one a pessimist, the other an optimist. They were about eleven years old. It was Christmas morning. Their parents had decided to teach them a lesson. They gave the pessimist a lot of toys and clothes, but set out a box of horse manure for the optimist.

At 6:00 A.M., the boys rushed downstairs to see what they'd get.

"What'd you get?" the optimist asked, excitedly.

"Oh, phooey," the pessimist said. "I got a model erector set, a battery-operated robot almost as tall as I am, twelve Brooks Brothers shirts, a gross of Matchbox cars, a color TV set, a dozen LP's and a portable hi-fi, two pairs of gym trunks and a bathing suit, and a leather-bound set of Tarzan books."

"What's wrong with that?"

"I can't use the darned erector set because I'm no good with my hands. The batteries in the robot are going to burn out before the day is over. Who wants twelve of those corny Brooks button-downs? Matchbox toy cars are for little kids and older men. On the color TV, the people are always green. Two pairs of gym trunks? They know I can't take gym because of my asthma. Bathing suit? I can't swim. A leather-bound set of Tarzan books is square. Frankly, Bruce, the whole bit put me down. What'd you get, anyhow?"

The optimist produced his odoriferous box. "I think I got a pony!" he cried happily, "but I can't find it!"

A small boy woke up in a terrible state on a Sunday morning. He hit his sister, kicked his tricycle, and refused to eat his oatmeal. His mother wheedled, coaxed, and begged him to eat it.

"You're a five-year-old boy," she said, "you *must* eat it. If you don't, God is going to be angry."

"I won't!"

"I tell you, God will be angry."

The tot went upstairs to brush his teeth, take off his pajamas, and change into his best Sunday suit to go to Sunday School. While he was changing, a terrible thunderstorm arose. The house was struck by lightning.

Trembling, the boy got his clip-on bow tie in place and went downstairs to the kitchen. "I never thought," he said to his mother, "God would make such a big deal over a little bowl of oatmeal!"

The little girl, just home from Sunday School, asked her father when her baby brother would be able to talk. The little boy was eight or nine months old.

"He won't be able to talk until he's about two years old," the father said.

"It was much better when they were writing the Bible," she said.

"What makes you think that?"

"They told us in Sunday School. In the Book of Job, it says, 'Job cursed the day he was born.'"

A noisy little girl was home from school.

"What did you do today?"

"Well, we did some reading, and then we ate lunch, and then we had pottery baking, and then we looked at some nice pictures from the Metropolitan, and then we went to the gym."

"I see. Were you a good girl? Didn't talk too much?"

"Oh, no!"

"Are you sure?"

"You should have heard me, I was so silent!"

According to a camp counselor, this letter arrived at a boy's house:

Dear Mom and Dad:
Please send some food. It is nice here, and my new friends are just fine. They come from all over . . . there is one boy who comes from Weehawken. But for Heaven's SAKE, please send some food. I am starving to death. All they give us here is breakfast, lunch, and dinner.

Yours,
Sidney

Grandmother, very old and sweet-natured, sat most of the time at a sunny window in her room reading her Bible. The grandchildren often took their little friends in to see her. After one of these visits a small boy asked:

"Why is your grandmother always reading, Phillip?"

"She's crammin' for her finals!"

"Tell me, son," the anxious mother said, "what did your father say when you told him you'd wrecked his new Corvette?"

"Shall I leave out the swear words?" the son asked.

"Of course."

"He didn't say anything."

"Junior," the old woman shouted to her grandson, "when that terrible Jones boy threw stones at you, why didn't you come and tell me instead of throwing them back at him?"

"Oh, what good would that do?" said the boy. "You couldn't hit the side of a barn."

A mother was trying to interest her five-year-old in the beauties of nature. "As we walk out into the countryside on a freezing winter's day," she said, "and look about us, what do we see on every hand?"

"Gloves," answered the child.

Grandparents are people who come to the house, spoil the children, and then go home.

"You're crying!"

"I'm not crying—my eyes are perspiring!"

"What are you drawing, honey?"

"That's God . . ."

"But no one knows what God looks like."

"They will now."

"Where's little sister?"

"In the next room."

"See what she's doing, and whatever it is, tell her to stop it."

L.A.

Los Angeles really knows how to make you feel at home. I heard a story recently about a young couple living in Van Nuys who had just gotten married, received a lot of wonderful presents, and settled down in their new home. One morning in the mail they received two box-seat tickets to the Hollywood Bowl with a note that said, *"Guess who sent these?"*

When the night for the show came they went to the Bowl, had a marvelous time, and returned home late in the evening. When they opened the front door they discovered that their house had been cleaned out. Every present was gone, everything of value.

On a bare table in the dining room they found a note that said, *"Now you know!"*

LABOR DAY

Day of Daze

Sure they made the open highway large
Enough to be too small
When the cars jam-pack it tightly 'til
They've slowed down to a crawl.
And they set gas stations carefully
So they'd be out of sight
When tires go flat or fuel tanks dry,
Or children cry at night—
Then, they sprinkled it with road dust
Just to add to all the gloom
When you hit the crowded beaches where
There's only standing room—
And to try it on the public
And find out how hair turns gray:
Sure they picked the hottest time of year
And called it LABOR DAY!

—Helen G. Sutin

Chickens

At last we know why a chicken crosses the road:
To lay an egg
For the government to buy
To keep the price
Of eggs too high

I see where the last sweat shop in the United States finally closed last week. There's just no market for sweat these days.

LANDLORD

The tenant of a new house was complaining to his landlord about its condition.

"It's disgraceful! Why, there's grass coming up through the floorboards in the drawing room!"

"Oh, we'll soon settle that," said the landlord. "I'll send a man round with a lawnmower."

LANDLORD: This castle has stood for six hundred years. Not a stone has been touched, nothing altered, nothing replaced.
VISITOR: They must have the same landlord we have.

"I'm the landlord and I want the rent."

"Some nerve! That's why we left the other place."

CALLER: Excuse me, madam, but do you believe in the hereafter?

LADY: Of course I do.

CALLER: Well, I'm here after the rent.

"I tell you I must have at least part of the rent. I've got some bills to pay."

"Then take this ten dollars and pay your electric bill."

"My landlord ought to be hung."

"Not hung, my boy, hanged."

"I say hung. Hanging is too good for him."

There were fourteen Russians, with three that could speak English. The other eleven did the talking.

"Ah! *Mai oui!*"

"May we what?"

"May we have a drink?"

"Why don't you learn how to talk English?"

"It's taken me thirty years to learn to say 'You all,' and I can't learn to say 'Youse guys' in two weeks."

Gene Lees, editor of *Jazzletter,* and one of the nation's better lyricists, wrote to me recently to share a couple of examples of his sister's superior sense of humor:

I have said for years people like you—and my sister, Pat, about whom more in a moment—have the odd ability to hear things sideways. It is a matter of hearing not puns but LITERALLY what language says, of interpreting LITERALLY something that someone else says. For example, some years ago in Toronto, I heard some weird grinding noise in my car, and visited the GM dealer to find out what it was. The mechanic said my air conditioner was shot. I asked how much a new one would cost. He said—this was 1972— that it would run about $350. I got bugged and told him to simply disconnect it. Driving home, I muttered to my sister, "Jesus, I can buy a room air conditioner for that."

She said, "Yeah, but the price of the cord'd kill you."

Another time she hit the brake of her car to avoid running down a very pregnant woman who had stepped into the street. My sister leaned out her window and said, "Hey, lady, you can also get knocked *down*."

LAS VEGAS

There's a method for going back home from Las Vegas with a small fortune. Go there with a large fortune.

LATENESS

SHE: Meet me at the library tonight at seven o'clock.
HE: All right; what time will *you* be there?

I'm always late. I never do anything on time except buy furniture.

The dealer hires a boy to be at his shop every morning at three o'clock to deal with the truck farmers. He himself gets there at eight. One night after a late party the dealer decided to check up on the boy, and dropped by his shop at 2:30 in the morning. Three o'clock came—no boy; 3:05, no boy. At 3:07 the boy hurried in.

"So?" yelled the boss. "Bankers' hours, eh?"

LAW

The warden of a penitentiary was looking over the new arrivals. Among them was a small, seedy-looking individual who seemed to take his situation very hard. He sighed so deeply that the warden asked, "What's the matter, son?"

"It's that sentence the judge gave me," mourned the new arrival. "I just can't do all that time."

"How much are you doing?" inquired the warden.

"Life!"

"Well," said the warden, helpfully, "just do what you can of it."

During a court trial a pompous Kentucky colonel was being questioned by the district attorney. Unable to weaken the testimony of the old fellow, the prosecutor first tried ridicule, then sarcasm.

"They call you 'Colonel,'" he sneered. "In what regiment, and in what war, pray tell, were you ever a colonel?"

"Well, suh," drawled the witness, "it's like this. The 'Colonel' in front of my name is just like the 'Honorable' in front of yours. It's purely complimentary—and doesn't mean a thing."

When a shoplifter was caught stealing a ring in a jewelry store, he pleaded with the manager, "Please don't call the police. I'll be glad to pay for it."

When the manager presented him with the bill, he said, "That's a little more than I'd planned to spend. Could you show me something less expensive?"

A man arrested for murder bribed a not-very-bright fellow on the jury with a hundred dollars to hold out for a verdict of manslaughter. The jury was out a long time and finally came in with a verdict of manslaughter. The man later rushed up to the dishonest juror and said, "I'm much obliged to you, my friend. Did you have a hard time?"

"Oh, yes," said the dope. "A hell of a time. The other eleven wanted to acquit ya."

A young lawyer attended the funeral of a financier.

A friend arrived late, sat down beside the lawyer, and whispered, "How far has the service gone?"

The lawyer nodded toward the clergyman and whispered back, "Just opened for the defense."

Old-time comedian Willie Howard, a man with a long and mournful face, did a famous sketch in the Ziegfield Follies of the mid-thirties in which he played a judge. An hysterical woman rushed into court with complaints about her husband.

She began to shout the instant she got on stage. The first word was *husband!*—which was followed by many incoherent phrases, such as "beat me up," "hit my kids with sticks," "kicked the dog," "tried to choke the cat," "said I'd hidden his booze," "punched the mailman in the nose," "threw out all my copies of *True Confessions,*" "drank a whole half-pint of bourbon," and "told my mother to pack!"

This went on for at least three minutes, during which Judge Willie looked alternately solemn, concerned, and sympathetic, and kept saying things (with his usual straight face) such as, "Is that so?," "Hmmm," and "Why, that's shocking."

The female character continued to rave for another few minutes. Howard remained silent all through the tirade. When she stopped, he let fifteen seconds elapse before he spoke:

"Tell me, madam, who's got the automobile now?"

A none-too-bright Mafia hoodlum was on trial. Told by the court clerk to hold up his right hand, he responded by hoisting a left. "Mr. Moretti," said the clerk, "I told you to hold up your right hand."

"If it please da court," said the hood, "I'm left-handed."

A man about to take an oath as trial witness in an English court suddenly asked to be excused.

"My wife," he said, "is due to conceive this afternoon, and I would like to be there."

The presiding justice said, "Sir, I think you've got that wrong. You must mean that your wife is about to be delivered of a child. But, whether I am right or you are right, I certainly think you should be there."

A bedraggled individual heatedly denied that he was intoxicated when the arresting officer testified that he had found the prisoner lying in the street.

"Very well," retorted the versatile judge, "you're fined for parking more than six inches from the curb."

"What is your age?" the intimidating magistrate asked. "And remember, you are under oath."

"Twenty-one years and some months," the woman replied.

"Be specific," the magistrate urged. "How many months?"

"One hundred and eight."

NO SWIMMING, read the sign posted next to the small pond in the park. A patrolman came walking by, and noticed a man swimming about in the water.

"Hey, you," the officer cried, "don't you see that sign? I'm going to arrest you as soon as you come out of there."

The man began laughing at the cop and told him, "I'm not coming out—I'm committing—I'm committing suicide!"

Whether a story is offensive to a particular ethnic group often depends entirely on who is telling it. If an Irishman told the following story, few Jews would find it amusing, but in the hands of a master storyteller like Myron Cohen, it's amusing.

A Mr. Garfinkel happened to be visiting a popular country club and strolled out on the grass of the golf course just as a member was teeing off. The man's drive hit Garfinkel squarely in the head.

"What do you think you're doing?" the injured man shouted to the surprised golfer. "You can't get away with carelessness like that. I'm going to sue you for five thousand dollars."

"But," protested the golfer, "I said fore."

"I'll take it," Garfinkel said.

A: What is statutory rape?
B: Raping a statue.

LAZY

That fellow is so lazy he staggers home and pretends he's drunk so his wife will put him to bed.

He could turn his head completely around . . . from looking for work.

She's so lazy she puts popcorn in the pancakes so they'll turn over by themselves.

"I'd like to get a horse to do part of my work."
"Why don't you get a jackass and let him do all of it?"

I need to sleep ten hours, but eleven feels so good I usually sleep fourteen.

"He's so lazy that yesterday he found a gold watch and he threw it away."
"He found a gold watch and threw it away?"
"Yeah, it wasn't wound."

"How is it that your uncle is always sitting at the window?"
"Well, somebody has to look out for the family."

LIAR

He doesn't lie exactly. Let's say he handles the truth economically.

A lawyer was questioning a farmer about the truthfulness of a neighbor.

"Wal," said the farmer, "I wouldn't exactly say he was a liar, but I tell ye, when it comes time to feed his hogs, he has to git somebody else to call 'em for him."

An oil well is a hole in the ground, owned by a liar.

"There's only one thing that saves you from being a bare-faced liar."

"What?"

"Your mustache."

A truthful woman is one who doesn't lie about anything except her age, weight, and her husband's salary.

A man from the East was telling an Irishman in Cincinnati that Boston was bigger than his town. The Irishman said, "I believe you, sir . . . but I believe you're lying."

LIGHT VERSE

Ever since at the age of six I discovered a book of humorous verse for children I've been addicted to the form, both as reader and writer. When I attended Drake University in 1941–42, on a journalism scholarship, one of my assignments was to cover sports for the school newspaper. That required me to attend what I still think is the most astonishing football game ever played, in which Drake was soundly defeated by Washington U. What was wild about the game was that it took place not just in a heavy rain—that's not a particularly newsworthy factor—but the heaviest downpour I've ever seen. The few thousand people who attended must have done so in the hope that at some point the rain would stop. But it did just the opposite; it kept getting worse. It was very difficult to even see the players on the field and close to impossible to figure out where the ball should be placed after each down because the field resembled what it had become, a six-inch-deep muddy pool in which no yard lines at all were visible.

It seemed pointless to try to report the facts of such a game in the conventional way, so I resorted to the following method:

'Twas a rainy autumn evening, and a goodly crowd was there

Which well nigh drowned as torrents formed Niagaras in the air.

Oh, the boys who led the cheering heard it turn to croak and cough,

And when the team picked up five yards they had to scrape it off.

For the mud was on the football, and a dozen times the huddle

Had to be detoured because someone near drowned beneath a puddle.

Yes, they stumbled and they fumbled, and they couldn't see the ball.

Why, they gained less with the end-around than the Australian crawl.

The referee had troubles on the slipp'ry, swishy sward,

Three times he blew the whistle, and declared "Man overboard!"

The cheerers wetly shouted as the finish nearer drew,

"Yeah boat, yeah boat, water we gonna dew?"

But the Bears splashed to a touchdown, to the Bulldogs' great chagrin,

Though the score might have been different if the tide had not come in.

For there was a crucial moment in the second half, you know,

When the ball was on the twenty—drown two and three to go.

A center plunge—a fumble—a pile-up—and a shout!

Six men fell in a puddle, but only five came out.

Oh, they're looking still for Harvey, they're looking still for Jim,

For it seems the lad went in the game, but never learned to swim.

The Bulldogs' victory ship was up the creek without a rudder
But we'll be kind to all the boys; each man is someone's
mudder.

A rhyme from the skilled pen of Morris Bishop:

A scholar annoys Syracuse
By pouring libations to Zeus,
And thunder replies
From radiant skies,
Which is thrilling, but no special use.

More from Morris Bishop:

A ghoulish old fellow of Kent
Encrusted his wife in cement.
    Said he, with a leer,
    "I was careful, my dear,
To follow your natural bent."

Another dumb poem, but one I'm rather fond of. It may appro-
priately be introduced during hay fever season:

I sneezed a sneeze into the air;
It fell to earth, I know not where,

But hard and cold were the looks of those
In whose vicinity I snooze.

I often pause and wonder,
At Time's peculiar ways.
Nearly all our famous men
Were born on holidays.

The birds are flying South,
The days are getting chill.
If taxes haven't busted you
Then Christmas surely will.

Ogden Nash, the poet, once wrote one of his rambling rhymes in which he told how to go down to the beach and throw rocks at sea birds.

"I do not ever like to leave one tern unstoned," he said.

Here's a dumb little verse of unknown origin and long circulation. For some reason it always makes me laugh:

Mary had a little lamb,
A lobster and some prunes.

A chocolate shake, a piece of pie,
And then some macaroons.

It made the naughty waiters grin
To see her order so,
And when they carried Mary out,
Her face was white as snow.

The late Samuel Hoffenstein, genial author of *Poems in Praise of Practically Nothing,* is remembered by his friends for a couplet:

My heart leapt up when I beheld
A friend of mine named Katzenfeld.

Abe Burrows, who started his writing career by working for the old *Duffy's Tavern* show on radio and later became a comedian, playwright, and play doctor, used to have a number of parodies of clichéd popular songs that he performed at parties at the demand of other guests. He later recorded them for Decca. One was called "The Hospital Song":

I may be sick in the hospital,
But I'm not sick of you.
I think about you through all the tape and all the bandage;
I think about you every minute I can manage.
I may be stuck with adhesive tape,
But I'm still stuck on you.

Oh, honey dear,
When I get out of here,
Please let's be
As close as Doctor Kildare
And Doctor Gillespie:
I may be sick in the hospital,
But I'm not sick of—
No, I'm not sick of—
I'm not sick of
YOU!

Abe wrote many such songs. For a time he appeared in night-clubs. One number he wrote was "You Put a Piece of Carbon Paper Under Your Heart, and Gave Me Just a Copy of Your Love." Many of his songs were performed at the home of Frank and Lynn Loesser. (Loesser, it need hardly be said, was the composer and lyricist of *Guys and Dolls,* as well as many other musicals.) One that Abe recorded was a tribute to man's ability to get off the ground. As nearly as I can remember it went as follows:

Shapiro invented
The auto-gyro—
Cohen made the telephone;
But the greatest invention
That I've ever seen
Was Levene and his flying machine.
Up, up, up he goes,
Into glorious flight!
Did you ever see Levene

In his flying machine?
My God! What a horrible sight!

It isn't likely that Abe made much money from these songs, but he delighted his friends with them; we used to call for them over and over.

Take back that heart you gave me
The angry Prep girl cried
The butcher gave her liver
And she was satisfied.

Here lies the body of Old Sam Jones
Resting beneath these polished stones
Her name was Brown instead of Jones
But Brown won't rhyme with polished stones
And she won't know if it's Brown or Jones.

Early to bed and early to rise
And your girl goes out with other guys.

Mary had a parrot tame,
She killed it in her rage.

Because when Mary's boyfriend came,
The parrot told her age.

She passed.
I saw.
And smiled!
She turned
And smiled
An answer
To my smile.
I wonder
If she, too
Could know
Her underwear
Hung down
A Mile.

Give me a sentence with the word Diabetes.
Look out for Yale, the Captain cried,
They're aiming to defeat us,
And all their football team has sworn,
They'll either diabetes.

Make me a child again, just for tonight,
Once said a Scotchman and Scotchmen are right.

I am leaving tonight on a train for Kildare,
Oh, make me a child and I'll travel half fare.

Under the shedding chestnut tree,
Even as you and I.
With a hunk of bunk
And chunk of junk,
You're a better man than I am Old Black Joe.

Little Rollo full of glee,
Pushed his Papa into the Sea,
Mother said with look malicious,
You naughty brat,
You'll kill the fishes.

Rub-a-dub-dub,
Three men in a tub . . .
Crowded way to take a bath.

There was a young lady from Lynn,
Who was so exceedingly thin,
That when she essayed,
To drink lemonade,
She slipped through the straw and fell in!

There was a young lady from Trent,
Who said she knew what it meant,
When men asked her to dine,
She had cocktails and wine,
She knew what it meant, but she went.

Red lips parted, teeth of white,
Waist encircled with his right,
Glimpse of Heaven! Ecstacies!
When damn the luck, he had to sneeze.

Let poets sing their lilting songs,
And gaily smite the lyre.
Give me the man that can whistle when,
He's fixing a flat tire.

Three's a crowd and there were three,
He, the lamp, and lovely she.
Two is company, and no doubt,
That is why the lamp went out.

It was just the other day,
In a fortune-telling place,
A pretty maiden ready my mind
And then she slapped my face.

This poem is written in Iambic Speedometre.

Little Josie, quite distrait,
Fell into the fire grate;
Who'd have thought that little Josie
Could make the room so nice and cozy!

LIMERICKS

What Could Be Ha
There was a young man from Fla
Who was necking a girl in a Ca.
Then cried he in glee,
"I never did see
A place where the women were Ta."

One of my own:

There was a young man who ate lamp chops
When he wasn't frequenting lamp shops
He pulled down a shade
And sharpened his blade
And went and had dinner at Longchamps.

Si went to the circus one day
Resolved to get in without pay;
He crawled under the tent
No one knows where he went
For the elephants thought he was hay.

LINCOLN

As a boy, Lincoln worked in a quicksilver mine and was later promoted to section chief in the plant where they processed the quicksilver into mercury. Although it's never been officially recorded . . . he was probably the first Lincoln-Mercury dealer in the world.

I always honored Lincoln's Birthday. Every year I sent Raymond Massey a telegram.

LOAN

A: Loan me five dollars, will you?
B: Sorry, but I have only four dollars and seventy-five cents.
A: Well, give me that. I'll trust you for the other quarter.

A proud mother walked into one of the leading "Small Monthly Payments Interest on the Unpaid Balance Only" establishments, clutching a small monthly payment. She placed it on the Kredit Kounter contentedly.

"Here," she said, "the final payment on our baby carriage."

"And how is the baby?" asked the friendly clerk.

"Fine," she said, "just fine. He's getting married next week."

Smith and Jones, Ltd., received a letter:

"We are very much surprised that the money we have demanded so often has not yet arrived."

They replied shortly and to the point: "You do not need to wonder; we have not yet sent the money."

LONE RANGER

A cowboy struts into a bar and asks, "Who owns that big white horse outside?"

The Lone Ranger stands up and says, "I do. What's wrong with him this time?"

The cowboy looks him in the eye and says, "Nothin', but you left your Injun running."

LOVE

Line from an old Eddie Cantor film:

Let me run my fingers through your hair. There are no towels in the bathroom.

The "Advice to the Lovelorn" editor of a daily newspaper received this query from a young man: "Please tell me why a girl closes her eyes when a fellow kisses her."

The editor replied: "Let me see a recent picture of yourself and maybe I can tell you."

The old-fashioned girls would take two drinks and go out like a light; now they take two drinks—and out goes the light.

MAN: Suppose an ugly man tried to kiss you, what would you do?
WOMAN: Just try it and see.

"What do you want to see her about?"
"About five o'clock."

Imagine, it says here that last year over twenty thousand girls were lost. I couldn't find one.

"Do you drink?"
"No."
"Do you smoke?"
"No."
"Do you neck?"
"No."
"What do you do?
"I tell lies."

"The way she dresses I can't see what keeps her warm."
"You ain't supposed to."

She's an interesting girl . . . she was taken once for Dolly Parton, and twice for grand larceny.

"You say you were out very late last night?"
"Yes. Mother was so angry she made me go to bed without breakfast."

"I used to be ashamed of the way I behaved."
"What did you do?"
"I got over being ashamed."

GIRL: Would you call it mental telepathy if we were both thinking of the same thing?
GUY: No, just good luck.

"Will you love me when I'm old and gray?"
"Of course I do!"

"My husband stays out until five in the morning. What would you do in my place?"

"Let's go over to your place and I'll show you."

If I ever get married it'll be a companionate marriage.
No kidding.

He wrote his girlfriend a letter every day for two years . . . and she married the mailman.

She's a girl you would love to take home to Mother . . . you could trust your father.

HE: Well, good-bye, dear, I'm going out of town for a few days. What's your phone number? I'll call you when I get back.
GERTIE: Plaza 2121, and if a man answers, you stayed away too long.

A: What kind of man do you like?
B: Kind? Are there kinds?

A: Sure, for instance, do you like overpowering men?
B: Sure, if I can find one weak enough.

BOB: I love Beatrice more than I can tell.
SLOB: Neither would I.

In the old days you could write anything you wanted to a girl. But now you might just as well start your letter "Sweetheart and Gentlemen of the Jury!"

DAN: Boy, I went out the other night with a platinum blonde that would knock your eye out.
TONY: What happened?
DAN: I asked her for a kiss and she knocked my eye out!

HE: I'd go to the end of the world for you.
SHE: Yeah, but would you *stay* there?

It was Love. Blind, unreasoning love. The kind that comes to a woman only once . . . in a while.

HE: You gave me your hand. . . . You gave me your heart. . . . Now won't you give me your lips?
SHE: Hey, what are you doing . . . piece work?

"If you refuse me, I will die!" he said.
She refused him, and sure enough sixty years later he died.

Gee, that's a wonderful number. *(Fiddle with piano.)* Sorta reminds you of . . . old flames. I heard from an old flame of mine the other night, Joe. Would you believe it? We hadn't seen each other in eight years, but she's still carrying the torch. What? No, not for *me* . . . she's a welder at Lockheed.

"His interest in her was purely paternal."
"Paternal?"
"Yes. He wanted to become a father."

LSD

The drummer took a drink of it and then he ran over to the wall and drew a big picture of a car. The rest of us took a drink and we got in the car and he drove us home.

MAGIC

STOOGE: You're a magician, huh? Make me disappear.
MAGICIAN: Don't worry; I'm working on it.

(A button on vest is fixed up with a long length of thread with weight on end. Appear to remove the button.) "You don't want this anymore, do you?" (Hold it out, let go, and it flies back in place, as stooge makes a grab for it.)

"Take a card . . . tear it in half . . . now tear it in quarters . . . now tear it in one eighths . . . now in sixteenths . . .
(As you go on this way, the smaller you tell the person to tear the card, the funnier it gets. . . . When you see that it is getting impossible to continue:)
"What's the matter, no guts?"

Tie a string inside your pants from bottom of one pocket to the other so when you pull out first pocket, it may be pulled back in by pulling second pocket out.

Use a pack of cards and ask someone in the audience, or one of the musicians or the leader, to pick a card . . . then, replace it in the deck and tell him to shuffle the deck. Then, as you spell out his name, the last card is supposed to be his, as you say: "Your card is the (whatever card you wish to mention)." Naturally, he'll say "no" . . . then, you throw the entire deck of cards up in the air or out in the audience as you say: "Ah, the hell with it!"

Get a deck of cards, all the cards the same. (You can pick this type of deck up at any magic store). Repeat the procedure of having a card picked from the deck. Then, you tell the person to hold the card up in full view of the audience and you tell him the card. Naturally, he'll say you're right. Then, you turn around and show the audience the deck, spreading the cards, as you say: "You're damn right it's correct, every card in the deck is a (whatever the card is)."

MANNERS

A bird in the hand is bad table manners.

The nine-year-old New York boy won his first literary prize, for an essay entitled "Manners." We agree wholeheartedly with the judges that his entry had special merit, and we reprint it in full:

"I have good manners. I say good night and good morning and hello and good-bye, and when I see dead things lying around the house I bury them."

MARRIAGE

Some jokes sound as if they're going to be vulgar but happily they fool you. In this connection I think of the story of a woman who was making a cross-country trip on a train. Something went wrong with the car's heating system and before long the passenger was suffering desperately from extreme cold in her upper berth. Finally, maddened with discomfort, she leaned over and spoke to the male passenger who was occupying the lower berth.

"Excuse me," she said, "but are you as cold as I am?"

"I'm colder," he said, "something's wrong with this damned train."

"Well," the woman said, "would you mind getting me an extra blanket?"

Suddenly the man got an odd look in his eye and said, "You

know, since we're both so miserably cold, let me ask you a direct question. Would you like to pretend that we're married?"

"Well, actually," the woman said, "yes, I would."

"Good," the fellow said, "then get up and get it yourself."

Hollywood marriages are evidently losing their reputation for brevity. One producer liked one of his wives so well, he decided to hold her over for a second week.

A now classic story concerns the suburban matron who telephoned the builder of her house to complain about vibrations that shook the structure just as a train passed by two blocks away. "Ridiculous," he told her. "I'll be out to check it."

"Wait till a train comes through," said the woman when the builder arrived. "It almost shakes me out of bed. Just lie down there yourself. You'll see."

The builder accepted her challenge. He had just stretched himself out on the bed when the woman's husband came home. "What are you doing on my wife's bed?" the husband shouted.

The builder said, "Would you believe I'm waiting for a train?"

"My wife is always after me for money. Always. Day in, day out. She's always after me, always pestering," so spoke one tired salesman.

"What does she do with it?"

"Who knows? I never give her any."

A: Is his wife talkative?

B: Is she? He had lockjaw for six weeks before he even found out about it.

Two expectant fathers were pacing the floor in the waiting room. "What lousy luck," one said. "This had to happen during my vacation."

"You think you have tough luck?" the other said. "I'm on my honeymoon."

The customer goes to the tombstone man and says he wants something for his wife's grave.

"But didn't you buy one here about eight years ago?"

"Yes, but I remarried."

"Congratulations!"

A man came into work one morning in good spirits but with two black eyes. His coworker spotted him and asked, "What happened to you? Get in a fight?"

"Naw," said the man, "the little woman got mad because I used my paycheck to buy something for the house."

"What in the world did you buy that made her so mad?"

"Just ten rounds of drinks."

A man was sleeping peacefully in bed next to his wife when all of a sudden she shook him and asked, "If I were to die, would you get married again?"

"What kind of question is that to ask at this time of night?" the man mumbled.

"Would you get married again?" the wife persisted.

"Yeah, I suppose so," her husband admitted.

"Would you live in this house?"

"This is a ridiculous conversation," he protested drowsily, "but it's a nice house, why shouldn't we live here?"

"Would you give her my car?"

"Why not, it's practically brand new. Of course I'd give her your car."

The wife pushed on. "What about my golf clubs?"

"No," her husband answered quickly.

"Why not?"

"Because," said the man, "she's left-handed."

As the reader may know, I could easily do without about 99 percent of the "dirty jokes" I've ever heard. But occasionally you encounter one that is funny without being too pictorial or gross:

An unhappily married gentleman came home one evening to find his wife hurriedly packing her bags.

"Where are you going?" he asked.

"To Las Vegas," she said.

"Why?"

"Because," she said, "I've just found out, from a good authority, that I can make four hundred dollars for what I give you around here for free."

"That's fantastic," he said and immediately got out a few suitcases of his own.

"What are you doing?" his wife asked.

"I'm going to Las Vegas myself," he said. "I've got to see how you're going to live on eight hundred dollars a year."

Popular wisecrack of the 1920s: "I love my wife, but oh you kid!"

I love my kids, but oh you wife.

"That's the third night straight she's been out with her husband."

"Must be a publicity stunt."

Let's get married, and see how long we can stand each other.

"Sir, I wish to marry your daughter."

"Can you divorce her in the manner to which she is accustomed?"

"The man I marry must be a hero."

"He'd have to be."

I often wondered where my husband spent his nights. When the curfew came along I went home and there he was!

OLD GENTLEMAN *(bewildered at an elaborate wedding):* Are you the bridegroom?

YOUNG MAN: No, sir. I was eliminated in the semifinals.

SHE: Are you secretly married to her?

HE: No. She knows it.

There are just two kinds of people who make foolish marriages—men and women.

"What's the matter with my wife?"

"I think her dinner disagreed with her."

"I certainly admire its courage."

As Lebowitz opened the door, he heard Lena's gasps. There she lay breathing her last.

"You're just in time, Mischa—I'm dying—and now that I'm dying, I've got something to tell you—I've been unfaithful to you."

"I know it," answered Lebowitz. "Why do you think I poisoned you?"

MOVIE DIRECTOR: Unmarried?

APPLICANT: Twice.

"You deceived me before we were married. You told me you were well off."

"I was, but I didn't know it."

We have no divorces here, but a lot of husbands have taken up golf.

"Do your children live with you?"
"No, they're not married yet."

"For crying out loud; how did you get the new fur coat?"
"For crying out loud."

"Did you sew that button on my coat?"
"I couldn't find the button, so I sewed up the button hole."

MAN *(In prison garb):* Hide me quick! I'm an escaped wife-beater.
HENPECKED HUSBAND: Hide you nothing! I'll hire you!

A little advice to men. Never go around with a married woman unless you can go two rounds with her husband.

"So you married me for my money?"
"If I did, I earned it."

"If a man steals he'll live to regret it."
"You stole a kiss from me before we were married."
"You heard what I said."

HUSBAND: Let's go out and have some fun this evening.
WIFE: Okay, and please leave the light on in the hallway if you get home before I do.

He found a job . . . but his wife wouldn't take it.

He's the light of her life. She won't let him go out.

SHE: Why does a woman take a man's name when she gets married?
HE: Why not? She takes everything else he has!

My father married my mother . . . my aunt married my uncle . . . my grandfather married my grandmother. . . . Why should
I marry a stranger?

JUDGE: Were you present when the trouble started?
DEFENDANT: Your honor, I was a witness at their wedding.

HARRY: Are you still engaged to June?
JERRY: No.
HARRY: Good. How did you ever manage to get rid of her?
JERRY: I married her.

"Good morning, madam. I'm from the gas company. I understand there's something in the house that won't work?"

"Yes, he's upstairs."

JONES: You must feel badly about your very best friend running
off with your wife.
SMITH: Yes, I'll sure miss him.

My wife treats me like a Greek god. Every meal she places a burnt offering before me!

"I can truthfully say that I've never deceived my wife."
"That's a good record."
"Of course, I've tried."

Never let your husband do the housework . . . he may develop womanly traits and want to be the boss of the house.

"She's been lying to me. She said she was with Helen last night."
"Well, maybe she was."
"No. I was with Helen last night."

"Do you ever read in bed?"
"No . . . but I often lie awake listening to a lecture."

HE: If you marry me I'll take out a big insurance policy so you'll be well provided for.
SHE: Yes, but suppose you don't die.

"Mother, dear, what is an angel?"

"My darling, it is a little girl with wings, who flies away up in the skies."

"But Mother, yesterday I heard Daddy telling the maid that she was an angel. Will she fly away?"

"Yes, my darling, she'll fly the first thing in the morning."

SHE: I kicked you out last night, didn't I?
HE: Yes, but I came back to show you there were no hard feelings.

HE: If you refuse me, I shall never love another woman.
SHE: And if I accept you, does it still hold good?

Dear Editor:
Do you think a father of 50 should marry again?
Reply: Certainly not. Fifty children ought to be enough for any man.

BRIDE: What's the best way to protect a wedding ring?
MOTHER: Dip it in dishwater three times a day.

"How long have they been married?"

"About five years."

"Did she make him a good wife?"

"No, but she made him a good husband."

Try complimenting your wife, even if it does frighten her at first.

Marriage begins when he sinks in your arms and it ends with your arms in the sink.

HE: Darling, how could you buy another new dress? We're broke.

SHE: I'm terribly sorry, dear, but the devil just tempted me.

HE: But don't you think you should have discouraged him?

SHE: I tried to, dear. I said, "Satan, get thee behind me," and the next thing you know I hear a whispered voice say, "That dress is a dream from the back!"

HE: Don't forget, you took me for better or for worse.

SHE: Yeah, but you're worse than I took you for!

"You mean to say," asked the judge of the defendant, "that you threw your wife out of the second-story window through forgetfulness?"

"Yes, sir," replied the defendant. "We used to live on the ground floor and I forgot we moved."

He was a widower, getting along in years, and no longer handsome.

"You are the fifth girl I have proposed to without avail," he said.

"Well," said the young woman, "maybe you'll have better luck if you wear one."

He didn't like his wife very much so he had forty-two kids and tried to lose her in the crowd.

HE: When are you thinking of getting married?
SHE: Constantly.

STEVE *(to man in audience)*: Where's your wife tonight?
MAN: She's home.

STEVE: Folks, you've just witnessed a scene from the movie: *Fat Chance.*

A: Darling, the maid has burned the eggs. Wouldn't you be satisfied with a couple of kisses for breakfast?
B: Maybe you're right. Bring her in.

A girl may wear a golf outfit when she can't play golf, and a bathing suit when she can't swim, but when she puts on a wedding gown she means business.

I'm going to propose to my girl in a locked garage, so she can't back out.

A woman lecturer asked: "Is there any man in the audience who would let his wife be slandered and say nothing? If so, stand up."

A meek little man rose to his feet.

The lecturer glared at him. "Do you mean to say you would let your wife be slandered and say nothing?" she cried.

"Oh, I'm sorry," he apologized, "I thought you said 'slaughtered.'"

SHE: When we get married I'm going to cook, sew, darn your socks, and lay out your pipe and slippers. What more can any man ask than that?
HE: Nothing, unless he is evil-minded.

SHE: Engaged? But that means marriage . . . if we ever did get married, how could we manage? You have nothing. How would we live?
HE: Don't worry; I'm sure something would come along.
SHE: Yeah, and we'd have to feed that, too!

How did you meet your wife?

I won my wife on a TV quiz show . . . she wore a big white dress. I thought she was a refrigerator.

DENNY: What makes Jack look so worried and worn out?
PENNY: Oh, he's been contesting his wife's will.
DENNY: His wife's will? I didn't know she was dead.
PENNY: She isn't.

JUDGE: Will you tell the court what passed between you and your wife during the quarrel?

DEFENDANT: Yeah, a flatiron, a rolling pin, six plates, and a teakettle.

A: Nobody likes me . . . even my wife didn't like me. She used to sit at home night after night and read that magazine, *Better Homes and Gardens.* Then she ran away.

B: Who'd she run away with?

A: Some guy with a better home and garden!

"Everyone knows you married me for money."

"Sure, that's the only way I could get rich."

Two men who had been bachelor cronies met for the first time in five years.

"Tell me, Tom," said one, "did you marry that girl, or do you still darn your own socks and do your own cooking?"

"Yes," was Tom's reply.

When we were first married we hit it off swell. But as we were leaving the church . . .

"Will you go quietly, or will I get my wife to throw you out!"

WEN: Well, I've got something new that'll make your mouth water, Steve. Last night my wife cooked me a luscious, juicy, two-inch steak!
STEVE: You mean it was two inches thick?
WEN: No. Two inches long!

I lost my woman because of incompatibility. We were neckin' when in came Pat, and he had more ability.

Girls in Utah generally marry Young.

All the mothers in the world presumably are actual or potential matchmakers, particularly for their daughters, but some of the best matchmaker stories come out of Jewish society and culture. A middle-aged Jewish woman riding a city bus happened to find herself seated next to an attractive-looking young fellow. Being a friendly sort, she started a conversation by saying, "I don't believe I've seen you on this bus before."

"I guess you haven't, ma'am, but that's because I just came out of prison."

"Oh, is that right?" the woman said. "And what was the nature of your crime?"

"Well," he said, "I don't like to tell you this, but as a matter of fact I'd been convicted of murdering my wife."

Without a moment's delay, the woman said, "Oh, so you're single? Listen, there's a young lady I'd like you to meet."

MEDICINE

Myron Cohen used to tell the story of the Catholic, Protestant, and Jewish patients who lay dying in the hospital. Their doctor asked each to make a final wish. The Catholic wanted to make a confession; the Protestant wanted to see his family for the last time; the Jew said: " I want to see another doctor."

S. J. Perleman was being interviewed by a young woman who was at a loss for questions to pose.

"Have you ever had any diseases?" she asked.

"Yes," Perleman said. "I've got Bright's disease—and Bright's got mine."

A wit went to a psychiatrist, who showed him a large inkblot and said, "What does it mean to you?"

"It means," the visitor told him, "that you need a new fountain pen."

Speaking of doctor jokes, there's the one about the optometrist who pointed to an eye chart and asked his patient to read it.

"Gosh, doc," the patient said. "I'm afraid you'll have to read it for me. My eyesight ain't worth a damn."

A woman who was in analysis went to dinner in a restaurant with her husband. Her analyst appeared, and she introduced him to her husband: "Doctor, this is one of the men I've been telling you about."

A tough old Texas oilman got an urgent call one night from his family doctor.

"I'm calling you from the hospital," the doctor said. "Your wife is seriously ill and we need your permission to perform an exploratory operation."

"The hell with that," the oil driller shouted. "They ain't nobody gonna wild-cat on my wife!"

The man in the doctor's office was twitching and trembling, could scarcely talk. The doctor listened patiently to his all-but-incoherent recital of the marital problems that were gradually driving him up the wall, and finally said he would give him a prescription for some tranquilizers.

"How often do I take them, Doc?"

"Three times a day. Except *you* don't take them. You give them to your wife."

A doctor, going on his rounds in the hospital, stopped to make inquiries of a newly admitted patient.

"Are you eating well?" he asked.

"Yes," said the patient.

"Do you sleep okay?" the doctor inquired.

"Yes, I do."

"Well," said the doctor, "I'll give you something to put a stop to that."

Henny Youngman said he had a wonderful doctor. "I told him I couldn't afford the surgery he recommended. So he touched up my X-ray."

A poor woman, dedicated to her dying husband, was faced with a terrible predicament when his doctor told her that her mate must undergo a serious surgery. Not having the money to finance the operation, the woman didn't know where to turn until the doctor came up with a brilliant suggestion. He said, "We'll get a crew of the finest doctors in the world to operate on your husband, and all you have to do is to allow the procedure to be shown on live television, so the whole world can see how this very intricate operation is performed."

The woman saw this as a blessing, and they signed the contract. On the day of the operation, they wheeled the fellow into the operating room, and with six cameras and two directors present they started the operation, as the wife sat outside in the anteroom. In about a half hour the doctor came out and said, "I'm terribly sorry, but your husband just died on the operating table."

The poor wife sniffled and said, "Well, that's show business."

Two old maids ran a drugstore. A man walked in one day and said, "I'd like to see a male clerk."

One of the old maids answered, "I'm a registered pharmacist. You can tell me your troubles."

The customer explained, "I'd like some sort of pill to calm me down. I have a terrible habit. Every time I see a girl, I wanna make love to her. What can you give me?"

The old maid replied, "Just a minute. I'll discuss it with my sister."

About five minutes later she returned. "Well?" said the man.

"My sister and I," said the old maid, "decided to give you the drugstore and seven hundred dollars."

Science *has* made rapid strides. In the old days, with old-fashioned methods, a cold would last fourteen days. Now, however, with the new wonder drugs and treatment, the common cold can be completely cured in two weeks.

BILL: There's a fellow I'd like to see in the City Hospital.
ROSE: Why don't you go up to see him?
BILL: He's not there yet.

"He gave me some medicine to take after meals. But I can't take it."
"Why?"
"I ain't gettin' any meals!"

MEMORY

Did you hear the absent-minded professor fell down the stairs? When he hit the bottom, he picked himself up and said, "Now I wonder what all that noise was about."

I have loved her since time out of mind; and this time I'm really out of my mind.

"You know what-you-call-its daughter? Well she and whos-its son went to the whats-its and to the thingamajig to and got married! Didn't you hear about it?"

"Yeah, but this is the first time I've heard the details."

MILITARY

"I was in the navy for three years."

"Navy?"

"Yeah, I was in the laundry—I used to button the hatches."

Some humor does hold its quality over a long expanse of time.

Admiral Lord Howe, while at sea, was once hastily awakened after midnight by a Lieutenant of the Watch, who agitatedly informed him that a fire had started near the ship's magazine.

"If that be the case," said the Admiral, "we shall soon know it."

The lieutenant flew back to the scene of danger but returned shortly. "Oh, you need not be afraid, sir," he said, "the fire is extinguished."

"Afraid?" exclaimed Howe. "What do you mean by that, sir? I've never been afraid in my life." Looking at the young lieutenant intently, he added, "Pray, how does a man feel, sir, when he is afraid? I need not ask how he *looks*."

Another ancient but still funny story, evidently venerable in 1881, is still in common currency. A soldier, having been arrested and tried several times for drunkenness, was up once more before a stern magistrate.

"Soldier," said the judge, "you are undoubtedly guilty of habitual drunkenness. Have you anything to plead in the way of an excuse?"

"Nothing, your Honor," said the soldier, "but habitual thirst."

Moshe Dayan called his generals to a dawn conference. "Gentlemen, this morning we go to war with Egypt." Said one officer, "But what do we do this afternoon?"

A grizzled captain aboard a destroyer was quizzing a young sailor. "What steps would you take if a sudden storm came up on the starboard?"

"Sir, I'd throw out an anchor."

"And what would you do if another storm sprang up, aft?"

"I'd throw out another anchor, sir."

"And what if a third storm came up, forward?"

"I'd throw out one more anchor, Captain."

"But wait a minute, son," the captain said. "Where the hell are you getting all these anchors?"

"From the same place you're getting all your storms, sir."

Concerning a certain popular singer's war record, it is said that during World War II he spent three years being hidden in an attic by a sympathetic Italian woman.

And that was in Union City, New Jersey.

PRIVATE: I feel like telling that sergeant where to get off again.
SECOND PRIVATE: What do you mean, "again"?
PRIVATE: I felt like it yesterday, too.

STRANGER AT CAMP: What does "O.I.C." mean?
FRIEND: O.I.C. means "Officer in Charge."
STRANGER: OIC.

"Who goes there?"
"Private Stock, Company C."
"Advance private stock and be sampled."

"You'll get thirty days in the brig for this."
"What for?"
"For A.W.O.L., drinking while on duty, and ad-libbing with your superior."

"So you are joining the army," cooed the sweet young thing. "Will you get a commission?"

"No, just straight pay."

A colonel's wife sent the following note to Captain Greene:

"Colonel and Mrs. Browne request the pleasure of Captain Greene's company to dinner on September 15th."

To which she received the following reply:

"With the exception of five men on leave and three on sick leave, Captain Greene's Company will take great pleasure in accepting your invitation."

"Who are you to be kicking me?"

"I'm the General."

"Well, is that the any way to get new recruits?"

OFFICER: What's the big idea here? How come you men are climbing trees and crawling through bushes?

PRIVATE: Well, sir, we camouflaged the cannon before lunch— and now we can't find it.

A young private sought permission from his commanding officer to leave camp for the weekend. "You see," he explained, "my wife's expecting."

"Very well," said the officer, "I understand. Go ahead and tell your wife that I wish her luck."

The following week the soldier was back again with the same explanation: "My wife's expecting."

The officer looked surprised. "Still expecting," he murmured. "Well, well, my boy, you must be pretty bothered. Of course you can have the weekend off."

When the same soldier appeared again the third week, however, the officer lost his temper. "Don't tell me your wife is still expecting," he bellowed.

"Yes, sir," said the soldier resolutely, "she's still expecting."

"What in heaven is she expecting?" cried the officer.

"Me," said the soldier, simply.

SENTRY: I can't let you proceed without the password, sir.

MAJOR JONES: I've forgotten it, but you know who I am.

SENTRY: I'm sorry, sir, but I have orders—

MAJOR JONES: Now look here, young man—

VOICE FROM GUARDHOUSE: Don't stand there arguing all night—shoot him.

SARGE: I suppose when the war is over, you'll be waiting for me to die so you can spit on my grave.

WRETCHED ROOKIE: No, Sarge. After the war is over I never want to stand in line again.

An elderly woman out for a drive one day managed to get involved in some army training maneuvers. As she approached a bridge a sentry stopped her. "Sorry ma'am," he said, "you can't cross this bridge, it's been destroyed." Amazed, the old lady stared at the bridge through her glasses; it looked all right to her. Just then another soldier came along. "Excuse me," said the old lady, "but can you tell me what's wrong with this bridge?" The soldier shook his head. "Don't ask me, lady, I've been dead for two days."

SENTRY: Halt! Who goes there?
VOICE: You wouldn't recognize me anyway. I'm new here.

"We would never do for infantrymen," commented J. B. Priestley, registering with other 47-year-olds for national service, "but if you armor-plated some of us, we might do as tanks."

The army has a great system with its uniforms. If it fits—you're an officer!

"Friend of mine's in the army. But he's never dated a girl, shot crap, sassed a second louie, or smoked a cigarette."

"No kidding! How long's he been in the army?"

"About ten minutes."

A former soldier, now a civilian, wrote to his former CO, a studious young second lieutenant: "Dear Sir, now that I'm a civilian, it gives me great pleasure to tell you to go to hell."

In due time he received the following reply: "Sir, any suggestion or inquiries concerning the movement of troops must be entered on Army Form 1234, a copy of which is enclosed."

"They can't put you in the brig for that."

"They can't? I'm talking from there."

BOB: When you get into the army, look up my uncle Louie.

DICK: Louie, the midget?

BOB: Yeah.

DICK: How did he get into the army?

BOB: He lied about his height.

MONEY

"Lend me five dollars for a month, old boy."
"What's a month-old boy going to do with five dollars?"

I didn't say I'd pay on time, I said I'd pay *in* time.

"Money isn't everything."
"No, but it comes in handy when you're trying to live."

PROBLEM: If you had twenty-three dollars in one pocket and fifty-six in the other, what would you have?
ANSWER: Somebody else's pants.

MAN: I have an account in this bank. Why didn't you mail me a statement?
ACCOUNTANT: We didn't want to spend three cents to tell you that you have two cents.

People these days are always spending money they haven't yet earned, for things they don't need, to impress people they don't like.

ERNIE: Is that how you got your money?
VAL: That's how I got some of it.
ERNIE: How did you get the rest of it?
VAL: I haven't got the rest of it yet.

ERNIE: Well, they're paying us to talk about it.
VAL: Where's the money?
ERNIE: You see, we talk, and if it's any good, we get a check.
VAL: Why don't we get the check, and if it's any good we'll talk?

HUSBAND: You spent fifty dollars on a bottle of perfume?
WIFE: Oh, don't get so excited. You get a nickel back on the bottle.

I made sixty-four dollars on *Take It or Leave It*. When nobody was looking, I took it.

Her folks are in the iron and steel business. Her mother irons and her father steals.

MOON

SHE: Does the moon influence the tide?
HE: I don't know, honey, but it sure influences the untied.

MOTHER-IN-LAW

I worship the ground her slacks drag on.

HE: There's one thing about my mother-in-law. She's outspoken.
SHE: Not by anyone I know.

HE: But darling, you'll learn to love her in time.
SHE: I haven't got the time.

"Her mother-in-law's husband just died."

"What was he sick of?"

"My mother-in-law."

Adam had no mother-in-law. That's why they called it Paradise.

"Before he was married, he said he would tame his wife's mother, or die in the attempt."

"How did he come out?"

"In a black silk–lined box with silver handles."

SHE: Have you forgotten I was here?

HE: No, but I was trying.

"Are you an American?"

"Why yes, my mother-in-law was at the Boston Tea Party."

"She was?"

"Yeah, she was the bag they threw overboard."

My mother-in-law lives a stone's throw from me. I know because I often throw stones at her.

The Hollywood merchant's mother-in-law passed away, and the undertakers asked him, "Would you like the body buried, embalmed, or cremated?"

"Better do all three," declared the merchant. "I'm taking no chances!"

MOVIE STAR

The *Enquirer* says that Rudolph Valentino had a drinking problem. I've just written a new song titled "Rudolph, the Red-Nosed Valentino."

MUSIC

There was, early on in the history of jazz, a group known as The Mound City Blue Blowers. Its members consisted of its leader, Red McKenzie, who played a comb blown through a piece of newspaper, which he somehow managed to make sound like a muted cornet; Eddie Condon and Jack Bland, banjos; and Frank "Josh" Billings, who played with brushes on his own version of drums, a couple of suitcases covered with wrinkled brown paper.

The group became popular in Chicago during the Prohibition

era, and went east for what turned out to be a sensationally successful engagement in New York at the Bath Club, a speakeasy. "There often were more customers on the stand than there were musicians," Condon later recalled.

McKenzie, out of St. Louis, who had been a jockey, was a tyrant of the worst kind.

One night Condon found little Billings crying in the bathroom of the Bath Club.

"What's wrong, Josh?"

"That damned McKenzie."

"What did he do?"

"He bawled me out. He said my suitcases sounded hollow."

"Well, Josh, you know how Red is."

"Yeah. With him, it's 'When you're in Rome, do as they do in St. Louis.'"

Although music may indeed have charms that can soothe the savage beast—or is it breast?—there are nevertheless a few civilized breasts—or beasts—that are not soothed by it, particularly since the advent of electronically amplified rock music. The classic put-down in this category still belongs to Dr. Johnson, who once sat without expression during the performance of a piano sonata. A lady seated nearby took the liberty of asking the philosopher if he was fond of music. "Not particularly, madam," he replied, "but of all noises I think music is the least disagreeable."

The everyday language of musicians, black or white, has long had a certain snap and poetry to it. Much of the lingo of today's teenagers is jargon borrowed from the jazz culture of the 1930s. Such words as *man, dig, baby, groovy, cool, hip,* etc., have been in common use among musicians to my knowledge since the mid-thirties, and possibly before that.

I stopped one day at Charlie's Tavern, a Sixth Avenue saloon apparently frequented only by musicians and their associates. I am not a saloon-type, nor is beer one of my necessities, but having heard of Charlie's for so many years, I took advantage of the occasion of passing it to inspect its interior.

My lady companion and I had been seated at the bar for only a few minutes when a sot some distance to our right began to address the world in language heavily sprinkled with vulgar obscenities. Although he was directing his remarks to no one in particular, I naturally became uncomfortable that my friend was forced to listen to such language. After a moment, the bartender, sensing the lady's embarrassment, moved toward the drunk and handled the situation not like a bartender, but like a musician.

"Hey, man," he said very quietly to the loudmouth, "modulate."

To me stories based on truth are always funnier than fantasy jokes. I'm indebted to jazz critic and lyricist Gene Lees for recalling funny incidents that occurred over the years at another saloon frequented by jazz musicians, Jim and Andy's, in midtown Manhattan.

"Some of them," says Lees, "sprang from Zoot Sims. Zoot, a man of phenomenal stamina, and at the time a heroic capacity for alcohol, usually came in wearing a sweater and looking most casual. One noon he turned up impeccably accoutered in a dark suit, white shirt, and tie. 'Hey Zoot,' someone said, 'you're looking mighty dapper today. What happened?'

"Zoot looked down the length of his own elegance and said, as if puzzled, 'I don't know. I woke up this way.'"

On another occasion, Lees reports, "Zoot turned up during the morning after having worked until four or five A.M. He'd had no sleep, and he faced a heavy day of recording. Lamenting his condition, he asked if anyone might have a pill to help him through the day. The fiancée of a fellow musician offered him one.

"Zoot looked it over on the palm of his hand. 'I've never used this kind before,' he said. 'Is it strong?'

"'Sort of,'" the girl said. 'You can take half of it and throw the rest away.'

"'*What?*' said Zoot in mock indignation. 'Throw that good stuff away? Do you realize there are people in Europe *sleeping?*'"

My friend, columnist Don Freeman, has recalled a story they tell about Jascha Heifetz and Mischa Elman, both concert violinists of the top order in a bygone day. They were seated together at a big dinner when a waiter delivered a letter to their table. On the envelope were written these words: "To the Greatest Violinist in the World."

"It must be for you, Jascha," Elman said.

"No, you open it, Mischa," Heifetz said.

"No, no," Elman said. "You open it, Jascha."

They agreed to open it together.

The letter began: "Dear Fritz . . ."

To bring the musical theme into the present, surely you've heard about the teenager playing in the rock group who was asked if he could read music.

"I can read music a little," the kid replied. "But not enough to hurt our playing."

It's hard to disagree with critic Tom Shales's line, "Rock music was invented so that people without talent could be stars, too."

A writer asked the brilliant lyricist "Yip" Harburg, "Mr. Harburg, your lyric to 'April in Paris' is incredible and yet you've said you've never been there. How could you possibly write a lyric about a place you've never been to?"

"I've never been 'Over the Rainbow' either," Harburg said.

A young composer brought his latest composition to Igor Stravinsky to seek his opinion.

"This music is beautiful and new," said the Russian-born master, who was not usually generous with his praise.

The other was overjoyed.

"However," added Stravinsky soberly, "the part that is beautiful is not new, and the part that is new is not beautiful."

Violin virtuoso Mischa Elman began his career as a child prodigy and was still playing concerts when he was in his seventies. Once, during the latter period, he was asked how audience reaction differed from what it had been when he was a wunderkind.

"I haven't noticed any difference," said the violinist. "When I was a boy, audiences would exclaim, 'Imagine playing the violin at his age!' Today, they say the same thing."

He used to be an organist . . . but his monkey died.

Saxophone . . . An ill woodwind that nobody blows good.

After Wendell Noble's Song:
STEVE: Hurray, Noble! Ray Noble!
JUNE: You like to hear Wendell sing?
STEVE: No. I like Ray Noble.

SARA: Can you play the piano?
DICK: I don't know; I never tried.

"The only way to listen to good music is with your eyes shut."

"Did you ever try listening to it with your mouth shut?"

"Where's Tommy?"

"He's in the house, playing a duet. I finished my part first."

Say, if any of you folks are from out of town and feel lonely because you don't know anyone in Manhattan and have no one to talk to . . . I have the remedy. Get an old price tag and put it on your suit. Then all day people will be coming up to you to tell you that you have a price tag on your suit. You'd be surprised at the friendships that can start with conversations.

NEW YORK

The subway was so crowded this morning the people were packed in like sardines. It was even worse; at least the sardines have room to lie down.

One thing I never could understand: subway maps. You can never find one in a station. You find subway maps *inside* the cars, after you get on, so you can find out which subway you should have taken instead of the one you're on.

Did you ever notice how impatient New Yorkers are? They kill themselves trying to get a seat, and then they're in such a hurry to get off that they'll get up and stand by the door about four stops before their station.

There's a subway about every fourteen seconds, but these people continually risk their lives to catch one that's pulling out. The reason most people are in such a big hurry is that they want to get home and do nothing.

Twenty years ago I came to New York, broke and unknown. Then an idea came to me. I bought a typewriter on credit and I started a correspondence school course. And, now ... twenty years later, I still owe for the typewriter.

My name for the subway to the Bronx—Bronchial Tube.

An old joke of Fred Allen's:

I met a girl years ago on the subway ... we went steady for a while and even got engaged. I was living on 86th Street and she lived on 51st. But we had to call it off . . . my parents didn't want me to marry a girl below my station.

A man across from me had a seal sitting next to him. I asked the man if the seal was trained and he said, "Don't ask me, I don't know. He got on at Central Park!"

Michael Kanin brings the following to our attention from the *Jewish Daily Forward:*

"The garbage collectors in New York are paid up to $40,000 a year."

"Really? Then why are the street so filthy?"

"Well, you can't expect a man who makes $40,000 a year to fool around with garbage."

A spaceship from another planet, due to a flat tire, is forced to land in the Lower East Side of New York City. Looking for a spare, the captain of the vessel (green and with funny ears) roamed the streets until he came upon a delicatessen, the window of which seemed to have a pan of spares. Entering the shop, he pointed a feeler:

"I need a couple of those wheels," he explained. Pityingly, the counterman smiled down.

"They ain't wheels, kid," he explained. "They're bagels—eat one."

The visitor took a bite and stood deep in thought. Suddenly, his green visage glowed. "You know what this wheel would be awfully good with?" he asked. "Lox and cream cheese."

A thousand and one stories are told about Max Asnas, who for years managed the Stage Delicatessen on New York's Sixth Avenue. A congenitally generous man who never turned down a panhandler, Asnas, rather than embarrass the man by handing him some food and showing him the door, usually would give him fifty cents, tell him to sit down at a table, order something, and pay for it like a regular customer. As Max saw it, the technique accomplished two purposes. He got his fifty cents back in any event, but more importantly, the gesture helped to instill a bit of self-confidence in the unfortunates.

One freezing winter night a customer came in and put the bite on Asnas. Perhaps moved by holiday spirit, Max gave the visitor more than usual—seventy-five cents. The stranger took the money, sat down at a table as directed, and opened a menu.

In less than a minute he was in a heated argument with a waiter.

Asnas hurried over and asked what was wrong.

"Listen," the bum snorted, "where the hell do you get off charging sixty-five cents for a corned beef sandwich?"

NIGHTMARES

I had a nightmare . . . I dreamed I was lost on the Sahara Desert dying of thirst and I was surrounded by peanut-butter sandwiches.

He got to walking in his sleep so much we finally had to tattoo some underwear on him.

PATRIOTISM

SHE: What did you ever do for your country?
HE: I moved to the city.

"Do you believe this is a free country?"
"No, I'm a pedestrian."

PAKISTANI

In poor neighborhoods, living conditions are often crowded. A pollster visits the Pakistani district of Birmingham, England, and asks a Pakistani about the voting. "I can help you, sir," says Pak. "Thirty-three will vote Conservative, 64 will vote Labour, 7 will vote Liberal, 1 communist, and 15 have so far not yet decided. Of course, sir, I cannot speak for the people upstairs."

PERFUME

DAME: You'll love the perfume in this bottle. This is "Moonlight on the Mississippi."
STEVE: "Moonlight on the Mississippi," huh?
DAME: That's right.
STEVE: When did you make it . . . at low tide?

PHILOSOPHY

A man is a sort of roadhouse where his ancestors stop for a while on their way to become his descendants.

WILLIE: Dad, teacher says we're here to help others.
DAD: Of course we are.
WILLIE: Well, what are the others here for?

To quote a famous philosopher . . . *(Digs card from pocket, reads):*
The happiest life consists in ignorance. Before you learn to pravish, and rejoice, Ansit the inuxable with persistence and your

farration will turble the imprecations of fate. Unquote. *(Looks to see who said it):* This was said by . . . Morey Amsterdamus?

PHOTOGRAPHY

"Is this the expression you want?"
"Yes."
"Then snap quick . . . it hurts my face."

"Look pleasant now, pleasant—
All right. You may resume your natural expression."

"That's my father and mother before they were married."
"Who's the girl in the middle?"
"That's me."

PLUMBER

PLUMBER: Did you bring all the tools?
HELPER: Yes.
PLUMBER *(disgusted):* You would.

POLISH

A Russian official, visiting Poland, noticed a peculiar sight. A Polish citizen was jumping up and down on the sidewalk, saying, "62—62—62!" The Russian asked him what he was doing and the Pole explained that it was an old Polish custom, which always brings good luck. "Why don't you stand here and try it?" asked the Pole.

So, to be comradely, the Russian official stood next to him and started jumping up and down, saying, "62—62—62!" A trap door opened and swallowed him up, whereupon the Pole started jumping again, "63—63—63!"

POLITICS

Norton Mockridge relates that in his last year or so, New York Mayor John Lindsay had a good deal of opposition from residents of the borough of Queens to a particular housing development. When someone asked him if he was avoiding the borough except to get to JFK Airport, he said, "Well, I've had more trouble with Queens than anybody since Henry VIII."

Walter Hoops of the *American Rationalist* magazine shares the story that in Communist heaven the equivalent of St. Peter stopped one applicant at the gate and asked, "What are your qualifications for entering here?"

"Well," said the man, "on earth my father was a rich industrialist. My mother came from a family of middle-class tradesmen. Me, I was a successful writer. And finally, after inheriting a large sum of money, I married a baroness."

The gatekeeper was choking with rage by this time. "And those are your claims for entering the Communist heaven?" he spluttered.

Meekly the applicant added one more line: "I thought my name might help me," he murmured. "It's Karl Marx."

Vilovic Melor, in *L'Arme du Rive,* tells of former Polish party leader Wladyslaw Gomulka visiting a small restaurant to see how the masses were living. Sitting at the next table was a very old man who was ordering the most expensive dishes and wines on the menu. Pleasantly surprised, Gomulka remarked, "I'm delighted to see you ordering such a fine meal. But how can you afford it?"

"I'm retired," replied the old man. "But my two sons both have good jobs, and they're very devoted."

"And what do they do?"

"One is a locksmith; the other is a bricklayer."

"Marvelous!" Gomulka exclaimed. "This is what the Worker's Party has done for the working classes. Your family is a remarkable example of social progress. Now, what can I do for you?"

"I should like a passport so I could visit the United States—for just three weeks."

"What the devil do you want to do in the United States?"

"Well, you see, it's been a long time since I've *seen* my two sons."

I have the impression that politics is an even more difficult way of making a living than show business, which reminds me of the story of a fellow who, after a costly and bitter campaign, was elected mayor of a small town in the Midwest. A friend came to visit him one day and had occasion to stop into a number of places of business in the community before going on to city hall. In each shop there was strong criticism of the mayor, who was called "a phony, a crook, an idiot, a bum, a chiseler," and worse.

When the visitor finally sat down for lunch with the mayor, he said, "Listen, Bill, why on earth did you want to become mayor of this town?"

"Oh," said the mayor, "I took the job for the honor that's in it."

The late G. Graybill Diehm, a Republican leader in Pennsylvania, hired on a man who had been his opponent for many years.

"But Grabe, that man is a son of a bitch," a lieutenant protested.

"Yes, but he's *our* son of a bitch now," Diehm answered.

Twenty-five years ago he started out to be the President of the United States. He got as far as Cleveland.

RADIO

Hear Mr. Wilcox. The complete dope on the weather.

"What else have you done in radio?"
"I've done plenty. Worked on a lot of big shows. Have you ever heard of the *Lux Radio Theatre*? *Command Performance*? And the *Screen Guild Players*? Well, I've heard of those shows, too.

Here's a late news item right now. The Kaiser has just sent German troops into Belgium. What are you complaining about? Have you ever heard any news that was later?

A dramatist employed to write stories from the Bible in radio form was astonished, at the end of the broadcast, to hear the announcer say, "Will Cain kill Abel? Tune in at the same time tomorrow morning and find out."

To woman in audience: You look familiar . . . but not to me.

That's Bern Bennett, our announcer . . . you've probably heard him on many of your favorite soap operas.

Right now, he's doing a new one called: *Ruth and Gus . . . Two-Run-of the-Mill People, Who Run a Mill.*

SPONSOR: And you can make people laugh, can you?
COMIC: I always leave them laughing, sir. If they don't laugh, I don't leave!

Quatrain

The fact that the sun continues to shine on soap operas
and sponsors who back 'em
disproves for me the old belief in
nature abhorring a vacuum.

This about winds it up, and those of you that came in expecting to be bored I'm sure I didn't disappoint you. If you folks care to spend another depressing hour drop in again tomorrow night.

I hope you don't mind my disheveled appearance tonight. I took great pains this morning to get myself sheveled, but now I'm disheveled again, and it's awful.

You're listening to a little production called *The Steve Allen Show*, which reaches you six nights a week, if you want to be reached, from Studio 3 here at CBS in Hollywood. The studio I'm in is just a stone's throw from the Palladium. I'm sure of that because every so often the people over there start throwing stones at me.

I hope you don't mind if I sneak a peek at the evening paper here from time to time. The only chance I ever get to read anymore is when I'm on the air.

(Rustle paper) Let's see here. I see where Governor Warren is threatening to freeze rents here in California. But the landlords get even. Next winter they'll freeze the tenants.

The NAACP has formally complained about the new comedy show *Ignoramus and Andy.*

A: I tuned you in last week.
B: How did you like my program?
A: It's the first time I ever saw a radio change stations by itself.

Did I tell you there's a lot of commercial interest in the package? Uh—for the benefit of those not associated with the radio industry, the word *package* is used in the trade to indicate an actual radio program or an idea for a program, which has all the component parts of the show under the control of one agency or network. Thus, an advertising agency might create, say, a package for a sponsor, by hiring a comedian, a singer, an orchestra, a couple of writers, then puts them all together—and the whole works is referred to as—a package.

Almost everybody in Hollywood has some private little package deal cooking, and it's really quite impressive. One guy I know was wined and dined and invited to play golf one day after somebody thought they heard him say he had a package *for* Phillip Morris. It was only after a considerable length of time that it developed he must have said a package *of* Phillip Morris.

Today marks the end of my first three years here at CBS, and ya know, just now, thinking about it . . . I got a lump in my throat . . . I swallowed my bubblegum.

I remember my first appearance as a comedian. I had them rolling in the aisles. Then the usher came in and took away the dice.

Nancy, when you were a little girl, did you ever walk along the sidewalk trying not to step on the lines? Well, you should have, kid, you're sure stepping on a lot of lines on this program!

Friends, do you have personal troubles? Is there a depressing problem that's preying on your mind? If so, why not write to Dr. Allen's Court of Human Relations? Are your relations human? Seriously, write me about your difficulties. I won't be able to help you; I just would like to hear about the mess you've made of your lives.

Our contests without prizes seem to be going over pretty well . . . so here comes another one. I'm going to play a record, a fellow is going to sing a number, and if you can tell me the name of the singer and the song . . . I'll give you several wonderful prizes.

First of all, if you pick up your application blanks in Honolulu, you'll win an all-expense-paid trip to Rexall drugstore. Then you'll also win a five-year's supply of nylons . . . that's one pair with a needle and some thread.

Then, you'll also win a five-pound box of cement, five tickets to last week's broadcast of the Alma Seltzer news, and a set of tooth-less combs for people who are bald . . . or, if you prefer, you may have an invisible hair-net, which is great if you have invisible hair.

We will now have an old-fashioned cracker barrel discussion. (Two men sit around and discuss a cracker barrel.)

RAILROAD

"I want to be procrastinated at the next corner," said the man to the streetcar conductor.

"You want to be what?"

"Look in the dictionary, man. Procrastinate—to be put off. That's what I mean."

PASSENGER: When will the eight-twenty be in?
CONDUCTOR: About eight fifty-five.
PASSENGER: Great, it's early today!

REAL ESTATE

"Where's the house I bought?"

"It's the first real bargain on your left and then the second golden opportunity around the corner."

"I'm a real estate man."

"Yes, I see your samples under your fingernails."

RELIGION

If I didn't think all the jokes in this collection were funny I wouldn't have included them. But some are funnier than others, such as the story of a remarkably devout elderly Christian woman—a widow living alone—who was awakened by noises one night and discovered that a burglar had invaded her living room.

Acting on who knows what sort of inspiration she shouted, "Stop! Acts 2:38!" ("Repent and be baptized every one of you in the name of Jesus Christ for the forgiveness of your sins . . .")

The burglar, scared to death, was unable to move, which gave the woman enough time to call 911 and explain to the police department what had happened.

A few minutes later, as an officer was leading the handcuffed burglar away, he said, "I don't understand why you just stood there and didn't run. All that lady did was yell a scripture from the Bible to you."

"Scripture?" the burglar responded, "I thought she said she had an ax and two .38's."

There is the particularly ancient story of a clergyman who was a little deaf. He had got some new hymnbooks, and was anxious to introduce them to his congregation. He directed one of his elders to notify the audience. The elder, who also was clerk of the church, said at the close of the sermon, "All those who have children they wish baptized, please send up names immediately."

The pastor supposed that the clerk was giving out notice of the arrival of the hymnbooks. He said, arising, "I want to say for the benefit of those who haven't any, they can be obtained from me any day between three and four. The ordinary little ones at fifteen cents; special ones, with red backs, at only twenty-five cents each."

Outdoor sign on Easter at Faith Temple Church in Sioux Falls, South Dakota:

THE FIRST EASTER SONG? THERE WAS A ROCK AND THERE WAS A ROLL.

Excerpts from a "Then and Now" checklist for aging baby boomers:

Then: Long Hair.

Now: Longing for hair.

Then: Acid rock.

Now: Acid reflux.

Then: Getting out to a new, hip joint.

Now: Getting a new hip joint.

Then: Trying to look like Marlon Brando or Elizabeth Taylor.

Now: Trying not to look like Marlon Brando or Elizabeth Taylor.

—Rev. Joseph Breighner, *The Catholic Review*

FMC member Joseph Mattingly of Lexington, Kentucky, passed on the following list of patron saints, which appeared in *CUF Links,* newsletter of Catholics United for the Faith, Steubenville, Ohio:

- Patron Saint of Travel Agents . . . St. Martin of Tours
- Patron Saint of Bald People . . . St. Hedwig
- Patron Saint of Chocolate Milk Drinkers . . . St. John Bosco
- Patron Saint of Candy Makers . . . Our Lady of Mt. Carmel
- Patron Saint of Police . . . St. Prokop
- Patron Saint of Shippers . . . St. Francis de Sales
- Patron Saint of Mortgage Payers . . . St. Bernadette
- Patron Saint of Lawyers . . . Our Lady of Good Counsel

I've heard at least a dozen popular comedians tell this next story. None of us seem to have any idea where it originated. At a large public meeting, before the speakers and entertainment were heard, a man in the front row shifted about, craned his neck, and gave every evidence of being extremely uncomfortable.

After several minutes of such discomfiture, he stood up and said in a loud voice, "Is there a Christian Scientist in the audience?" A fashionably dressed woman across the aisle stood up and said, "Yes, I am a Christian Scientist."

"Fine," the fellow said. "I wonder if you would mind changing seats with me. I'm sitting in a draft."

The Rev. Fortunato Castillo, a Presbyterian minister working as relocation specialist for the Community Redevelopment Agency of the city of Los Angeles, once said that we could better understand the different philosophical approaches to the problem of poverty by observing how the relevant terminology has evolved in recent years.

"The poor man," he said, "used to be called simply poor. But an out-of-work fellow I knew said to me recently, 'A few years ago they stopped calling me poor. For a while I was referred to as needy. Then we went through a phase where we were referred to as underprivileged. After a time they changed the word to disadvantaged. I still haven't got a dime to my name, but I'm building a hell of a vocabulary.'"

George Slaff, Beverly Hills, California, attorney, tells a charming story about the rabbi in a poor section of Eastern Europe whose flock wished to honor him on his fiftieth birthday.

Being poverty-stricken, there was little of material value they could give him. So a number of the more thoughtful members of the community, knowing that the rabbi was in the habit of taking a nap each afternoon following his midday meal, decided to gather outside under his window, apparently by chance, and speak in loud voices about his many virtues.

On the appointed day they arrived, by twos and threes, and took up their positions below the window. For some time they spoke in glowing and loving tones about the man's honesty, his virtue, his spirituality, his wisdom, his sense of humor, his courage, and his charm. After awhile, assuming that they had done him suitable honor, they began to drift away.

Suddenly the shutters of the rabbi's window opened. He stuck his head out and said, "And what about my modesty?"

The story is told that in Libya a certain teacher once instructed her pupils that, "Khadafi takes care of us and Allah looks after Khadafi, so before every meal you must say, 'Thanks to Khadafi and Allah be praised.'"

One day a pupil asked, "Suppose Khadafi should pass away?"

"In that case," the teacher explained, "you simply say, 'Allah be praised.'"

While I am not a member of the Quaker faith, I sometimes think the world would be much better off if everyone else was, the Quakers being so truly dedicated to the cause of peace. It reminds me of the classic admonition addressed by an early Philadelphia settler to an insulting troublemaker, "Have a care, friend, lest thou run thy face against my fist."

A very loud and long-winded preacher was giving his sermon one Sunday morning, when halfway through a baby began to cry. A woman got up, holding the child in her arms, and started to leave the church. The preacher, fearful that it would seem as though his speech was driving the woman away, called out, "It's all right, ma'am, that baby isn't bothering me."

"That may be," answered the woman, "but you're sure bothering her."

Two inebriated cowboys were sitting behind two nuns at a ballgame and because of their habits, the cowboys couldn't see. So they decided to give the nuns a hard time. One says loudly, so the sisters were sure to hear, "You know, I think I'll move to Texas, they only have fifteen percent Catholics there."

"Oklahoma would be better," said his friend, "they only have ten percent Catholics there."

One of the nuns turned around, looked them square in the eye, and said, "Why don't you go to hell? They have no Catholics there."

Monsignor Arthur Tonne, in *Jokes Priests Can Tell, Volume 5,* relates the story of a Canadian pastor who leaves a distinctive calling card during visitation to delinquent churchgoers.

On one side is the name of the church and times of the services. The other side features a small black-lined square with the title: "Test Your Health Free of Charge!" The accompanying directions state: "Hold square to face and blow on it. If it turns green, call your doctor. If it turns brown, see your dentist. If it turns purple, see your psychiatrist. If it turns red, see your banker. If it turns black, call your lawyer and make your will. If it remains white, you are in good health, so there's no reason you shouldn't be in church next Sunday."

No one seems to know who the author of the following routine was, but it was submitted to the *Joyful Noisletter* by Sister Monique Rysavy of Owatonna, Minnesota:

What You Learn from Noah's Ark

Everything you really need to know can be learned from Noah's Ark:

- Plan ahead. It wasn't raining when Noah built the Ark.
- Stay fit. When you're 600 years old, someone might ask you to do something really big.
- Don't listen to critics. Do what has to be done.
- Build on the high ground.
- For safety's sake, travel in pairs.
- Two heads are better than one.
- Take care of your animals as if they were the last ones on earth.
- Don't forget we're all in the same boat.
- When the manure gets really deep, don't sit there and complain. Shovel!
- Stay below deck during the storm.
- Remember that the woodpeckers inside are often a bigger threat than the storm outside.
- Don't miss the boat.
- No matter how bleak it looks, there's always a rainbow on the other side.

Also from the *Joyful Noisletter:*

Does this describe *your* fitness program?
Jumping to conclusions;
Flying off the handle;
Beating around the bush;
Running down a lead;
Dragging your feet;
Dodging responsibility;
Passing the buck;
Climbing the ladder;
Wading through paperwork;
Pulling strings;
Throwing your weight around;
Bending the rules;
Pushing your luck.

The following joke was sent to me by a friend named Brad Curl. It concerns a preacher speaking on the subject of perfection:

"None of us," he said, "are perfect, although some people have the feeling that they are. Is there anyone here today who thinks he's perfect? If so, please stand up."

At first there was no visible response from the audience, but suddenly one old fellow in the back row rose to his feet. The preacher said, "Sir, by standing, do you wish to suggest that you are perfect?"

The old fellow said, "Oh no, sir; I'm just standing up on behalf of my wife's first husband."

A man, fed up with his life, decided to become a monk and live in an order where one was only permitted to say two words once every decade. After the first ten years, the head monk called the man into his office and said, "Well, you can say your two words now."

The man replied, "Food cold," and left the office.

Another ten years went by the man was once again summoned to the head monk's office where he was told to utter his two words. "Bed hard," the man said, and then quietly turned away. After another ten years, the man stood before the head monk and said, "I quit."

The head monk shook his head and replied. "I'm not surprised. You've been complaining since you got here."

A midget died and, since he had been a good Catholic, was given an appropriate wake and funeral.

When friends arrived at his house to pay their respects, the landlady said, "Yes, you can go up to see him, but make sure you close the door when you leave." At the second landing, they were halted by her cry again: "Be sure you close the door!" Again, at the third: *"Don't forget to close the door!"*

They went into the midget's room, said their prayers, and went back downstairs, only to be confronted again by the strident landlady.

"Did you close the door?"

"Yes, yes, we closed the door. What's all the commotion about?"

"Well, I *hope* you closed the door," she said. "The cat's had him downstairs three times this morning."

A woman finally decided to join the church. As the deacons plunged her into the river the first time, she gasped, "I believe."

After the second dip, she chattered, "I believe." Then they dunked her the third time, when she began screaming and yelling, "I believe . . . I believe, yes, I believe."

One of the elders said, "What do you believe, sister?"

She sputtered, "I believe you boys are trying to drown me!"

A hearse is a poor vehicle to start going to church in. Why wait?

The sister had distributed paper and crayons to the second-grade class and asked them to draw a picture of the Holy Family.

Among the many original portraits was Billy's. It showed four passengers in an airplane, three with halos.

"I recognize the Holy Family, Billy," Sister said. "But who is the fourth passenger in the plane?"

Billy looked up at her incredulously, "Sister, don't you know? That's Pontius, the pilot."

A minister in a little church had been having trouble with the collections. One Sunday he announced, "Now, before we pass the collection plate, I would like to request that the person who stole the chickens from Brother Martin's henhouse please refrain from giving any money to the Lord. The Lord doesn't want money from a thief."

The collection plate was passed around, and for the first time in months everybody gave.

A little boy asked his mother: "Hey, Mom, is it true that 'dust thou art and to dust returneth'?"

His mother said: "That's right, son!" To which the kid replied: "Well, if you'll look under the bed you'll see that somebody's either coming or going!"

Thanksgiving Day, Thursday, November 24, will be observed with the Service of Morning Prayer at 9 o'clock. The choir will sing appropriate music. There will not be a sermon. Let us thank God for our Blessings.

A safety-minded pastor, when asked to bless St. Christopher medals for the protection of his parishioners while driving, always reminded them, "This blessing is only good up to forty-five miles an hour."

Sign on bulletin board in front of church in small Wyoming town:

SUBJECT FOR THIS SUNDAY: DO YOU KNOW WHAT HELL IS? COME AND HEAR OUR NEW ORGANIST.

An evangelist and his singer were holding a revival in a west Texas town, which was attended mostly by cowboys. The singer passed the hat around and the cowboys only put clods of dirt into the hat. His singer placed the hat on the rostrum, which was full of clods. The evangelist said: "Let us thank the Lord."

"What for?" asked the singer.

The evangelist replied: "We got the hat back."

A party of Jewish soldiers from the Sixth Armored Division was being shown through an Italian convent by a hospitable Mother Superior.

The many mistakes made by the soldiers in this strange environment were patiently overlooked by their hostess. But one was too much for her altogether; so rounding up the party she made the following appeal:

"Boys, I didn't say anything when you lit your cigarettes with the holy candles. I didn't say anything when you filled your water bottles with the holy water. But there is one thing I just can't stand any longer. For mercy's sake, *please don't call me Mother Shapiro.*"

A minister closed his radio sermon with the admonition to "Cast your bread upon the waters." Whereupon an announcer stepped to the microphone for station identification and informed the audience that "This is the National Broadcasting Company."

A visiting minister, arriving at the church where he was to preach, was asked by the sexton if he had brought a surplice. "Dear me, no," was the reply. "Unfortunately, we have had nothing but deficits for the past five years."

A young minister told his flock that he had a "call" to go to another church. One of the deacons asked how much more he was being offered. "Three hundred dollars," was the reply. "Well, I don't blame you for going," remarked the deacon, "but you should be more exact in your language, parson. That isn't a 'call.' that's a 'raise.'"

A bishop attended a banquet, and a clumsy waiter dropped a plate of hot soup in his lap. The anguished clergyman glanced around and exclaimed: "Will some layman please say something appropriate?"

Heaven, Purgatory, and Hell—the original triple threat.

"Brethren and sisters, we are gathered together here today to pray for rain," said the preacher. He looked his congregation over a little sadly and added, "But before we begin, I'd like to ask you just one question—Where are your umbrellas?"

The modernists say, "There ain't no hell." The fundamentalists say, "The hell there ain't!"

"Do you believe in the hereafter?"
"Yes."
"Then hereafter don't bother me."

I never swear on Sunday—but tomorrow you can all go to hell.

DAUGHTER: I can't marry him, Mother. He's an atheist and doesn't believe there's a hell.

MOTHER: Marry him, my dear, and between us we may convince him that he's wrong.

Brookline, Mass.

June 23

Dear Steve Allen:

I have a suggestion, which I hope you will consider.

As you wrote a song, "Let's Go to Church on Sunday," the following might give you an idea for a song!

The poem I heard was given to an emcee a few months back; and it follows:

Every time I pass a church
I always pay a visit,
So when I'm carried in
HE won't ask, "Who is it?"

Sincerely yours,
Edw. J. Raulins
9 Sewall Ave.

RESTAURANTS

A diner rushed over to the manager of the restaurant. "I turned my head and someone stole my topcoat," he screamed.

"What kind of coat was it?" asked the manager.

"It was a brown tweed with a high collar," replied the customer.

"Mmm," mused the manager. "Come to think of it, I saw a man walking out of here with that very coat on."

"Quick!" demanded the customer. "What did the guy look like?"

"Terrible," sighed the manager, "the sleeves were too short for him."

WAITRESS: Haven't they given you a menu yet, mister?
STARVING CUSTOMER: Yes, but I finished that half an hour ago.

DINER: I can't eat this stuff. Call the manager.
WAITER: It's no use. He won't eat it either.

CUSTOMER: These clams are very small.
WAITER: Yes, sir.
CUSTOMER: And they're also not very fresh.
WAITER: Then we're lucky they're small, aren't we, sir?

A: Is this a good restaurant?
B: The best in town. If you order a fresh egg, you get the freshest

egg in the city. If you order hot soup, you get the hottest soup in the city.

A: Yeah, I know. I ordered a small steak!

Jimmy Durante ordered a plate of spaghetti in an Italian restaurant in Greenwich Village, saw a sign warning patrons to keep their eyes on their hats and coats; he watched his hat and coat so intently that someone stole his plate of spaghetti.

After waiting what seemed hours, the customer buttonholed the headwaiter. "Just as a matter of curiosity," he said, "did the waiter who took my order leave any family?"

After eating a large steak, a man asked the restaurant manager, "Do you remember me?"

"No," replied the manager, "I don't believe I do."

"I was in here about a year ago, ate a big steak, and you had to throw me out because I didn't have any money."

"Oh, yes," the manager agreed, "I remember you now."

"Well, sir," said the diner, rising, "I'm afraid I'm going to have to trouble you again."

I had lunch in a drugstore. I don't think it's too good a place to eat. I ordered a tongue sandwich and when I lifted the bread to put mustard on, the tongue went "tsk-tsk-tsk."

You've heard of this wonderful eating place called Hamburger Heaven? Well, I've discovered a place where they burn all the meat. It's called Hamburger Hell.

I like the atmosphere in this nightclub. Some clubs take you to Havana, some take you to Algiers. This joint just takes you.

This planked swordfish is a little difficult to eat. The sword is stuck in the plank.

HANK: I'd like my steak . . . rare. Very rare.
ELAINE: I'd like my steak well done.
DAN: I'd like mine medium. Very medium.

DINER: I'll have a hot dog, please.
WAITER: One hamburger in solitary confinement!

DINER: I think there's a fly in my soup.
WAITER: Think? I can't be bothered with rumors.

DINER: This is an outrage . . . roast beef—gone . . . corned beef—gone . . . chicken—gone. . . . Bring me my hat and coat.
WAITER: That's gone, too.

DINER: Is there any soup on this menu?
WAITER: No, I just wiped it off.

"Didn't I say two three-minute eggs?"
"Well, we only had one egg left, so I cooked it for six minutes."

He works at a gas station, and when he took his girl to eat he said to the waiter, "Fill her up."

"Waiter, there's a fly in my ice cream."
"Let him freeze. It'll teach him a lesson."

DINER: Is this a first-class restaurant?
WAITRESS: Oh yes, but we'll serve you anyway.

SHE *(hinting):* That roast duck in the window makes my mouth water.
HE: Then spit.

DINER: Are those doughnuts fresh?
WAITER: I don't know, madam. I've only been here two weeks.

DINER: Waiter, what do you call this stuff?
WAITER: That's mock turtle soup, sir.
DINER: Well, I think this is carrying mockery a bit too far.

"Why does this chicken have a leg missing, waiter?"
"It was in a fight, sir."
"Well, take it back and bring me the winner."

DINER: Waiter, your thumb is in the soup!
WAITER: Oh, it's all right, lady, it isn't that hot.

DINER: What kind of pie is this?
WAITER: What's it taste like?
DINER: Glue.
WAITER: Then it's apple. The pumpkin tastes like soap.

I had a rabbit dinner last night. Lettuce and carrots.

"This food isn't fit for a pig."
"I'm sorry, sir, I'll bring you some that is."

". . . I don't know officer . . . we were eating alphabet soup, and one word led to another."

She always brings my coffee half-and-half. Half in the cup and half in the saucer.

HE: This steak is awful tough.

SHE: What are you eating it for?

HE: I need the exercise.

DINER: I'll have an order of caviar.

WAITER *(to chef):* One tapioca pudding with smoked glasses.

Wherever there's smoke, there's toast.

DINER: I'll have tea without cream.

WAITER: Sorry, we haven't got cream. Will you take it without milk?

These lamp chops are nice, but who designed the paper panties?

SHE: Why are you eating with your knife?

HE: 'Cause my fork leaks.

DINER: Waiter, bring me a bottle of wine, a steak, and a dog.
WAITER: A dog?
DINER: Yeah, give the dog the steak!

ROMANCE

HE: Do your eyes bother you?
SHE: No.
HE: They bother me.

SHE: Kipling said that women are nothing but a rag, a bone, and a hunk of hair.
HE: Shake hands with a junk dealer.

"I've got a yen for you."
"All right, hand it over, but after this bring American money."

"I'll never marry a man that snores."
"Okay, but be careful how you find out."

Cleopatra couldn't read or write . . . but she made her mark.

"Did anyone ever tell you how wonderful you are?"
"Never."
"Then where'd you get the idea?"

As soon as things get shook down a bit I hope to have more time to miss you.

"Would you love Annette Bening if she kept throwing herself at you?"
"No, but what a way to play catch!"

She loves me for myself, but I haven't been myself for weeks.

I'd like to have you for my wife, but my wife would never put up with it.

"You don't kiss me like Clark Gable kisses a girl."

"No, and I don't get five thousand dollars a week for doin' it, either."

"Is this the Salvation Army?"

"Yes."

"Do you save bad girls here?"

"Yes."

"Will you save me one for tomorrow night?"

"Are you sure he's serious about you?"

"Oh yes! He even wants to find me a good job so he can marry me."

"She's a sensible girl. I like her attitude."

"Her longitude ain't bad either."

HE: Let's get married or something.

SHE: Let's get married or nothing.

I was engaged to a man with a wooden leg, but I broke it off.

"I was out with my girl; it cost me three dollars."

"That's not much."

"That's all she had."

"Do you like talkative women, as well as the other kind?"

"What other kind?"

"There's Sophia Loren. You know, I feel like going out with her again."

"Again?

"Yeah, once before I felt like it."

"You've kissed worse-looking guys than me . . . I say you've kissed worse-looking guys than me."

"I heard you the first time, I was just trying to remember."

"Is it easy to kiss Mable?"

"Like falling off a log."

"Where'd you get the black eye?"

"I fell off the log."

HE: Will you marry me, dear?

SHE: No, I don't want to get married for a long time.

HE: Okay, we'll get married for a short time.

"I just got a letter from a man telling me if I didn't stay away from his wife he'd shoot me."

"Well, all you have to do is stay away from his wife."

"But he didn't sign his name."

Dolly Parton asked me out—I was in her house at the time.

"Were you ever disappointed in love?"

"Twice. The first girl jilted me, and the second one didn't."

HE: You have beautiful hair—lovely eyes—a cute little nose—

SHE: What about my mouth?

HE: I'm coming to that.

"He's got money to burn."

"Well, she's a good match for him."

A Swiss bell ringer loved a girl. They both said they would lay down their lives. They were dead ringers for each other.

BOB: She said there wasn't another man in the world like me.
JIM: That's flattering.
BOB: Yes, and she said it's a good thing, too.

HE: Do you remember me?
SHE: No, I don't.
HE: Sure. I'm the guy who told you twelve years ago that I couldn't live without you.

I've never loved anyone like I love you—and I've loved lots of 'em.

MABEL: I told him I didn't want to see him anymore.
RUTH: What did he do?
MABEL: He turned out the light.

BOB: When I took her in my arms the color left her cheeks.
BILL: Yeah, may I see your shirt . . .

"They say money won't buy you love."
"Maybe not. But it'll tide you over until you find it."

"You think your girl is true to you?"
"I don't *think,* I *know.*"
"I don't think you know, either."

"Irene, I have a bone to pick with you."
"Sorry, Tim, I'm not hungry."

"You are an apt boy. Is your sister apt, too?"
"Oh, yes, if she gets a chance, she's apt to."

"You're all the world to me."
"Will you marry me?"
"Not until I see some more of the world."

LAVERNE: I like a man who'll take me in his arms and over-whelm me . . . and crush me, crush me . . .

BOB: You don't want a man. You want a steamroller!

A gentleman checked out of a hotel and, when a few blocks away, remembered his umbrella. Returning to the hotel, he learned a newly wedded couple had taken the room. As he approached their door, he heard a kiss from within and the bridegroom say, "Whose little mouth is that?"

"Yours," she cooed.

"And whose little neck?" he asked.

"Yours, of course, sugarplum," she replied.

"And whose little hands?"

"Yours, all yours," she murmured.

"Listen here, you folks!" the man in the hall called out, "when you get to the umbrella, it's mine."

SAILOR: I'd like to have some good old-fashioned loving.

GIRL: Okay, come on over to the house and I'll introduce you to Grandma.

"Are you looking at my ankles?"

"No, I'm above that."

You been going with my daughter for twenty-three years. People are beginning to talk.

GUY: I could go fer you!

GAL: And I could go fer you!

COMIC: There's a couple of "Gophers" if I ever saw any!

CORPORAL: What did you tell that bleached blonde?

SARGE: I told her to take me or leave me.

CORPORAL: Which did she do?

SARGE: Both.

"Do you love me, darling?"

"Of course I do, Herbert."

"Herbert? My name's Arthur."

"Why, so it is. I keep thinking today is Monday."

That's the way it is—give a woman an inch and she makes a miniskirt.

I'd like to marry a tattooed woman with St. Vitus' dance—if I couldn't sleep nights I'd sit up and watch the moving pictures.

SHE: Haven't I seen your face somewhere before?
HE: Possibly; I lose my head once in a while.

Elmer, aged thirteen, was puzzled over the social problems and discussed them with his pal, Mortimer.

"I have walked to school with this dame three times," he told Mortimer, "and I have carried her books. I bought her ice-cream sodas twice. Now do you think I ought to kiss her?"

"Naw, you don't need to," said Mortimer. "You've done enough for that dame already!"

She was only a drill sergeant's daughter, but she knew when to call a halt.

A: Does she ever walk home from rides?

B: No, but sometimes she rides home from walks.

A: Say, what became of that girl you made love to in the hammock?

B: We had a falling out.

A: Want some chewing gum?

B: Thanks.

A: Wanna neck?

B: Nope.

A: Gimme back my gum.

Mrs. Gray and I met often on the sly. One evening we arrived there to find that the sly had been torn down by her suspicious husband.

"The way to fight a woman is with your hat—grab it and run."

—John Barrymore

It was a whirlwind courtship—we met in a tornado and went around together for a while.

He loved me with abandon—in fact, I never saw him again.

You can never get in trouble chasing women. The trouble starts when you catch one.

Walt Morrissey is a big ladies' man—he goes out with the biggest ladies in town.

GIRL'S FATHER: Young man, we turn out the lights at 10:30 in this house.
YOUNG MAN: Gee, that's darned nice of you.

HE: Hello cutie. Where have you been keeping yourself?
SHE: What do you mean, cutie? And what makes you think I've been keeping myself?

SHE: Stop that man, he tried to kiss me.
HE: Don't worry; there'll be another along in a minute.

SHE: Pardon me, are you looking for someone particular?
HE: No, I'm satisfied if you are.

JAYNE: You look nice.
STEVE: I *am* nice.

ANXIOUS MOTHER: Young man, you have been keeping company with my daughter for six months. Now tell me what your intentions are.
SERGEANT: Honorable, but remote.

"Is Mary your older sister, my little man?"
"Yep."
"And who comes after her?"
"You and two other guys."

WEN: Boy, at the amusement park yesterday I went through the tunnel of love . . . it was pitch dark in there . . . boy, it was fun!
JUNE: Did you have your girl with you?
WEN: What for? I ain't afraid of the dark.

He sent his girl a jigsaw photo of himself, so she could get used to his face gradually.

RUGS

I didn't want to get wool carpeting for my mew apartment because I was afraid of moths, so I got carpeting made out of cotton. It has been completely destroyed by boll weevils.

RULES

AGENT: You know my rules! No drinking!
FIRST MAN: No drinking.
AGENT: No smoking!
SECOND MAN: No smoking!
AGENT: No girls!
THIRD MAN: No smoking.

RUNNING

A man entered a restaurant from the pouring rain, and as he put his umbrella in the rack by the door, he took out a pen and piece of paper and wrote the following note: "This umbrella in the stand below belongs to the champion heavyweight fighter of the world. He's coming right back."

After fastening the note to the rack he proceeded to relax and enjoy lunch. When the man came back to the rack, his umbrella was gone, and in place of his earlier note, there was this one: "Umbrella now in possession of the champion marathon runner of the world. He is *not* coming back."

RUSSIA

Two Russians were discussing the chances of war. One said that if it came, Russia would win.

"As soon as we develop the atom bomb, we will send six or seven agents to America, each with an atomic bomb in a suitcase. They will set off their bombs simultaneously in the great cities. That will finish the war."

"We couldn't do that," said the second Russian.

"Why? Don't you think we shall have the atomic bombs?"

"Oh, we'll have the bombs," replied the skeptic, "but where are we going to get the suitcases?"

A real estate developer paid a visit to an Indian Chief on his reservation, hoping to convince the tribe to allow part of their land to be used as a housing development. The developer was led into the Chief's private council, where he began to outline his plans.

"We will build you houses, parks, and excellent recreation centers," boasted the developer.

The Chief looked at the visitor, nodding his head and grunting, "Oom gawa."

"You will become rich beyond your wildest dreams," continued the fast-talking visitor.

"Oom gawa," the Chief answered.

"I promise you a better life and prosperity for your children."

The Chief continued to nod and replied, "Oom gawa."

The developer, delighted at this easy sell, thanked the Chief and hurried out of the teepee to survey the land for his new development. He looked off into the distant field where a herd of cattle were grazing. "Do you mind if I just walk over to the field and take a look?" the developer asked a nearby Indian brave.

"Not at all," answered the brave. "Just be sure you don't step in the Oom gawa."

A man selling the 44-volume encyclopedia finished his pitch with a hearty, "Yes, ma'am, you just put a tiny deposit down and don't pay another penny for six months."

The prospect looked surprised and asked, "Who told you about us?"

A real estate salesman spent almost an entire Sunday showing a young couple one model home after another.

"And here," said the realtor, weary at the eleventh home, "is the hobby room. Do you folks have any hobbies?"

"Oh, yes," replied the wife. "On Sundays we look at model homes."

Anyone who goes to auctions will love this story:

During heated bidding at a Wilshire Boulevard art gallery in Los Angeles, the activity was momentarily halted when the auctioneer said, "Ladies and gentlemen, a man in the room has just lost his wallet containing $25,000 in cash. He offers $500 for its return."

There was a brief pause, after which a voice from the back of the room cried, "$525!"

One of the best stories about Hadacol, the patent medicine, that legends have spread throughout the country, is of the salesman who reported to the owner of the company that Hadacol had had its first fatality.

"She was ninety-two years old, and had been taking Hadacol regularly for many years, but she died," sighed the salesman.

The owner was shocked by this distressing news, and the salesman hastened to console him with: "But we saved the baby!"

SCOTTISH

A Scotsman invited a friend to his birthday celebration. He told the address of the street in Glasgow where he lived, and mentioned the various ways of getting there, giving instructions for the proper buses, trains, and taxis.

"When you get to the front door of my apartment, push the bell with your elbow, and when the buzzer sounds, shove the door open with your right foot."

"Why do I have to go to all that trouble?"

"Why not? You're not coming empty-handed, are you?"

SECRETARY

BOSS: You should have been here at nine o'clock this morning.
NEW STENOGRAPHER: Why, what happened?

"I seem to remember that girl. Who is she?"

"She was my typist last year."

"She's charming! Why did she leave you?"

"She was too conscientious for me. One day I proposed marriage to her, and what do you think she did? She took all that I said down in shorthand and brought it, nicely typewritten, for me to sign."

SHAKESPEARE

Shakespeare once wrote a play about Popeye called *The Merchant of Spinach.*

SHOES

These shoes are really something. I said: "Do you have anything like size 11?" He said: "Yeah . . . size 14." I think these were formerly ballet slippers for a kangaroo.

An after-Christmas customer at local shoe store:
"How much are your ten-dollar shoes?"
"Five dollars a foot."

Comic puts shoes on while legs are crossed, and as long as legs are crossed, shoes look perfectly normal. When comic straightens legs out, it is seen that he has shoes on wrong feet.

SHOPLIFTING

Warning to small businessmen: The Better Business Bureau announces that there is a wave of shoplifting going on and urges all store owners to nail their shops down securely.

SHOPPING

"Gracie, what's this check stub, one pullover, $25? I don't want to sound like a cheapskate, but isn't that a lot of money for a pullover?"

"The man on the motorcycle said it was the regular price."

"You got it from a man on a motorcycle?"

"Yes, I went through a red light and he drove up and said, 'Pull over!'"

Burns and Allen

SHOW BIZ

There has been so much written about Samuel Goldwyn, including a book by Alva Johnson, that I hesitate to include a Goldwyn story here. To our knowledge, this one never has been printed.

Andre Previn, the pianist, arranger, and composer, tells it. He was working on the Goldwyn lot. Every morning he had to have a conference with the old gentleman. One morning he noticed that

Goldwyn seemed excessively nervous. Same thing the next morning, and the next.

On the fourth morning, Previn, thinking that perhaps his work was not up to Goldwyn's standards, inquired hesitantly if there was anything wrong.

"Yes, yes, there is," Goldwyn said. "My wife has a birthday coming. I don't know what to give her. Jewels, no. She has all she wants. Paintings, no. Another car? No. Luggage? No."

Previn did not know what to suggest. He turned in his work of the day before and went back to his studio.

The next day he found Goldwyn in a state of relaxation. "I've solved the problem," Sam said. "I know what I'm going to give Frances for her birthday. You know, Frances has lovely hands. I love to look at them, they're so graceful."

Previn said, "Yes, I've always admired her hands."

Goldwyn said, "Well, I was thinking about her the other day, and I came to the conclusion. For her birthday, I'm going to give Frances a bust of her hands."

Previn has another Goldwynism that never has been printed. He and the old man were on their way to the commissary when they encountered actress Ann Blythe. It was noontime.

"Hello, dollink," said Sam, as she embraced and kissed him. "Come along and have lunch with us."

She explained that she was on her way to the makeup department, and couldn't have lunch with them. Off she went. Sam gazed after her fondly. He turned to Previn. "There goes the cutest two things on feet," he said.

Something else Goldwyn once said made me laugh heartily, although I suppose that was because he said it to me.

We were guests at the same Hollywood dinner party some years ago and, although I had met Mr. G in passing once or twice earlier, I had never really had an extended conversation with him. This particular evening I was pleased to have that opportunity and we chatted about one thing or another for quite some time. A couple of hours later, as the group was breaking up, Goldwyn approached me as I neared the front door. "Good night," he said. "I just wanted you to know how much I enjoyed talking to you tonight, Ed."

The old Tim Costello's bar, at 44th Street and Third Avenue in New York, was a favorite hangout for writers. One Monday morning there were convened Sam Boal, now deceased; Lester Cooper, later a TV producer and writer; and Ring Lardner, Jr., one of the Hollywood Ten, all of whom had gone to federal prison for a year for refusing to testify before the House Un-American Activities Committee as to their previous Communist Party activities. One who had testified against these men had been Budd Schulberg, author of *What Makes Sammy Run?* It was in part his testimony that, in fact, had sent the Ten to prison.

Budd had had a collection of short stories reviewed in the *Times* the day before. The reviewer had said that Budd "has nothing to say."

On this day in Costello's, Lester Cooper said, "Isn't that a terrible thing for a reviewer to say? That Budd has nothing to say?"

Sam Boal said, "Well, he doesn't have anything to say." Ring Jr., who had just spent ten months in prison, quietly said, "Except when he goes to Washington."

Ernie Kovacs was once a guest panelist on *What's My Line?* The Mystery Guest was auto magnate Henry J. Kaiser, and after some questioning, the panel determined that he was an automobile manufacturer who had named his car after himself. "Are you Edsel Ford?" One panelist asked.

"No."

"Are you Henry Ford, Jr.?"

"No."

Kovacs then asked, "Are you, by any chance, Abraham Lincoln?"

David Merrick had seven shows he had produced in New York and London running simultaneously. A press agent who was working for Merrick got to loathe him for various reasons: his spurious show of virtue, his sneaky pretense of honesty, and his staging of public relations stunts, which mainly were rigged by his press relations counselor, my funny old friend Jim Moran.

Eventually Merrick became famous enough to have a nickname bestowed upon him around Broadway. People called him "The Abominable Showman."

Jim Moran was a large, amiable man, who ran for the unfinished term of the dead Hiram Johnson in California with the slogan, "What this country needs is a good five cents."

One day, when a friend was visiting him, the telephone rang. "No," Moran said. "A hundred and fifty bucks is too much to pay for a man trap." He put down the instrument. "Imagine that," he said to his visitor. "Some guy wants to sell me a trap to catch a man." Later, he explained that mantraps had been in common use in England to catch poachers.

Examples of early 1940s radio humor:

SHIRLEY ROSS: It looks like rain.
BOB BURNS: Not in California!
SHIRLEY ROSS: But look at those clouds up there.
BOB BURNS: They don't mean nothin'. They're just empties comin' back from Florida.

Always fascinated by complicated machines, Moran used to invent them himself. One of his better ones, introduced to the world on my original *Tonight Show,* was called he "Fatolater," which had a number of pistons, gears, wheels, and lights.

"One of the primary laws of nature," Moran said, "is that matter can be neither created nor destroyed. Now millions of people are going on diets these days. The fat they're losing must be going somewhere. I have discovered it is going into the atmosphere, so I have developed a machine to render it out."

Moran turned on the machine. It whirred and growled, and a wisp of blue smoke came up from it. The lights flashed on and off. After a moment, a chime sounded, and the machine stopped.

Moran faced our cameras dramatically. "Notice this small drawer in the Fatolater," he said. "When I open it, I will remove a small ball the size of an English walnut, resembling pure lard. This will be fat from people who have lost weight, rendered from the air around us."

Deliberately, he opened the little door to the drawer. With much ceremony, he took out a small piece of steak. "Good Lord!" he shouted. "Somebody around here is losing meat!"

Moran used to like to create strange animals and birds. One Thanksgiving, he and a butcher spent hours sewing four extra legs on a turkey. He presented it to TV host Dave Garroway.

"Where did you get this?" Garroway asked, understandably mystified.

"I mated two three-legged turkeys," Moran said.

On another occasion, Moran invited some friends to his apartment to see what he described as the world's only fur-bearing turtle. There it was, hirsute as anybody could imagine, crawling around the place. "I call it the Furtle," he explained.

He later confessed to a friend that he had glued an opossum's skin to the turtle's back.

The late Richard Maney, the press agent, went to work for Jed Harris, the fabled producer, who at the age of twenty-four had four plays running at the same time on Broadway. He was called The Boy Wonder. It was a wonder to his associates as to how he could find any spare time to write so many memoranda. Presently,

Richard Maney grew tired of Harris's habit. One day he decided to send Jed a memo:

To: Jed Harris
From: R. Maney
Dear Jed: What time is it?

Moss Hart, who with his partner, George S. Kaufman, wrote some of the funniest plays produced in the '30s, was forever falling wildly in love, swearing he was going to marry the girl of the moment. Then, after a few weeks or months, he would break up and go on to another affair.

Eventually he met and fell in love again, this time with Kitty Carlisle. "Oh, this is it," he said to Kaufman. "This time I really am going to get married."

"I see," Kaufman said.

They arranged to meet in Sardi's for supper after the theater one night. Hart came in with Miss Carlisle on his arm.

"Here comes Moss," said George to his companion, "with the future Kitty Carlisle."

Hart did marry Kitty Carlisle, but that did not prevent Kaufman from continuing to make japeries about him, as he had done from the beginning of their collaboration. After their first success, Hart decided to become a country squire. At that time, the "in" place to move to from New York was Bucks County, Pennsylvania. Both land and houses were cheap there. It was quiet; it looked to city-folk writers like an ideal place to work. Josephine Herbst and John Hermann had led the march down; Dorothy Parker and Allen

Campbell had followed, and all four, when they got back to New York for weekends, would urge their literary friends to follow.

Immediately after Hart's first hit with Kaufman, the former went to Bucks County, took a house, had it remodeled, spent a lavish amount on landscaping, and hired a great many servants. It was the most elaborately furnished house in Bucks County, and was the one that most impressed New York writers who went down to visit.

Kaufman was not especially impressed. "It shows," he said, "what God could do if he had money."

Dining in Sardi's, an actor discovered at the end of his dinner that he had left his wallet at home. He said to Vincent Sardi Jr., "I'll have to sign."

"No," said Vincent, "you won't have to sign. I'll just write your name on the wall over there, and the amount under it."

"But that'll be so embarrassing! All my friends'll see it."

"No, they won't."

"Look, I'm in a big hit now. All my friends will see it! They'll all think I'm as broke as I used to be."

"They will not see it," Vincent said. "I'm going to put your overcoat right over it."

There used to be a number of famous wits in Hollywood, all of who used to supply the old-line women columnists with material, which they could not dig up themselves. Vince Barnett was one, Jim Henagan was another; Ken Englund was one, and so was Bill Morrow, though scarcely any of the people who laugh at Jerry

Lewis and Red Skelton movies would recognize their names. Vince Barnett was a "ribber" who contrived elaborate practical jokes. Jim Henagan was a press agent who contrived elaborate schemes. Ken Englund's name might be recognized; he and a partner wrote several of the early Danny Kaye films. Bill Morrow wrote for Bing Crosby and Jack Benny for many years. He wrote in partnership with a man named Eddie Beloin. They made up what many considered the funniest radio joke of all time. Benny was being held up, at a time when it was well established that he was a tightwad. The script went as follows:

HOLDUP MAN: Your money or your life.
JACK BENNY *(long silence):* I'm thinking it over.

Now at last we get around to the man who is regarded in the film industry as perhaps the funniest—Billy Wilder. His humor is both contrived and spontaneous: contrived for his films, spontaneous for his friends.

Wilder, who was born in Vienna, regards the human race, and himself, with a detachment that is a mixture of pity and irony. Verbally he is merciless, but internally he is kind.

"I was nominated for the Academy Awards twenty-three times," he has said. "My films and me. I got only eighteen nominations. Five times they robbed me."

Wilder was positive that *Suddenly, Last Summer,* the first picture to deal with contemporary cannibalism, would not be a success. "In this movie business, you learn that you do not offend pressure groups. Do not offend the Jews, the Catholics, the Protestants, the dentists, the Seven-Day Adventists, the Rotarians, the Lions, or any other group. That picture will flop," explained Wilder, "because it will offend vegetarians."

George Axelrod, the playwright, had had a long-running Broadway play in *The Seven-Year Itch*. Billy Wilder bought it and Axelrod went to Hollywood, taking the original script with him. He said he thought they might use it "as a guide."

"Fine," Wilder said, dropping it to the floor. "We'll use it as a door-stop."

"We shoot only from angles that tell the story and push it along," Wilder said. "None of that overhead stuff. When someone turns to his wife or neighbor and says, 'My, that was beautifully directed,' that's proof that it was not."

"The deals out here, these days, are for pictures in cycles," Wilder said. "Western cycles, gangster cycles, all kinds of cycles. There is a cycle of Freudian pictures coming along. I would not be surprised if they make *Hopalong Oedipus,* or *Frontier Mother-Lover.*"

Wilder had a bad back for a time. "How did you get it?" A friend asked.

"I have been to famous doctors everywhere, for years," he said. "They could not tell me anything about it. Finally I came to my own conclusion. I got it from trying to make love to girls in hallways, in Vienna, when I was a boy. Some nights there were no girls—just hallways."

Wilder made *Some Like It Hot* with Marilyn Monroe, who showed up late most of the time and sometimes never came to work at all.

Wilder said he'd never make a picture with her again in the United States. "But I would do it in Paris," he said. "While we were waiting for her, we could all take painting lessons on the side."

The following letter was actually received at the offices of the Federal Communications Commission in the nation's capital:

Dear FCC,
Please make Walter Cronkite stop saying "That's the way it is" at the end of his news program. He don't know how it is. He only thinks he does.

Since his days in Germany, Wilder always had been known as a man who is willing and extremely able to tinker with and improve others' work when they feel they are in trouble. Even when he was in the middle of shooting, he took time out of his busy schedule to help a friend untie some knot.

One day Otto Preminger, a gentleman who played a Nazi in *Stalag 17*, was quarreling with Samuel Goldwyn. Wilder was brought in as umpire.

Preminger began yelling.

"Calm down, Otto," Billy said. "I've still got relatives in Germany."

An unusually conceited Hollywood actor did about a forty-minute monologue on the subject of himself, hoping to impress a young starlet. At last he said, "But enough about me, my dear. Let's talk about you. Tell me, how did you like my last picture?"

John Barrymore, while playing Hamlet in London, was asked by a matron whether she thought Hamlet had ever had sexual relations with Ophelia. "Only in the Chicago Company, madam," Barrymore replied.

At a testimonial dinner honoring Cary Grant, Frank Sinatra read wires from MGM's Kirk Kerkorian, Lord Olivier, Nancy and Henry Kissinger, and Grant's former costars, Ingrid Bergman, Audrey Hepburn, and Princess Grace of Monaco. NBC's Tom Brokaw recalled that Grant had given the "best response to a writer's question." To a wire from *Time* magazine asking "How old Cary Grant?" Grant had replied, "Old Cary Grant fine. How you?"

Five teams of writers were working for a well-known comedian. They had been working for him so long, they had all their jokes numbered.

"Seven!" one would shout, and the man at the typewriter would write "Seven" into the script.

The head writer would beam with approval.

"Three!" yelled another.

The head writer again would smile.

"Twenty-two!"

"Fine," the head writer said. "Keep it up, boys!"

"Sixty-eight!"

"Great!"

"Ninety-six!"

"Next week, you'll find a bonus in your envelope!"

Everybody was laughing up to this point. Then one of the writers intoned, rather solemnly, "Eleven."

The laughter stopped. The room was silent. The head writer looked gloomy. It was a full minute before he spoke.

"Sorry, Irving," he said. "We can't use that in this script. You just don't tell it right."

To be a comedian you've got to suffer—suffer! You . . . not me!!

Arthur Godfrey got a letter from a CBS fan saying: "Dear Mr. Godfrey: I know you're famous for not using a script in your broadcasts, so in the future please don't rattle it so loudly at the microphone."

All right, everybody, hold hands; we'll have a community sleep.

My old pal from TV's *What's My Line?* Bennett Cerf used to tell the story about playwright Moss Hart meeting an old school chum by chance one day while visiting New York's Delancey Street. The friend was selling hot dogs.

"Say, aren't you Moss Hart?"

"Yes, I am," Moss said. "And your name?"

"Abe Melman. Listen, Hart, what are you doing now?"

"Well," said Hart, "I write plays for a living. In fact, I have two hits running on Broadway right now."

"That's marvelous," said Melman. "Tell me, from these hits, how much are you making?"

"Well," said Hart, "at present it's adding up to something like two hundred thousand dollars a year."

"Two hundred thousand a year from writing plays?" Melman cried. "My God, why didn't *I* think of that!"

Saw you at that big benefit. Wotta night! All the big stars were there. Frank Sinatra sang, Bob Hope told jokes, and Boris Karloff strangled three customers to death . . .

He was sort of a pantomime heckler. . . . He made faces at the stage.

This picture was not released; it escaped.

We want you to have fun here tonight, and when you laugh I want you to go all out. And if you don't you can all go out.

SIGNS

"See that sign KEEP OFF? That means you."
"Me? How did they know I was coming?"

On a "super" service station:

ONLY EXPERIENCED MEN WORK ON YOUR CAR HERE

And just below it:

HELP WANTED

NO EXPERIENCE NECESSARY

PLEASE DON'T THROW CIGARETTES IN THE WATER FOUNTAIN. THEY GET SOGGY AND HARD TO LIGHT.

Sign in a washroom:

GEORGE SCHLEPPINGTON WASHED HERE

Sign on bridge:

NO DOGS ALLOWED ON THIS BRIDGE

"How did the dog get across?"
"The dog couldn't read."

SIN

Sin covers a multitude of charities.

SINGING

Now don't forget . . . if you forget the words just say "Tum-Tum-Tummy-Tum," or something like that until the words come back.

(Sings): And she wore a wreath of roses 'round her Tum-Tum-Tummy-Tum.

After listening to Tallulah Bankhead struggle through a song, Jimmy Durante confided, "I think you ought to have your tonsils out."

"I've already had them out," she replied.

Durante suggested: "Then put 'em back in."

A: Do you know "The Road to Mandalay"?
B: Shall I sing it?
A: No, *take* it!

I've been advised by my physician not to sing in public . . . in fact, I've been warned.

"Carry me back to old Virginia." That's the only way they'll ever get me there.

I'll now sing you a medley of songs from Broadway shows I'd like to be in.

"False-etto?" No! My etto is the real thing.

Vic Damone got his start when he was an elevator operator in the Paramount Theatre. He stopped Perry Como between floors and sang for him. He'll never forget Perry's encouraging words, "Four, please."

He was a street singer. When he'd start singing in the house, they throw him out in the street.

A: I know a girl who can sing "Honeysuckle Rose" for two hours.

B: That's nothing . . . I can sing "The Stars and Stripes Forever."

Some women who sing in nightclubs are addicted to one deplorable practice, which serves exactly the opposite purpose to that which they intend. They approach your table and sing to you personally.

SKEPTIC

Our idea of a skeptic is a man who sees twenty people waiting for the elevator and then goes up and pushes the button.

SLEEP

His bed looked as if a herd of buffalo had run through it during the night.

I've been trying to read a book titled *How to Fight Insomnia* but I can't seem to get interested in it. I keep falling asleep.

Early to bed and early to rise.
And you'll never have red in the whites of your eyes.

The fluffer:

He spends six of his eight hours whacking at his pillow. He lives alone. His wife left him when, for the third time, he accidentally fluffed up her head.

The get-readier:

This type spends three-quarters of an hour getting "all set" for bed. Everything is within reach: book, magazine, milk, cake, pipe, radio, reading lamp . . . then he finally climbs in . . . and falls right to sleep.

SLOT MACHINES

A Chicagoan went to a roadhouse near French Lick recently, and after dinner dropped $50 worth of quarters in the slot machine without getting a return. Turning to the attendant, he inquired how often the jackpot paid off.

"I couldn't say, sir," said the lad. "I've only been here two years."

SMILE

Every man likes to see a broad smile, especially if she's smiling at him.

SMOKING

"Do you mind if I smoke?"
"You can burst into flames for all I care."

SOCIETY

Mayflower—a small ship on which several million Pilgrims came to America in 1620.

SONG TITLES

"I Want to Take You with Me Wherever I Go . . . 'Cause I Can't Stand to Kiss You Good-Bye."

The name of this song is "La Vie en Rose."
Oh, I'm sorry. It was written by Levy and Rose.

We will now have a songfest . . . and some of the songs these days sound as though they've been allowed to fester.

(Sings): "And for Bonnie Annie Laurie I'd lay me down and die."
"Is Miss Laurie in the house?"

"Before I Pop the Question, Dear, I'd Like to Question Your Pop."

"If You Knew Susie, Like I Know Susie, You'd Go Out With Sadie."

"Strolling Down the Osteo-path."

I'd like to dedicate this next tune to a wealthy girl that I used to go with back in Chicago. Her father was a junkman and he died and left her a pile. It's called "Nobody Knows the Rubble I've Seen."

You've heard of Al Jolson's "My Mother's Arms"? I've just written a song called "My Father's Legs."

Richard Rodgers' instrumental "If They Asked Me I Could Drive a Truck."

"I'm Dancing with Tears in My Eyes 'Cause the Girl in My Arms Stole My Watch."

I'm working on a new tune about a tired brewer. It's called "The Night Anheuser Got Bushed."

COMEDIAN: Tex Beneke and the Glenn Miller Band were doing "My Heart Is a Hobo."

STRAIGHT MAN: Is your heart a hobo?

COMEDIAN: No, but my pancreas has been on the bum lately.

Drinking song: "Succumbing Thru the Rye."

Parody on "Say It Isn't So":

Say it isn't snow . . . say it isn't snow, tell me that it must be popcorn falling . . . say it isn't snow. Here in Southern Cal . . . every boy and gal . . . knows the stuff that falls from out the sky is orange juice, you know.

Once upon a time. Rain was quite a crime. Then the city fathers worried all about the smog and grime.

Now the mercury has dropped way down—that stuff has got to go. It's raining dandruff . . . Say it isn't snow!

Song for a racetrack sketch: "And Then My Horse Stood Still."

(Sings): "Is it true what they say about Dixie?"

"Yes, it is. I was out with her last night."

"She Was Only a Bachelor's Daughter." Which sounded fishy to me.

Here's a song title from an irate taxpayer: "I Wish I Had a Paper Dollar I Could Call My Own!"

"When It's Tomato-Blossom Time in Heinz-ville I'll Ketchup with You!"

"Waltz Me a Little Faster, Max, They're Playing a Charleston."

"You Must Have Been a Beautiful Baby, But Baby, What Went Wrong?"

"The Moon Is Yellow—and I'm Pretty Chicken Myself"

A lot of hit songs are named after novels such as "I Cover the Waterfront" and "Gone With the Wind." How come nobody ever wrote "Tom Swift and His Flying Machine."

"You Didn't Want Me When You Had Me . . . And Now That You've Lost Me and Haven't Got Anyone Else . . . And You Cry Every Night and Don't Know Which Way to Turn . . . You Still Don't Want Me"

"No Knife Can Cut Our Love in Two, When We Spoon By the Fork in the Road"

"Who Threw the Chowder in Mrs. Murphy's Overalls?"

"Was It Malice, Alice, When You Stepped on My Callous?"

"You Had What It Takes but Someone Took It"

"Why Look Around for an Ideal Man When It's Easier to Find a Husband"

Don't Come Back to Sorrento, Vito, There's a Price on Your Head"

"They Kem-Toned the Church with a Holy Roller"

"The Nite I Made You Say Uncle in the Ante-Room"

I've just written a sequel to "Careless Hands" called "Sloppy Feet."

You've heard of Peggy Lee's "Don't Smoke in Bed"? I just wrote "Don't Sleep in an Ashtray."

Love song of the apes: "Gorilla My Dreams, I Love You."

"He Was Bred in Old Kentucky, But He Was Just a Crumb Out Here"

Combining proven hits of yesteryear and the more progressive music of today:

"Ooh Blah Dee . . . Oodle Yuh Coo . . . How Come You Do Me Like You Do, Do, Do?"

"I've Got My Electric Blanket to Keep Me Warm"

"Things Were Very Blue for Father 'Till We Loosened His Collar"

"Early to Bed, and You'll Wish You Were Dead"

"She Was Only a Real Estate Man's Daughter but He Liked Her Lots"

"I'd Like to Get You . . . on a Fish Boat to Catalina."

"This Can't Be Love . . . Because I Hate Your Guts"

"You May Be a Good Skate, Baby, but You Cut No Ice with Me"

"My Girl Has Everything a Man Could Want . . . A Crew Cut, a Mustache, and Money."

"I May Be Square but I've Been Around."

"You May Have an Hourglass Figure Baby, but It's Later Than You Think"

"You Were the Cream in My Coffee but the Whole Thing's Sour Now"

"I Left My Sugar in Salt Lake City, So I'm Getting My Lumps By Mail"

"She Sued Her Husband for Flat Feet. They Were Always in the Wrong Flat."

"When You Kick Me Out in the Cold Again, Please Give Me the Old Soft Shoe"

"Don't Take Your Love From Me—Leave Her Here"

"Lover, Come Back to Me—You've Got the Keys to the Car"

"Now That It's October, I Try to Recall My Youth, but the Army Won't Release Him"

"Dear Old Pal of Mine, You're Always Around When You Need Me"

"Disc Jockey Blues" . . . (Listen to this lyric): "Baby, you look like a perfect stranger since your face got caught in my record changer."

SONGWRITING

It's fascinating to see how the great songwriters often experiment with a particular idea before deciding on their final version. The great Seymour Glick once wrote a song called "Tea for Six." A good enough idea, but it just didn't feel right. Then he wrote "Tea for Five." Again nobody was interested. Then, within a few weeks time, he wrote "Tea for Four" and "Tea for Three."

And then, all of a sudden—like a flash of lightning—he wrote his biggest hit; *(sings):* "I'm Alabamy Bound . . ."

SOUP

How do you expect to win the spelling bee if you don't eat your alphabetic soup?

RESTAURANT DINER: I just found a collar button in my soup.
WAITER: I wondered where that was.

I'll have a bowl of unexpurgated alphabetical soup, please.

SOUTH

When I was very young, I lived for a time in the South. My father and I worked on a cotton gin together, as a matter of fact; I took care of the cotton, and Father took care of the gin.

Two men from El Paso met one day:
"Where did you go?"
"I went to Dallas."
"Have a good time?"
"No, I never did like them Yankees."

SPANISH

"Adios, Señor! Hasta Mañana!"
"And Don Ameche to you!"

SPANKING

Little Bobby ran to his mother sobbing as though his heart would break.

"What's the matter, honey?" she asked.

"Daddy was hanging up a picture and he dropped it on his toe."

"Why, that's nothing to cry about; you should laugh at that."

"I did," sobbed Bobby.

SPEECH

As I look into your sea of upturned faces . . . I see your . . . upturned faces, and it gives me great pleasure to be called upon to speak on such a suspicious occasion. First I want to congratulate you on the magnificent job you've been doing. I'm not going to tell you what you've been doing . . . because you know what you've been doing . . . and it has been a magnificent job.

Your chairman showed me some figures, tonight, while you were coming in . . . and they were interesting figures. I think they show conclusively that as figures go, we are all growing bigger together. And that 2002, by and large, will be the year you looked forward to . . . in 2001.

I think, too, you were extremely fortunate in your choice of . . . er, chairman. I know of no other man, woman who could fill his seat, the way he does. I mean of course, *(bows)* Mr. George Sma— *(coughs . . . chokes . . . drinks water),* I think he is generally recognized as one of the greatest authorities on . . . his own particular field, in the world today.

And I can assure him that it is a great pleasure to be able to advance the interests of a man who has done so much to . . . to— to— advance the interests of, of— everything he has.

I met your chairman this afternoon, and I can say that ever since I've known him, he has proved to be a tireless worker, with his shoulder to the wheel, and his nose to the grindstone, his feet on the ground and . . . er . . . his back . . . against the wall.

I've also been speaking to your treasurer, and I believe that there is a man to be watched. And emulated.

Since he has been handling the treasury, the parathet has more than trebled the finjan and never before have so many owed so much . . . er, to so few.

I think we ought to give the Devil his dues . . . and pitch right in, fork over and er . . . help in his great work so nobly advanced.

The human brain is a wonderful thing. It starts working the moment you are born, and never stops until you stand up to speak in public.

We find him speaking nightly before great crowds in Madison Square Garden. All Manhattan was familiar with his ringing voice, his commanding air: "Programs, programs. You can't tell the players without a program!" But he quit because nobody wanted to tell the players anything anyway!

The late supervisor, James B. McSheehy, was one of San Francisco's most beloved and colorful public figures. During his six terms as a member of the board of supervisors, from 1918 to 1941, he delivered many memorable speeches, which he invariably punctuated with picturesque phraseology, including many a mixed metaphor.

Who could forget the afternoon, in the midst of a heated debate over a city transit issue, when Supervisor McSheehy declared:

"We should grab the bull by the tail and look the issue square in the face!"

Always sit down ten minutes before you think you are finished.

I've just been handed a note from the Committee, which asks me to remind you to pay Mr. Blivet your two dollars on the way out. The proceeds of tonight's dinner go to the Fund for Getting Better Speakers for the Dinners.

I think its one of the best examples of Billie Holiday's inimitable style.

By the way, for those of you who have trouble saying the word *inimitable,* I've discovered a handy shortcut that almost always works out. As you say the word, run your forefinger up and down over your lips twice, that is—once up . . . and once down. The labials mix with the dental sounds in just about the right combination to make the word come out right.

Friends of Rocky Graziano, the fighter who was always trying to improve his English, urged him to say *three* instead of *t'ree.* Despite the urging, Rockabye Rocky was telling them the other day about a certain fight and said: "The bum only lasted t'ree rounds with me."

"How many?" demanded his tutor.

"T'ree," said Rocky.

"How many?" repeated the instructor.

"Two," said Rocky.

The Society of After-Dinner Speakers owes a debt of gratitude to Dr. Robert A. Millikan.

The famed scientist, after waiting through more than three hours of preliminaries to give a speech at a Chamber of Commerce dinner, finally got up to say:

"At this hour, I fear the mind is too weary to listen to the speech I have prepared. I had intended to discuss one of the chapters in my new book, 'The Road to Peace.' Any of you who are interested may read the book."

The chairman of the committee was addressing a meeting at a teachers' institute:

"My friends, the schoolwork is the bulhouse of civilization, I mean—ah—"

He began to feel frightened.

"The bulhouse is the schoolwork of civ—"

The painful smile could be felt.

"The workhouse is the bulschool of—"

He was evidently twisted.

"The schoolbul is the housework—"

An audible snigger spread over the audience.

"The bulschool—"

He was getting wild. So were his hearers. He mopped his perspiration, gritted his teeth, and made a fresh start.

"The schoolhouse, my friends—"

A sigh of relief went up. Richard was himself again!

He gazed serenely around. The light of triumphant self-confidence was enthroned upon his brow.

"Is the woolbark—"

And that is when he lost consciousness.

"Mr. Johnson is well read. He repeated a wonderful quotation last night."

"What was it?"

"I can't give you the exact words but he said he'd rather be something in a something, than a something or other in a something else."

I accepted because where else can so many people see me without turning me off.

One of the most fabulous after-dinner speakers was George Jessel. George probably spent more time on the celery circuit than he did in strictly professional pursuits, and I have always suspected that he is a little sorry that he wasn't around to make an after-dinner speech after the Last Supper.

Public appearance idea: Start off speech by saying "—in conclusion."

PROFESSOR: "Can you give me the derivation of *auditorium?*"
PUPIL: "From *audio,* to hear: and *Taurus,* bull: A place where—
PROFESSOR: "That will do, that will do."

"It gives me pause . . . it behooves us . . ."

SPELLING

"Spell *weather.*"

"W-e-t-h-c-h-e-r, weather."

"That is the worst spell of *weather* we have had for some time.

Can you spell *snapping-turtle?*"

"Yes siree, horse and buggy!"

"Let's hear you."

"S-n-a-p, snap, snip-snap; take a straw, tickle him in the jaw, t-u-r-t-l-e, snapping turtle."

SPIRITS

"That was the spirit of your uncle, which turned the table over and made it do such queer stunts."

"I believe you. He always had very bad table manners."

Some English spiritualists once persuaded Charles Dickens to attend one of their séances.

"Now, Mr. Dickens," they inquired, "what spirit among the departed would you like us to summon?"

The author considered the question, and suddenly thought of a celebrated grammarian who had died when Dickens was a youth.

"Summon Lindley Murray," he suggested.

Soon they told him, "Lindley Murray is in the room."

"Are you Lindley Murray?" asked the doubting Dickens.

"I are," came the ghostly reply.

That was Dickens's last experiment in spiritualism.

SPRING

Spring breaks into town when no one is looking and hides in Central Park.

Ah! Spring is here. I woke up the other morning and found a Blue Jay on my big toe.

STARS

"Every night my girl and I would sit in the hammock and we'd look up to the Big Diaper."

"You mean the Big Dipper."

"You don't know what was hanging in our backyard."

STATE NAMES

Most of our states have Indian names. Translated, they sound rather silly. Massachusetts is from words meaning "big-little-hill town." The Indians had something in mind, but we don't know what. Another state name is from *"alba aya mule,"* which means, "I open the ticket." We call it Alabama, for some reason. Iowa was named for the Aiouez, or "Sleepy Ones," but don't mention it in Des Moines. Kentucky is from *"ken-tah-the,"* and means "Land of Tomorrow." Idaho, "Light on the Mountains." Minnesota means "sky-blue water." Texas means "friends," while Mississippi is *"maesi-sipu"*—"Fish River."

Names not Indian are mostly Spanish or English. Florida just means "Easter Sunday." California was named by Spaniards from a popular novel called *Las Serges de Esplandian.* In the book it was a balmy isle. Nevada is "snow-clad," if you believe in names. Maryland was so named in honor of Queen Henrietta Marie of England, who owned some land in France called "Maine."

—J. W. Holden

STEAM ROLLER

PHOTOGRAPHER: Have you ever seen a steamroller?
IRISH: No, how does one roll steam?

STENOGRAPHER

"Take a letter."

"Yes, sir."

"Just a minute, who ever heard of a typist taking a letter standing up? Come over and sit on my lap."

"Miss Gilmore," said the boss, "you doubtless have noticed how you girls today are getting your hair cut, smoking, swearing, and doing other things like we do."

"Why, yes—of course."

"Well, I wish you'd learn to spell like that man Webster."

Executive ability is the art of convincing your wife that you hired your pretty stenographer on account of her experience.

STOCK MARKET

How did I make out on the stock market today? Oh, I made a near killing. What? Yeah, my brother-in-law gave me some bad advice and I near killed him.

Stock Market Report: United Umbrella and American Elevators are still going up, but writing papers and envelopes remain stationery.

A speculator on the Stock Exchange was sitting in a friend's office, and during the conversation, which was mostly about stocks and bonds, he informed his friend that he had picked up a cheap thing during the winter.

"It stood at thirty-three then, and yesterday it touched eighty-four!" he said.

"By jove! You are lucky. What is it?" asked his friend.

"A thermometer."

"Bought it at 8 and sold it at 11. Only had it for three hours."

STOCKINGS

Another woman came in and called for a pair of silk stockings. I showed her a pair for twelve dollars. She said, "My goodness, but they come high." I said, "Yes, and you are one tall woman."

STRIKES

A man is walking with a sign on his back with the word STRIKE on it, and nothing else.

"What's the strike for and where is it?" somebody asked.

"I don't know yet, I'm looking for a sponsor."

I see there was another wildcat strike today up in San Francisco. Three wildcats at a zoo went on strike for more red meat.

Under the heading of chutzpah, comedian Harry Hirshfield used to tell the story of the woman who phoned the owner of a store and said, "Would you please call my husband, Mr. Klein, to the phone?"

"We have no Mr. Klein working here," the owner replied.

"I know," the woman said, "he's outside picketing your store."

STUTTERING

I need a pair of spec-rimmed hornicles. I mean sporn-rimmed hectacles, or heck-rimmed spornicles.

No, I got it. Him sporned rectacles.

SUPER BOWL

At the Super Bowl, a Texan placed a few bets and won five thousand dollars. The first thing he did was to phone his minister at home. "Preacher," he said, "I just won five thousand dollars on the football game. Isn't that the damnedest thing you've ever heard?"

The minister said, "Yes, but you should be more careful with your language."

"Okay," the man said, "but I want you to know I'm giving all the money to the church."

"The hell you say!" the preacher said.

SUPERSTITION

ME: Is it bad luck to have a black cat cross your path?
YOU: It all depends on whether you're a man or a mouse!

"I'm not superstitious."

"Then why are you throwing salt over your shoulder?"

"'Cause I've got a hamburger in my backpack."

STREETCAR CONDUCTOR: I can't let you on the car.

RIDER: Why not?

CONDUCTOR: There's twelve on here already and I'm superstitious.

Don Freeman, TV-radio editor of the *San Diego Union,* said to a friend one day, "Astrology is a lot of nonsense. I don't believe a word of it."

"That's very typical of an Aries," his friend replied.

SHE: Are you superstitious?

HE: Not at all.

SHE: Then can you lend me 13 dollars?

"Did you notice how he eats his soup?"

"Yes, he sounds like a drowning man going down for the third time."

TAXES

The *Denver Post* tells us that James Golden, regional program manager of Tax Payers Services in the Internal Revenue Service, says the agency receives conscience money sent in by anonymous taxpayers who believe they cheated on their income tax returns.

Golden said that five $100 bills fell out of an envelope with no return address. It also contained an unsigned letter, which read, "I cheated on my income tax return and I can't sleep at night. P.S. If I still can't sleep, I'll send you $500 more."

A mild-mannered little man sauntered into the Internal Revenue office and introduced himself to the receptionist. "What can we do for you?" she asked. "Oh, nothing," he replied. "I just want to meet the people I'm working for."

I've saved the money to pay my income tax. Now all I have to do is borrow some to live on.

A Bob Hope line:
Crosby never files a return, you know. Bing just calls Washington and asks, "How much do you need?"

Pitcher Dazzy Vance filed a return. And so much for "The Return of Philo Vance."

The sales tax would probably be a good thing if there were any sales to tax.

I was just thinking . . . if they didn't deduct so much for social security, welfare funds, unemployment insurance, and old-age pensions, we wouldn't *need* social security, welfare funds, unemployment insurance, and old-age pensions.

TELEPHONE

A: What's an operetta?

B: It's a girl who works for the telephone company.

A *(on phone):* Hello, hello, hello! Well, well, well! Good, good, good! Yes, yes, yes! Is that so? Is that so? Is that so? Well, good-bye, good-bye, good-bye!

B: Who was that?

A: The McGuire Sisters.

Getting wrong numbers over the telephone is not always the fault of the operator. Faulty enunciation is more often to blame. This incident illustrates one of the difficulties an operator has to overcome in answering calls.

An Englishman speaks over the telephone:

"Yes, this is Mr. 'Arrison. What, you can't 'ear? This is Mr. 'Arrison . . . Haitch, hay, two harrs, a hi, a hess, a ho, and an hen . . . 'Arrison."

Prank call:

VOICE ON THE PHONE *(3 A.M.):* Mr. Smith?

SMITH: Yes.

VOICE: Is your house on the bus line?

SMITH: Yes.

VOICE: Well, you'd better move it; there's a bus coming.

STEVE: After my last show the switchboard was jammed.

BOB: Lots of calls?

STEVE: No, the switchboard just got jammed.

The usual signal that people employ to indicate they are about to terminate a phone conversation is the phrase, "Well, listen . . ."

A (on phone): Hello . . . the time? Why, it's 2 after 10 . . . you're welcome (hang up).

B: Who was that?

A: Mr. Bulova!

WEN: You? Working at the telephone company? What do you do?

STEVE: When people try to dial a ten-cent number on a five-cent call I'm the little guy who picks up the receiver and goes: "WOOOO-ooooo-eeeee-oooo!"

A Kansas editor's definition of a woman is one who reaches for a chair when answering the telephone.

TELEVISION

You've heard of Ralph Edwards's *This Is Your Life*. I'm doing a new program, sponsored by Forest Lawn. It's called *This Is Your Death*.

We now present Mel Torme and Steve Allen in the *Mel Allen Show*.

We started the program cold. The janitor was on strike.

I have a note here about a new TV program. You've all heard of *Meet the Press*. Well, the Hot Dog Stuffers of America are going to put on a show called *Press the Meat*.

They got a new contest on television. They give you a bottle of Scotch, and after you finish it, the contest starts. You have to guess who *you* are!

Sometimes I sit at home for hours watching my television set. When this gets monotonous, I go over and turn it on.

When you're on television we can't get my husband away from our TV set. He's afraid somebody will turn it on.

Due to a peculiar pigment in my skin I photograph handsome. The only trouble is, in person I look like a kinescope.

We bought one of those new wide-screen TV's. I didn't realize it was so big until I saw all the cars lined up in front of my house. They thought it was a drive-in theater.

You can laugh, but the first night I made 20 bucks selling popcorn.

You're not supposed to have anything white on you when you're on TV. When I first signed up to do this show they wanted to pull all my teeth out.

They had great shows in the 1950s—*Time for Beany* . . . *Ding Dong School* . . . *Kukla, Fran, and Ollie*—and, of course, there are programs for children, too!

Television set commercial:

"You see . . . the handsome cabinet opens at a *(struggle)* at the flick of a—crowbar."

Buy the new Stromerg-Carlson set. See Arthur Godfrey, big as life. So close you feel you can reach right out and touch him.

Buy the new Fangschleister TV set. See Steve Allen so big you can hardly stand it. So close you feel you can reach right out and slap him in the mouth.

The Jigsaw Puzzle Manufacturers of America have just voted me the comedian most likely to go to pieces.

Comedy writer Goodman Ace once said he discovered how really to enjoy television. "We do it all with a six-foot screen," he explained, and when his visitor expressed astonishment, he added: "It's a Japanese screen, and we place it directly in front of the television set."

"I think my little boy is taking that Western television serial too seriously!"

"Why?"

"He's been going around branding all the furniture with his father's soldering iron, just so the neighbors won't rustle it!"

Some of these doctors on TV get carried away. I saw a doctor on TV last week perform a very skillful tonsillectomy. . . .

The applause from the gallery went to his head, so for an encore he removed the patient's appendix.

I was watching a cowboy movie on television the other night. The hero had a six-shooter. It would only fire 38 times without reloading.

It's nice to see you gentlemen in person. Both men from the network-owned stations . . . and those from the . . . er . . . dis-owned stations.

I know we're all sorry to hear that Walter Damm is retiring.

We've all looked up to him for many years. In fact, you might say he's been regarded in radio and television circles as something of a god.

And so this God Damm—I mean this . . . Oh, well . . . you know what I mean.

Referring to newspaper article titled "2000 in Argentina See Caesarean Birth on TV":

This could get to be a bad thing . . . women like to talk about their operations and also show their operations to other women. Now when one gal comes up to another and says, "Wanna see my operation?" the other gal will say, "No thanks . . . I caught the show."

We'll dolly in and then with the second camera we'll pan over. Now I've got a Dolly and a Pan, and when I put the dolly in the pan I want you to pan in on the dolly and dolly on the pan.

Examples of forgetting last word in an overly familiar series: Sears and—ah—Roebuck . . . C-B—ah—S.

Man, is my television set in bad shape. I tuned it in last night, and you know what I got? The Turpin-Robinson fight pictures. Ordinarily this wouldn't bother me . . . but it was Ben Turpin fighting Edward G. Robinson.

The reason radio- and television-studio audiences applaud at the mention of geographical place-names will always remain a mystery. One day I asked a woman in my audience a few questions about her personal life and in doing so elicited the information that she was the mother of twelve children. This bit of intelligence was greeted by the other members of the audience with nothing more than broad smiles, but when the lady announced that she was from the Bronx, the studio was shaken with lusty cheers. The important thing seems to be to live someplace; it doesn't much matter what you do there.

One of my favorite TV shows used to be the *Missing Persons* program. I often wonder why the show went off.

They probably ran into people.

Imagine a routine about the show's advertising agency getting into a panic because no people are missing. They assign a special kidnap squad to keep the show on the air.

I have two television sets at my house. Very interesting. The other night, on one set Milton Berle cracked a bad joke . . . and Hopalong Cassidy jumped out of the other one and shot him.

Color television will be here soon. I can't wait to see *Sam Spade, Private Eye,* brought to you in glorious blood-shot.

I see that NBC has been so pleased with the *Howdy Doody Show* that they're thinking of starting two new shows . . . one for the kids up to three years old and one for men over thirty: they're calling them Howdy Diddee . . . and Howdy Daddy.

Accidents are always occurring to mar the professional smoothness of TV shows. On one recent telecast a camera picked up a furtive prop man sprinkling ketchup on a corpse.
To make it look as if nothing were out of the way, he ate it.

What's the sense of buying a television set if you're going to listen to it with your eyes closed?

One of the big problems of television is makeup. I happen to have a very heavy beard. What is scientifically known as a *four-thirty* shadow. Without makeup I televise like a passport photo of Phil Silvers. Well, CBS wanted me to look pale and wan (like a native New Yorker) so they had a platoon of makeup men in for a treatment. They tried every powder in Max's box, but I still came over like Bluebeard. Finally, one genius came up with the perfect formula. Six cups of sifted flour and two teaspoons of baking soda. It's true. That's what I have on now. The only thing wrong is that if I stay under hot lights for too long, I break out in biscuits.

Comedian/writer Paul Pumpian recalls the story of a window washer who falls off the ledge of a 47-story building. As luck would have it, two workers below are carrying a mattress; the window washer falls onto the mattress, bounces high in the air through an open window, and lands on a pile of foam rubber.

People rush up and say, "My God, you're the luckiest man in the world."

He says, "Oh no, Regis Philbin is the luckiest man in the world."

TEXAS

A Texan in London was trying to impress some Brits with the size of his home state. "Do you know," he said, "that in Texas you can hop on a railroad car at eight in the morning and still be in Texas after riding twenty-four hours?"

"We," replied the Brits, "have trains like that in England, too."

THANK-YOU NOTE

A little girl's thank-you note: "Thank you for your nice present. I always wanted a pincushion, although not very much."

THEATER

I shouldn't complain about this theater too much, though. We have air-conditioning. When conditions are right . . . we have air.

To give you some ideas as to how old this theater is, the first show they put on here was called *Benjamin Franklin's Talent Scouts*.

I wouldn't exactly call this theater a barn, but where else did you ever see a piano stool with three legs?

I worked the Colonial Theatre here in Dayton years ago. The very fact that you people showed up here today means that you don't remember me.

Did you ever see the play *Hook and Ladder?* They had a great idea for a third act curtain. They set fire to the theater.

I played in a theater so rough the programs were printed on sandpaper.

JOE: I used to be a play-doctor.
BILL: When I was a kid, I used to play "Doctor" myself.

THEATER TICKETS

A young lad of thirteen was waiting to get into *South Pacific,* when he was spied by one of his father's friends.

"Hello, Paul," said the man. "How did you happen to get here tonight, you lucky kid!"

"Oh, I came on my brother's ticket," said the boy.

"And where's your brother?"

"Home looking for his ticket, I suppose," said Paul.

It's kind of tough to get tickets now. I can get you one seat . . . but it's not together.

THIN

He looks like an advance agent for famine.

She was so skinny she had to put lead in her pockets to keep from blowing away.

THRILL

A: Do you want to see something swell?

B: Yes!

A: Fine, drop a sponge in water.

TIRED

Worn-out as a woodpecker in a petrified forest.

TOAST

"I drink to your health when I'm with you, I drink to your health when I'm alone. I drink to your health so gosh-darned much, I'm afraid I'm losing my own."

Well *(man lifts glass),* here's . . . here's . . . here's my drink.

A toast from *The Widening Stain,* a detective thriller, by W. Bolingbroke Johnson:

"Champagne to my real friends, and real pain to my sham friends."

TONGUE TWISTER

In promulgating your esoteric cogitations or articulating your superficial sentimentalities, and amicable philosophical or psychological observations, beware of platitudinous ponderosity. Let your conversational communications possess a clarified conciseness, a compacted comprehendedness, coalescent consistency, and a concatenated cogency, eschew all conglomerations of garrulity, jejune babblement, and asinine affections. Let your extemporaneous descantings and unpremeditated expatiations have intelligibility and voracious vivacity, without rodomontade or thrasonical bombast. Sedulously avoid all polysyllabic profundity, pompous prolificacy, ventriloquial verbosity, and vain vapidity. In other words, say what you mean, mean what you say, and don't use big words.

TOUGH NEIGHBORHOOD

The other kids used to play Cops and Robbers around the block while I was doing it downtown—*with real cops.*

It was such a tough school, even the teachers played hookey.

TOWN

And, in case you've never been in one, a hick town is where, if you see a girl dining with a man old enough to be her father . . . he *is!*

It was a lovely little Swiss village, high in the Alps. On one side of the street I saw an old shoe cobbler, cobbling shoes. And a short distance away I saw a peach cobbler, cobbling peaches.

Small Town:

. . . Oh, yes, I've been there, that's where the old people go to visit their folks.

I understand that town is so dead the police department has an unlisted number.

"What is the best thing you ever saw in Wilmington?"
"The train to Baltimore."

TRAFFIC

The streets are sure tied up with traffic. I was in a cab this morning and everything was moving so slow that when my driver stuck out his arm to signal a left turn, a driver coming the other way stole his wristwatch.

I wouldn't say that the cars in New York were exactly riding bumper-to-bumper, but a friend of mine ran out of gas at 39th Street and didn't know about it until he reached the George Washington Bridge.

TRAINS

An old lady said, "Conductor, does this train stop at Chicago?"
He said, "Yes, providing the air-brakes work all right."
She said, "In case they don't work, where will we go?"
"That will depend altogether on how you have lived in this world."

Just as the train pulled out, the compartment door flew open . . . a man flung himself into the nearest seat; he was heaving and puffing, all out of breath. An elderly gentleman in the opposite corner put down his paper. "Young man, you must be in very poor condition. At your age, I never panted after a little exercise." The young man found his breath. "Listen, Pop . . . I'll have you know I missed this train at the last station!"

When I got off the train the other day, I was walking on air. The porter forgot to put the steps down.

MAN: Is New York the next stop?
PORTER: Yes, sah, brush you off, sah?
MAN: No, I'll get off myself.

Junior's first train ride was rough. He climbed on top of vacant seats, turned the aisle into a racecourse, and made himself generally obnoxious.

His father finally succeeded in grabbing his shirttail and hissing in his ear, "Sit down and be quiet—or I'll smack you."

"You hit me just once, Pop," Junior screamed, "and I'll tell the conductor how old I am."

HE: If I knew the tunnel was that long I'd have kissed you.
SHE: Good heavens! Wasn't that you?

"Is this Schenectady?"

"No, I'll tell you when we get to Schenectady."

But the old lady took no chances. At every station she would ask the conductor if this was Schenectady. Finally when they arrived, the conductor went to the old lady and told her it was Schenectady, but she didn't move. The conductor went to her and said, "This is Schenectady, don't you want to get off here?"

The woman said, "No, my daughter told me when I got to Schenectady not to forget to take my medicine."

TRAMP

A tramp knocked on the door of an inn known as George and the Dragon. The landlady opened the door and the tramp asked, "Could you spare a hungry man a bite to eat?"

"No!" replied the landlady, slamming the door in his face.

A few minutes later the tramp knocked again. The landlady came to the door again. This time the tramp asked, "Could I have a few words with George?"

SHE: I don't give money to people on the street.

HE: What do you want me to do, open an office?

TRAMP: Could you give a poor fellow a bite?
LADY: I don't bite myself, but I'll call the dog.

A beggar is a thief who has lost his nerve.

TRAVEL

"I want a ticket for Florence."
"Where in the devil is Florence?"
"Sitting over there on the bench."

SHE: It's nice in California right now. It was 80 when I left there.
HE: I was 30 when I left there.

Frank Morgan, in the play *The Band Wagon,* says, if you are lost in the Arctic and haven't seen a soul for days, take out a pack of cards, start playing solitaire, and pretty soon you'll be surrounded by kibitzers.

A fashionable lady had just returned from a trip to Europe and was busy impressing her friends with the beautiful things she had seen and the wonderful places she had visited, when a woman asked, "Did you by any chance see the Dardanelles?"

"See them?" the traveler replied, "why, my dear, we had lunch with them!"

EXPLORER: Once when I was lost in the South American jungle, I came across a tribe of wild women who had no tongues.
LADY: Great heavens! How could they talk?
EXPLORER: They couldn't—that's what made them wild.

TROMBONE

She used to play the trombone when she was a kid; then she let it slide.

HE: How about donating a dollar to bury a poor trombone player?
SHE: Here—take three dollars and bury a couple more.

. . . as tough as playing the "Flight of the Bumblebee" on a trombone in a telephone booth.

TUBA

While I was playing the tuba a strong wind came up and screwed me six feet into the ground.

TWINS

"I hear your wife presented you with twins? Boys or girls?"
"I think one is a boy and one a girl, or it may be the other way round."

UGLY

We call her Hesperus because she looks like a wreck.

He had two daughters—one was good-looking, and the other he could trust any place.

She's so ugly; when she gets ready to go to bed the guy across the street pulls down the shades.

UNCLE

He was in an auto accident. He fell out of a patrol wagon.

UNDERTAKER

"I just found out your uncle's an undertaker. I thought you told me he was a doctor."

"Nope. I just said he followed the medical profession."

UNEMPLOYMENT

One guy got so used to having everything done for him, he just went out and married a widow with six children.

UNICYCLE

"I'm so glad to see Freddie working again," said Allen. "Now he'll be able to afford another wheel for his bicycle."

USEFULNESS

Well, she's a pretty good girl, for one thing."
"Oh, what's the one thing?"

VACATION

"We went to a place called warm mattress."
"Where is that?"
"Just a little above hot springs."

"Yes, I had a wonderful holiday. No regular hours for meals! No extra charge for baths! As much food as you could eat, and no tips to waiters!"
"Swell! Where did you go?"
"I stayed home!"

He winters in Miami, summers in Canada, and springs at girls!

One of the preliminaries to going on a vacation is reading the travel folders and booklets describing hotel accommodations. The unsuspecting tourist will require some interpretation of the terms used:

Conducive to complete relaxation: The place is dead.

A charming atmosphere of rustic simplicity: No inside plumbing.

25th season under same owner-management: Haven't been able to sell the place.

Bathing nearby: The hotel has no swimming pool.

Spacious grounds—350 acres: You've got to walk two miles from your bungalow to the dining hall.

VACUUM CLEANER

Gus Swanson, the master salesman, waxed eloquently about the merits of his vacuum cleaner, but the small-town housewife was not impressed.

She suggested that he talk less and show her what the machine could do.

That was right down Gus's alley. Beaming broadly, he rigged up his cleaner and then reached his arm into the chimney of the open fireplace and brought out a handful of soot—then another. He spread the mess over the carpet and then, for good measure, added a shovel full of ashes, taken from the grate. "Now," Gus said, smiling triumphantly, "I'll show you what this vacuum cleaner can do. You'll be surprised, lady. Where's your electric switch?"

"Electric switch!" echoed the surprised lady. "We burn gas!" And that knot has been on Gus's head ever since.

MAID: There are half a dozen men downstairs with vacuum cleaners. They say they have appointments to give demonstrations.
MISTRESS: Yes, I sent for them. Put them in different rooms and tell them to get busy.

VALENTINE'S DAY

Dear Mr. Allen—
Your name belongs to Fred or Gracie
Your wardrobe comes from Penny, J.C.
Your specs are Dave's or Robert Q's
Your voice is like a lovesick goose
Your lines are limp, your tunes are looney
Your dancing's strictly Mickey Rooney
Your basketball stars play accordions
You're insulting to the audience
You pass out quips and joolry

And with every Dick and Harry engage in Tomfoolery . . .

You chatter with chimps and palaver with ponies

When you're not eating Shishlak you play ball with baloneys.

Your appetite is quite astronomic

You're a real gastronomic comic

You get paid for taking a haircut

Or learning how to give cards an unfair cut

Your, pardon the expression, format

Would shame a self-respecting doormat

With your hansom cabs and racing cars

Thank goodness you're nobody's fool but ours.

For in spite of your rating and your higher I.Q.

We find we cannot help but like you

VAUDEVILLE

"The weight-lifting Olsens had trouble at rehearsal yesterday. Olsen accidentally stepped on his wife's face."

"That's tough luck. Will they be off the bill long?"

"You can't tell. Athlete's foot is a serious thing!"

Old Vaudeville joke:

Ladies and gentlemen, our next attraction needs no introduction. What they need is an act!

My mother, a well-known Vaudeville comedian of her day, broke into show business by working as an aerialist with the old Barnum and Bailey Circus before the turn of the century. This fact had not yet been revealed, and so I announced to a guest on my show one evening some years ago that "my mother worked in the circus for years and she never once used a net."

"What did she do?" the guest asked.

"Sold popcorn," I replied.

WEALTH

A nouveau riche woman flaunted her wealth at every opportunity. One day she instructed her chauffeur to deliberately drive her through her old neighborhood in a sleek black limousine convertible. Her infant daughter, swathed in the latest, sat beside her. At a stop sign an admiring passerby looked at the child and said, "Can she walk?"

"Thank God she doesn't have to," the woman replied.

WOMEN'S LIB

He had a fight with Aunt Margi because he believes in women's suffrage. He said women had just as much right to suffer as men.

WORK

A very industrious, but not particularly bright, man was hired to paint a yellow line down the center of the road. After his first day on the job he reported back to the foreman and told him that he had painted a three-mile line. The foreman was very impressed. "Usually a good day is only two and a half miles," the foreman told the hardworking man.

The second day the man reported to his foreman that he had added only two miles to the line. "Well," said the foreman, "you have good days and bad days."

But the next day the worker came back from the road and told the foreman that he had only painted one more mile on the line.

"I'm sorry," said the foreman, "but each day you paint less and less. We're going to have to let you go."

On his way out of the office the disappointed man turned to the foreman and said, "Well, it's not my fault. Each day I get farther and farther from the paint can."

I work in fits and starts. If it fits, I start.

I believe it was Mark Twain who said that when a man boasts about his ancestors, he is suggesting that the best representatives of his family are those long dead. A certain stuffy gentleman was asked by the associate of a large firm if he could give a character reference or recommendation for a certain young applicant.

"Certainly," the New Englander wrote back. "Young George

Epworth is the grandson of Senator Epworth, the nephew of General Epworth, a third cousin of Lord Hodgkins, the nephew of Professor Epworth, and can boast of several other distinguished forebearers as well."

A company representative wrote back, "Thank you for your letter of recommendation about George Epworth, but may I point out that we were interested in him for work in computer programming, not for breeding purposes."

I've never seen him work so conscientiously—come to think of it, I've never seen him work!

I knew a really nervous girl once who tried to become a manicurist, but she had to give it up . . . she kept biting the customers' nails.

"Looking around for work?"
"I can't . . . I've got a stiff neck."

A: I have two versions of my life. Which one do you want?
B: What's the difference?
A: In the first version, I'm a hardworking, industrious young man with many virtues.

A: And in the second version?
B: I tell the truth!

I worked in a mill once. I was quite a dude. Mildewed, they called me.

WOMAN: I'm paying you by the hour, but I don't hear any noise in there!
PAINTER: Lady, if it's noise you want, I won't apply this paint with a brush. I'll nail it on with a hammer!

WRITING

A four-year-old girl was diligently banging away on her daddy's old typewriter. She informed him that she was writing a story.
"What is your story about?" he asked.
"I don't know," she replied. "I can't read."

"I wrote a book called *Boomerang* and sent it to a publisher."
"What happened?"
"It came right back."

Y2K

Larry King told me this one recently.

"Do you know what caused the Dark Ages?"

"No, I don't," I said.

"Y-1-K," Larry said.

MISCELLANEOUS

People who disparage puns generally don't know much about humor. Here's a marvelous multiple-pun fresh off the Internet.

Mahatma Gandhi walked barefoot most of the time, which produced an impressive set of calluses on his feet. He also ate very little, which made him frail, and with his odd diet, he suffered from bad breath. This made him what?

Answer: A super-callused fragile mystic plagued with halitosis.

From Henny Youngman's files:

Two hipsters were crossing the ocean. One said, "Yeah, man—and that's only the top of it!"

Henny Youngman: "Want to drive a guy nuts? Send him a wire that says, IGNORE FIRST WIRE."

Knock-knock jokes still persist, even though their original vogue ended in 1938. As with most jokes, nobody knows how this form of humor originated; certainly, nobody could find the person who made up the first knock-knock any more than anybody could write a definitive biography of Joe Miller.

Knock-knock.
Who's there?
Fortification.
Fortification who?
Fortification dey went to da Catskills.

Or

Knock-knock.
Who's there?
Orange juice.
Orange juice who?
Orange juice going to the party?

Vibraphonist Terry Gibbs told me the story of a man lost in the Arizona desert who hasn't had a drink of water in a week and is near death from thirst. Suddenly he sees a car coming along a deserted road and in desperation jumps up and flags the driver down.

"What do you want?" the driver says.

"Can you give me some water to drink?" the guy says. "I'm desperate; I'm dying of thirst."

"Do you wanna buy a tie?" the driver says.

"What the hell are you talking about?" the man says. "Here I'm practically half-dead from thirst and you're trying to sell me a tie. No, I don't want one of your damn ties, I want a drink of water."

"All right," the guy says, "relax. Back about 300 yards down the road you'll find a little cafe. Lots of luck."

So the man staggers back down the road, his throat parched, shaking with weakness. He finds the cafe, knocks on the door. The proprietor looks out and says, "Yeah? What do you want?"

"Please," the guy says, "I'm desperate for water. I've got to have it. Can I come in and have a glass of water?"

"You can't come in without a tie," the proprietor says.

If you are ever asked which particular joke is most often included in anthologies, it is probably the one credited—at least in *The Jestbook,* published in 1909 by MacMillan and Company, London—to Daniel Purcell, the famous punster. Although Purcell's fame would not seem to have survived the crossing of the Atlantic, he was presumably known in the nineteenth century for his ready wit and the ability to create humor spontaneously upon demand. One day one of his friends asked him to make up a joke on the spot.

"On what subject?" Purcell asked.

"The King," said his friend.

"My dear fellow," Purcell answered, "the King is not a subject."

He has a decided accent. I haven't decided what it is . . . but—

She looks like something that just fell off a ventriloquist's lap.

"Her coming-out party was a success."
"Well, she's still out."

"She spells atrociously."
"She must be very bright. I can't spell it."

I opened my eyes and felt for my watch—it was gone. I felt for my pants—they were gone. I felt for my shoes—they, too, were gone. No wonder. I was in bed.

"My alarm clock woke me up for the first time in a month."
"Is that so!"
"Yeah, my brother hit me over the head with it."

And remember, always put off tonight what you're going to put on in the morning.

A firm of shipowners wired one of their captains: "Move heaven and earth; get here on Friday."

Just as they were becoming very anxious they got this reply: "Raised hell and arriving Thursday."

"How did you get those black and blue marks on your shins?"
"I forgot what was trumps."

"That clock goes eight days without winding."
"How many days if you do wind it?"

JOE: I'm a man-about-town.
MIKE: I can't find an apartment, either.

"Did it take the artist long to paint you on skates?"

"Oh, about three sittings."

HE: Wanna fly?

SHE: Sure!

HE: Wait here and I'll catch one for you.

"What do you call a person from Michigan?"

"A Mishugena."

CHARLIE: How's chances to get a dime for a cup of coffee?

JIM: Coffee only costs a nickel.

CHARLIE: I know, but I'm keeping a woman.

Tulane University—look at all the highways named after it.

My uncle used to run and jump . . . he used to run Rum and jump Bail.

"So, you like Pensacola?"

"Yeah. But I like 7-Up just as well."

"Do the people next door borrow much from you?"

"I feel more at home in their house than in my own."

SHE: I can hardly hear myself talk.

HE: You're not missing much.

Monologues, Sketches, Essays, Etc.

MONOLOGUES AND SKETCHES

Radio Soap Operas

At the risk of alienating some of my fellow actors who have become rich and famous by appearing on TV soap operas, I've never gotten hooked on them, possibly because the daylight hours are worktime for me. Oddly enough, I did enjoy soap operas back when they were available only on radio. In those days an announcer, on the assumption that most listeners had missed some installments, would bring us all up-to-date on recent story developments. Possibly because my mind occasionally wanders, those updates always sounded like this to me:

Yesterday, you'll remember, Agatha paled when Roger entered the library. It seemed as if only days before he had gone out of her life, vowing never to return. And now, here they were, strolling along the beach, arm in arm. As they climbed the flagpole David spoke to her, softly.

Flinging the book into the fire, Elizabeth stood for a moment, poised against the window, then—with a suddenness that took Richard's breath away—she strode to the table and began putting the puppies back into the suitcase.

It was then that they both saw it. A tiny drop of blood on the man's shirt front. It could mean only one thing. And not a drop of liquor in the house.

As Helen pulled the speedy, low-slung Mercedes McCambridge into the drive-in, she felt a sudden sense of weariness, and almost without thinking threw back the covers and got out of bed. When the phone rang she let it ring for a long while, and then— very carefully—she spat out the tobacco, vowing never to return.

Would Dr. Carvel arrive on time? Samantha did not know, and couldn't care less. Not for her, ever again, the long walks in the country. Suddenly, lashing out with the lash she always carried, she slapped William full in the face. Then, primly confident, she turned on her heel, let it run for a while, and then turned it off.

As the curtain opened, a nervous titter ran through the audience. Dr. Gillespie whipped out a titter pistol and shot it.

Now, on with today's installment . . .

From *Seymour Glick is Alive But Sick*

Most people don't realize that six years before Cole Porter wrote "I've Got You Under My Skin," Seymour Glick had provided what I've always thought was the real source of Porter's inspiration. This brings up the tragic fact that Glick was dyslexic, which, perhaps fortunately, never became widely known.

Anyway—Seymour, too, started to write a song titled "I've Got You Under My Skin." Unfortunately, because of his problem, it came out "I've Got You Under My Sink."

But Seymour, ever resourceful, used the number anyway in a musical he was writing about the plumbing business. Now you know where Cole Porter got the idea for the line "Like the drip, drip, drip, drip of the drainpipe."

Disc Jockeys

I'm not the dumbest person in the world, but I'm having great difficulty figuring out exactly what some radio rock jocks are talking about.

There are a number of exploratory factors, of course. And we should always ask, "Compared to what?" Well, compared to disc jockeys of earlier times. There was never any difficulty in understanding a man who said, "And now here's Frank Sinatra to sing 'Stardust.'"

But these days not only do bands and groups have purposely bizarre names, but so do many of the songs.

Another factor is that old groups keep disappearing and new groups show up, literally every few days. So when I listen to these radio people now I don't know where the sentences end, or what the subject of the sentence is, or what the object (if there is one) is. It all sounds like this to me:

Hey, deputy Wizouck—say, hey, that was pate de foix gras and Shell Quick-Charge, jammin' it, whammin' it and stuffin' it on the Pomona Freeway label, with Don't-even-think-of-parking-here, Peeling Asbestos, Down and Dirty, John 3:27, and how's your sister this Friday night? Yeah! Arsenio's ratings are down, from the corner of whoop-te-dee and Beelzebub, rub-a-dub-dub. There's no tricky-city with Sally Jesse and the Raphaels, Con Mucho Incoherence, Mama, and Dep and dis and dat and de other ting.

Comin' atcha, gotta scratch ya!

In a minute Charlie Pope and the Cardinals excommunicate their drummer, alright? As they sing "Switchblade, Baby, You're Gonna Get The Point!"

What the hell are these people *talking* about?

Hairdo Monologue

I don't know about you, but I think we're seeing more weird hairdos on men and women than we ever have before.

Sometimes where the hairdressers go wrong regards the factor of exaggeration. They start with something creative, a cute little twist or curl or line. The first people who wear it look okay, but then other people say, "Hey, that's wild. I'm gonna do that and a little *more* of it," and at that point things go all to hell.

I saw a white guy at the airport the other day who had about nineteen pounds of hair sticking straight out the *back* of his head. Now that would be a marvelous hairdo if you dig looking like a hydrocephalic.

And—listen carefully now because I don't want to hear any nonsense about racism. Let's talk about the hairdos that *some* black folks wear.

I didn't mind when, about five years ago, some of the black athletes began wearing the flat top. Actually, it looked like what the U.S. Marines used to wear back in World War II, and it had the advantage of looking trim and neat. But then somebody got the idea of getting rid of the sideburns so that what some of the cats were wearing looked like they were totally bald, with a hockey puck on top of their head.

My vote for the worst-looking hairdo in the country is the one Sinbad used to wear on one of my favorite programs, *It's Showtime at the Apollo*. This man looked like his head was run over by a Goodyear tire.

And—to go back a few years—the cornrow was cute, particularly on pretty women, whether they were black or white. Well, come to think of it, almost everything looks good on pretty women.

That, of course, is why they never hire ugly people to work as models.

But as soon as the dreadlocks look came in, I checked off the bus. If that's authentic—in other words, if you're from Jamaica, play in a reggae band, and have marijuana soup for breakfast—then it's a legitimate look for you.

But I'll tell you right now, if I go to see my dentist or my stockbroker and he's got a dreadlocks haircut, he's not going to do a hell of a lot of business with me.

I happen to think that Whoopie Goldberg is a funny woman. How she's managed to read cue cards all these years with her hair down in her eyes I have no idea, but I hope, just for her fans' sake, she'll eventually try some *variation* on the hairdo because—to speak frankly—it does not look too gorgeous.

Incidentally, there's no sense putting down punk rock hairdos because the whole *point* is to look weird, just as the whole point of punk music is to *play* weird.

Probably 90 percent of the American people put it down, but I'll say this for punk, it's given a lot of ugly kids a chance to be popular.

So again—it's okay if you *want* to look rotten and sicko. Knock yourself out; it's a free country. But the pathetic thing is when the people who want to look sensational do dumb things to their hair. I'm sure nobody who knows Spike Lee could possibly accuse him of being anti-black. He's brilliant and our country should listen to what he's saying. But I think the funniest line in his movie *Do the*

Right Thing is where those three middle-aged cats, who are sitting against the bright redbrick wall commenting on life like a Greek chorus, have a conversation with the young loudmouth, who is the chief troublemaker in the story. You might recall the scene where this jerk tries to get the three older guys to take part in his boycott of the Italian pizza joint. One of the guys says, "Never mind that, man; what you *ought* to be boycottin' is the barber who did that to your hair."

Appropriate Attire at the Improv

Steve walks on-stage dressed in Levi's, a navy turtleneck under a blue work shirt (with the sleeves rolled up), an open black vest, and jogging shoes.

Hi, good evening. I probably look a little *strange* to you, being dressed like this on a big, important television show. Ordinarily you'd expect to see me in a tuxedo, as befits my station. But the Improv is a hip, funky place and this is the way most young comics dress who work in joints like this.

I saw a young comedian walk in here one night wearing a nice-looking, three-piece suit.

He was thrown out of the club.

They thought he was a *narc*.

The philosophical rationale of dressing like this when you do comedy is, first of all—I guess—to inspire *sympathy*.

You identify with the proletariat.

You look like you can't *afford* a tuxedo.

You look like it's not even definite that you're in show business at all.

You were just walking by the club, on your way home from the car wash, and you heard people laughing, so you stuck your head in, and the next thing—*wham!*—you're on stage, getting screams, dressed like a guy on welfare.

But do you know why comedians dress like this? I checked into it and have actually discovered a reason.

It's because about twenty-five years ago a lot of the hippie folk singers and rock singers were always wearing overalls and Levi's and dumb country clothes, either because they were poor, or they had no taste. I wouldn't want you to think, however, that they originated this kind of clothing. I had an uncle who, forty years ago, was dressing like this. Of course he was a bum. . . .

But then they began to have hit records.

So they were booked to perform in the city, and on television, and all the young kids who wanted to be in show business saw these hicks walking around in these rube clothes. So the first thing that happens is that all the *big-city* singers—all the Irish guys and Jewish guys and black guys, who wouldn't know a cow from a tree stump—they start dressing like hicks. And using phony hick *voices* when they sing. *(Sings):* Well-uh, mama, wanna getta sumpin'—" And it works for them. They become millionaires.

So now the comedians think, "Hey, to heck with class and style and sharp threads. I'll start dressing like I just flunked out of junior college; maybe it'll work."

Fads and Fashion

Historians of the future are going to have quite an easy time telling what life was like in the present period because we are leaving behind such a massive accumulation of evidence—movies, television tapes, recordings, newspapers, magazines, etc. But I don't think that people a thousand years from now will have an absolutely accurate picture of how we *dress*—what we actually wear on the streets and in our homes. The reason I say this is that I read what are called fashion magazines: *Vogue, Glamour, Harper's Bazaar, Gentlemen's Quarterly.*

These magazines do *not* show you how actual human beings dress. They do not even show you how professional models dress. All they show you is what professional models wear when they are working in fashion shows or in front of fashion photographers' cameras. I've known some models over the years, and I know some at present. On the street they dress the same as you and I. Men, particularly, do *not* dress like the male models in *Gentlemen's Quarterly.*

Then why, you might ask—if you are paying attention—has such a peculiar state of affairs come about? The answer is quite simple. If *Gentlemen's Quarterly* showed how men actually are attired, they would go out of business in six months because men's fashions change very slowly. I'm talking, of course, about typical American males—not punk rockers or other weird people.

Oh, lapels get a little wider or narrower every few years. Neckties get a little wider or narrower. But, for men, that's about it.

Occasionally young guys will wear stuff that's a little far out, but they don't get their ideas from *Gentlemen's Quarterly.* They get them from entertainers, or from the movies. For instance, if Michael Jackson wears one white glove, suddenly three million young jerks have to wear one white glove.

A few years ago it became hip for about one percent of young guys to wear very cheap-looking sports jackets with the sleeves pushed up to the elbow. Now these jackets have to be cheap and skimpy because if you're wearing a good, classy Brooks Brothers or Ralph Lauren tweed jacket, you can't push the sleeves up, they'll fall right down again. But if you make a jacket out of polyester and unborn linoleum, then, when you push the sleeves up, they stay up . . . at least until you take the jacket off.

Now, if your jacket sleeves are pushed up all day, they're gonna be wrinkled as hell when you take the thing off at night. What do you do? Run out to have them pressed and start the whole process all over?

That thought occurred to me a year or so ago when I was emceeing a Lenny Bruce comedy special on HBO. I pushed the sleeves of my jacket up and said to the audience, "What the hell is supposed to be so hip about this?"

A woman in the audience yelled out, "It's not hip anymore." And she was right. Sleeves pushed up were out, for about six months. Then they became slightly hip again, at least if you're a rock singer.

To use Michael Jackson as an example again—he usually wears white socks with dark pants onstage. For the last fifty years, the only people in America who wore white socks with dark clothes were members of the Teamsters Union from Columbus, Ohio. The look was considered the squarest of the square. Now it's supposed to be hip, simply because Michael does it.

Don't you people have minds of your own?

Product Names

The lady who asked the question about the name *Roach Motel* does have a point; lots of products do have strange names. For example, did it ever occur to you that *Hotpoint* is a very peculiar name for a refrigerator?

*Cold*point I could figure, but *Hot*point? Another weird name for a product is *Smuckers*. Do they sell Smuckers jams and jellies in this part of the country?

Incidentally, let me make it clear that I'm not knocking these products themselves. The Smuckers company makes terrific jams and jellies. But old man Smucker, whoever he was, must have been a real ego case, to insist on putting a name like *Smuckers* on his labels.

By the way, did it ever strike you that *No-Nonsense Pantyhose* is a sort of weird name for a pair of stockings? I mean, the implication is that if you're not wearing that particular brand, then there's something nonsensical about whatever brand you are wearing.

I'll tell you what—let's take a little survey right now. Will all those of you who are wearing pantyhose at this moment—all you ladies—or even you gentlemen, for that matter—but will all of you who are wearing pantyhose please applaud. *(Applause.)*

Thank you. Now I put a second question to you: Will all of you who are wearing a brand of pantyhose *other than* No-Nonsense Pantyhose please applaud. *(Scattered applause.)*

Very well. *(Picking out one particular woman who has just applauded.)* Now, the lady right down here. I don't wish to embarrass you in the slightest, but we have just established (a) that you are wearing pantyhose and (b) that they are *not* No-Nonsense. Is that correct?

Very well, then I put the simple question to you: Is there any particular sort of nonsense going on under there?

Another thing I sometimes buy—and I know many of you do—is Crazy Glue. That's the name of it. But I bought a brand of glue the other day that was *really* crazy. When I took the top off the tube, I heard little voices going, "Brhhhh-Buhhhhhp-Boo."

And then a little blob of the stuff came out and went *(sticks thumbs in ears and wiggles fingers)* at me.

Now that glue's really crazy, you have to admit. They ought to lock up glue like that. I mean it just shouldn't be allowed to stick around.

And how about that brand of coffee that's so big in the East—Chock Full O' Nuts?

As coffee, it's as good as any other, but the name always sounded strange to me.

"Say, Jim, there's something wrong with this can of coffee. How the hell did all these *nuts* get in here?

And there's a kind of inexpensive candy which, in my opinion, has a stupid name—*Milk Duds*. I doubt that anybody ever actually got dressed during a snowstorm and said, "Honey, I'll be back in about an hour and a half. I'm going out to pick up some Milk Duds." No, you usually buy them at a movie theater while you're hanging around the lobby. But what a name for a product. The *milk* part of it I can understand, although I'd like to know what actual percentage of milk is in the candy. But *duds?* I can just see the guys inventing this stuff at the original candy factory. "I'm sorry to break the news to you, Chief, but that new milk chocolate you've invented has turned out to be a real dud."

And how about *Intensive Care* hand cream? "Yes, your husband is in the hospital, Mrs. Johnson. We picked up his body about an hour ago. No, he seems to be coming along just fine. Oh, there is one thing, his hands are in intensive care. We'll do our best, but you know what intensive care means."

"Lincoln's Gettysburg—Like—Address"

The misuse of language in our society at present is so notorious that a number of books have been written about it. It sometimes seems that the coherent, grammatical English sentence should be added to the list of endangered species. Even our leaders are not immune from the virus of careless communication.

The other day I was entertaining the fantasy that if perhaps our greatest speaker among American presidents, Abraham Lincoln, were alive today and was going to deliver his immortal Gettysburg Address—well, it occurred to me that it might come out sounding like this:

Four score and—uh—*you know,* seven years ago—our fathers *like,* brought forth on this continent, a new nation, conceived in liberty, and dedicated to the—uh—*you know,* proposition that all men are, *like, wow*—created equal.

Now we are engaged in a—*you know*—great civil war, *all right?*—testing whether that nation, or, *you know, like* any nation so conceived and so dedicated, can, *like,* long endure, *you know what I'm saying?*

We are met on a great battlefield of that war. *You know—been there; done that. Basically* we have come to dedicate a portion of that *you know, field,* as a final resting place for those who here did *the give-your-life thing* that that nation might live. It is altogether fitting and, *like, you know,* proper, that we should do this, *okay, if you see where I'm coming from? Whatever.*

But, *hey, let's face it,* in a larger sense we can not dedicate—we can not, *like,* consecrate—hallow—this ground. *Give me a break.* The brave men who struggled here, have, *like,* consecrated it, far above our poor power to add or, *you know what I mean,* detract.

The world will little note, nor long remember, *hey, it couldn't care less,* what we say here. *Listen, we're history*—but it can never forget what they did here, *man.*

Anyway, the *bottom line* is that it's for us the living, rather, to be dedicated to the unfinished work which they who, *like,* fought here have thus far so nobly advanced, *you know—the whole nine yards.*

You know what? It is rather for us to be here dedicated to the great task remaining before us, *and was that task great or what?—* that from these honored dead we take—*you know, like* increased devotion—that we here highly resolve that these dead shall not have died in vain—*let's not go there*—that this nation, under—*you know, the man upstairs*—shall have a new birth of freedom—and, *you know,* that government of the people, by the people and—*guess what?*—for the people, shall not perish from the earth!!

I'm outta here.

Women of the Street

You know, we live in a time of general collapse of standards, and I'm sure none of us need to be reminded of the dreadfully serious problems that trouble our society.

Recently, public officials have been giving attention to one particular problem by cleaning out the red-light districts of certain major cities, trying to make the streets safe once again for just plain folks.

Well, that's all right with me, but it doesn't answer one question: What do you do about all the—shall we say—women of the streets, who will be left unemployed? Since ours is a society in which pretty much *everything* is for sale, I propose a modest solution, which would work something like this *(walks over behind a somewhat higher pitchman's counter):* A going-out-of-business sale at a house of ill-repute. . . .

Yes, folks, *everything* must go—blondes, brunettes, redheads, baldies, wildies, hippies, junkies! Come on down, and if you mention my name before next Friday, you'll get a 15 percent reduction!

We've got *new* models, *old* models, models in all colors. I mean we've got whites, blacks, Orientals, half-breeds . . . you name it!

Why *rent* when you can *buy* at these once-in-a-lifetime low-low-low bargain prices?

Say, men, be the first guy on your block to own a strumpet! Imagine, a brazen hussy you can keep around the house for those days when the TV is on the blink and the ballgame's been rained out.

Help clean up your community! Get the women *of* the streets *off* the streets! Be a good neighbor. Take a hooker to lunch. Or—and this is for you real bargain-hunters—buy six and go into business for yourself!

Yes, men, no more wasting valuable money on expensive magazines and crummy porno movies. Get the real thing, at these low, low, lost-our-lease sale prices!

My Opening Monologue for Merv Griffin, Fall, 1985

The last time either Jay Leno's or David Letterman's writers won an award for comedy writing, I swear that about twenty people got up out of the audience and ran up on stage to receive their award statuettes. Programs of that sort no longer have the traditional few, but a platoon of writers.

In the context of that fact, guess how many people I had writing for me when I started the Tonight *show back in the early '50s in New York?*

The answer is: none.

A few months later I met a very talented fellow named Stan Burns and added him to our staff, and not long thereafter Stan brought in Herb Sargent, another productive creator of jokes and sketches. Somebody recently interviewed Herb about his having

*worked with me and he was kind enough to say that he didn't think
I actually needed writers.*

*That was very modest of him, but of course if we're talking
about formal sketches, a writing staff is always very much a ne-
cessity. But because of the peculiar way I work, I sometimes get
bigger laughs ad-libbing on the basis of whatever is my situation
or predicament at the moment. A perfect example is the monologue
that follows, which I did one night when I got a late-afternoon call
from Merv Griffin's office asking if I could possibly help them out
by filling in for Merv that night because he was not feeling well. I
got to his theater, on Vine Street, not long thereafter, but it was too
late for his staff people to prepare anything for me. I told them not
to worry about that, but I would appreciate some food, and fast,
because I was missing my dinner hour. They sent out for a hamburger, but it was late in arriving, and in fact was given to me, literally, as I walked on stage after having been introduced.*

The following is the transcript of my remarks.

Hi, folks. Thank you very much.

This is a hamburger. It's not a comedy prop. A woman just came
up and thrust it in my hand, and that's how it is. I propose to eat it
during the show because I'm starving. This is not a comedy routine. I'm just sharing a little reality with you.

When they called today about this, they said, "Do you want
food?" I said, "Yes." So it's only just now arrived.

Anyway, good evening, ladies and germs. Look what you
laughed at. Comedians always say this. I think Milton Berle was
the first one—*(public address system comes on)* Ah! There we are.
Now we can all hear each other.

As I say, Milton Berle was the first person to say "ladies and
germs," but tonight I *mean* it because *(coughs)*—Oh, boy! Now

you know what I'm talking about, right? I have not been in contact with very many ladies today but lots of germs.

As a matter of fact, it's ridiculous that I am replacing Merv on the grounds that he is sick, because I am much sicker than Merv is.

Merv's always sick. I said to him years ago, "Merv, you're sick. You know that?"

He didn't take umbrage.

How many of you know what the word *umbrage* means? Would you just put a hand up? That's what I thought. It was a five-hundred-dollar question. Sorry, you're too late, sir.

Anyway, Merv—*(spits something accidentally)* Oops! That was a peanut.

I don't entertain. I just let you watch me live for about an hour. That was really a *piece* of a peanut. If it was the whole peanut you'd get sick looking at me.

But I finally said, "Where's my cheeseburger?" and they said, "Here's a peanut," so I ate that. And it came out. I guess now that I've got the burger, I didn't need the peanut anymore anyway.

Anyway, Merv called me about an hour ago. He said, "I've lost my voice." He really did. I said, "You've lost your voice?" He said, "Yes." And I said, "Then through what portion of your anatomy are you communicating with me at this time?"

And he laughed, good-natured slob that he is.

Well, actually, it was not Merv who called me, because—figure it out—if he'd lost his voice, he couldn't be calling me.

But the producers had been looking high and low for Merv's voice, and *they* called me. I'm not kidding. They did look high and low. But nary a trace—Do you know any other comedian who uses words like *nary?* None at all. That's right. That's why they're all in Vegas making a million tonight, and I'm stuck here. But that's all right.

Anyway, the producers were really looking high and low for Merv's voice. One of them was high, the other was low.

And neither of them could find it. So I finally listened to this nonsense, and I said to them, "Get lost."

They were so desperate one of them actually did get lost. And the other went and looked for him. That's why there was no warm-up for the show tonight. But that's all right.

Anyway, they thought they'd invented a new game called Hide-and-Seek.

(To man in front row): Where are you from? I'm sorry, sir, your time is up.

That was a hundred-dollar question. You have to pay attention.

I'm just warming you up because it wasn't done earlier; later people are gonna come out here and expect laughs.

I'm already secure. I don't need laughs *(coughs),* I just need a hospital. But they said Merv is under the weather, and I said, "So am I. And there isn't room under there for both of us."

And they said, "But the show must go on."

I said, "I don't care. My pants must come off. Really, I'm not joking with you. I'm sick as a dog."

They said, "We'll order dinner for you."

I said, "Fine."

They got me Gravy Train.

See, now you're laughing at garbage! The good stuff went right over your head. But that's all right. We'll arrive at an understanding in a few minutes.

I said, "I'm really not kidding. I just got up out of a sick bed to answer the phone." They said, "A sick bed?" I said, "Yes, it's a Chippendale. And if you've ever had a chip in your dale, you'll know . . ."

Do any of you have *any* idea what I'm talking about? I don't. So that makes two of us.

Oh, there were some question cards here. They're under a glass of—is this a glass of water? Is that some superstition of Merv's? You put cards under water and they turn into something else?

Some of you folks wrote questions. They thought of this at the last minute, too, so there was no time to get your names and addresses and your thumbprint and all that.

Be that as it may, where is Bill Sweeney? *(man waves)*

Hi, Bill, nice to have you with us. He writes, "Steve, what's it like being married to a beautiful woman like Jayne Meadows?"

It's interesting that what you actually wrote was "beautiful wom*en* like Jayne Meadows." Did you know you wrote that? That's what it's like! No—there's a lot to Jayne. No, no, no. I didn't mean it that way. I mean there's a lot to her. She's very versatile. She's in Northville, Michigan, right now, making a speech about great women of history.

(Man yells out): I'm from Michigan!

You're from Michigan?

Yes.

Who cares? *(laughter)* No, I just said that to see if something would wake you people up, and look what did it—rudeness. Comic brilliance went right over your head, but at rudeness you laughed right away. That's terrible.

Bad cess to you. And bad cess to the Roto-Rooter man, now that I think of it *(man laughs)*. Thank you, sir, but what is your opinion against that of thousands? One man down here is hysterical.

Jane Sweeney. Hi, Jane. Oh, you're with the gentleman from Michigan. Nice to have you with us. She writes, "Where do you live, Mr. Allen? Do you have a place on the ocean?"

Yes, I have a place on the ocean. It's called a raft. That's a silly answer, but the question wasn't too great either.

I live in Santa Monica. I don't *want* to live in Santa Monica, although it's a lovely community. But I had to get out of my other house. It was burned about a year ago. It was in all the papers. They were burning, too.

"How long have you and Jayne been married?" We've had twenty-four happy years *(applause)*. We've been married thirty-six, but . . . *(laughter)*. You laugh at old stuff. We'll get to some more of those a little bit later.

I think I'll sing now. Who's to stop me? I'm six-foot-three, I weigh two hundred pounds, Merv is home in bed sick, so who's going to stop me?

Book Publishing

I've decided I'm now going to become a book publisher.

Of course book publishing is a business where it's very easy to lose your shirt.

So is the laundry business, for that matter.

I obviously don't see myself successfully competing against Random House, Scribners, Doubleday, Harper and Row, Starsky and Hutch, or any of the other big firms.

But I've analyzed the field, and I can see what kind of books are making money right now, especially in the field of nonfiction.

The secret is that publishers and authors are simply picking up some popular issue or question and then saying exactly the opposite of the traditional or popular view on it.

For example, take divorce. A real tragedy, right?

Sure. But now they're bringing out books that say divorce can be "creative."

Getting fired—kicked out of your job—need no longer be considered a real bring-down. It can now be looked upon as a new beginning. The doorway to freedom.

There are books about understanding child-abusers, apologies for the Mafia, all kinds of these reverse switches.

So that's what I've decided to do as a publisher. I've contacted some other authors and I have here a little press release telling about some of the books I'll be bringing out in the next twelve months.

The first one is *The Joy of Death,* by Reginald Lishness, M.D., Ph.D., RIP. This is an uplifting eye-opener by the noted English physician, dead now for twelve years, who explains why death is preferable to pain.

With his remarkable wit, and the spiritual insight for which he is noted, Lishness patiently explains the pleasurable aspects of occupying a small space, being covered with dirt, wearing the same underwear every day, and being completely oblivious to bills, pollution, the energy shortage, and other of the problems that perplex the living.

The second book I'm bringing out is *Ecology Makes Me Barf,* by Cyril Klaveman.

It's a refreshing and terrifying view of how Mother Nature will destroy us all if she gets half a chance.

Klaveman, an ivory importer and fur dealer, advances impressive statistics, and has obviously done his homework, in demonstrating that Kool-Aid is much better for humans than pure water.

He also reveals the startling information—so far well suppressed—that if left unchecked baby fur seals will conquer the world by the year 2050! Klaveman, noted for his spiritual insight, also reveals that the great majority of forest fires are started by Almighty God, who uses lightning as his instrument.

Says the *New York Times Book Review,* "I never knew until reading this startling book why Nature is called a mother."

The third book we're bringing out is titled *I'm Adolph—Love Me* by Freida Kraus and Heinrich Dorfman.

In this remarkable study, the former shoeshine boy and masseuse of the Führer himself explodes the myth originating with the OSS propaganda department during the war, that Hitler was criminally insane and given to violent rages.

With a brief but poignant text and heretofore unpublished photos the authors warmly chronicle the private life of "an odd but kind of nice man"—a true gentleman who always apologized profusely after pistol-whipping his dinner guests, who insisted on testing torture devices on his own mother before turning them on the public, and who never drowned a puppy unless it happened to chew up one of the hand-made lampshades with which his quarters were decorated.

Says a reviewer for the *New York Post:* "Listen . . . we all make mistakes."

The next book is really inspirational. It's titled *Laughing Your Way Through Leprosy.*

World-famed naturalist and advocate of living the simple life, Fred DeCordova describes that, by a remarkable coincidence, just at the point of his life where he had begun to give away excess books, record albums, clothing, and other belongings, he began to notice a few other things were falling by the wayside as well.

In his usual crisp, repertorial style, DeCordova describes how he discovered his new condition one day: "I happened to reach for a cigarette: I took hold of it and walked to the other side of the room—then realized that the cigarette was still in the ashtray and I was still holding it."

Laughing his way past that remarkable discovery, DeCordova explains, brought him face-to-face with the realization that we can all do without and learn to like it.

Bra Monologue

Things like brassieres were once called "unmentionables." Remember that? Now they're mentioned every time you turn around. Shall I turn around? I guess not.

Anyway, the first successful attempt to liberate women from the tight confines of the corset came in 1910. And then they all moved across the hall to 1911 and tried it again before they got thrown out.

But all seriousness aside, in 1910, Otto Tizling, a German-born American who worked in his uncle's corset factory—he pulled down about 300 a week—made a bra to aid a young opera singer, Swanhilde Olafsson. That was her name. The very name bespeaks amplitude of pulchritude.

With her remarkable measurements, Miss Olafsson had found it painful to sing Puccini locked in a corset. Once liberated, however, she sang like a freed bird. And if you've ever had your . . . whatever. But anyway, the first bra company, I'm sorry to tell you, went bust.

After World War I, however, fashions—and attitudes—changed. Soon adorable little women the country over were hooked on—and into—this new contraption. It was truly the start of something big. Or small. Or medium.

Right-Wing Minister Monologue

Given the increasing emphasis, in recent years, on vulgarity, schlock, and general sleaze in television entertainment, I'm often asked if I personally have ever been subjected to censorship. To the best of my recollection this happened only in one case, and so far as I am aware it was not NBC program executives but the production staff of the Tonight *show that made the decision. I had written the following monologue, which was clearly aimed at a certain kind of extreme right-wing clergyman who, far from concentrating on truly religious subject matter, chose instead to use his pulpit—on or off the air—to make political points. Preachers of this particular sort, in reality, seem invariably to speak with Southern accents, a point easily explained if we have any degree of familiarity with the last 300 years of American history, particularly as regards to race relations.*

Parenthetically, at one point on the Tonight *show when I was delivering the routine, one couple in the audience were observed to stand up and walk out of the audience, with rather stern expressions. Oddly enough, they were not Southern whites, but an attractive-looking middle-aged black couple who seemed to have missed the point that my own bias was on their side of the question, and were shocked by one of the terms employed.*

(Steve moves behind a lectern, behind which is a vaguely religious stained glass backdrop or lighting effect. Church-style organ plays softly in background.)

Brothers and sisters—I am calling upon you tonight to rise up in your wrath and smite the forces of ungodliness! Do you agree?

(Drummer does rim shots. Audience shouts "Yes!")

The Lord spoke to me the other day and told me what we must do. If I tell you, will you do it? Lemme hear you say, "Yay-uh."

(*Audience says, "Yayuh."*)

That's good. That's very good.

Now the Lord said to me, "Brother Jerry-Jim—I want you to speak unto the people and tell them to go about the world with the Good Book in one hand."

And a rifle in the other.

We've got to keep guns in our homes against the day that the Communists come knocking on our doors.

Now some people say that Communists don't come knocking on your door.

But I say you can't be too careful.

Last week I knocked off three delivery boys and the Avon lady.

Now let me say a word about those bleeding hearts, the environmentalists.

We read in the Book about the cursing of the fig tree. And I tell you tonight, brothers and sisters, that we ought to do that to trees ourselves. Because they do cause pollution, just as President Reagan says they do.

Now a lot of people ask me, they say, "Dr. Jerry-Jim, isn't woman inferior to man? And if so, how can she demand equal rights?"

Well, I don't like to say that woman is inferior to man. But this much I do know. Man is certainly superior to woman! I say, look to what wise men have said on this question. And I like to quote the words of Butch Stone,* who said, "Keep a smile on your face and your big mouth shut!"

People say to me, "Dr. Jerry-Jim, can we ever trust Fidel Castro?"

---

* Vocalist with Les Brown, who sang "A Good Man Nowadays Is Hard to Find."

Well, I'll tell you, my friends, I never even trusted Desi Arnaz.

And consider, my friends, consider the case of the woman taken in adultery. Where was she taken?

And did they have reservations?

Now, some people say that any form of sex is all right, as long as it's between consenting adults.

I say no! I am sick and tired of all this talk about things being okay as long as it's between consenting adults.

And I know what I'm talking about, too—because I got *in between* two consenting adults one time.

You wouldn't believe what was going on in there! Now, one of my colleagues said the other day that the Lord does not hear the prayers of the Jews. And, my goodness, the terrible criticism he took for expressing this ancient truth, my friends.

Though I personally have nothing against Jews.

I think Jews are very cute people.

And I'm absolutely confident, my friends, that I speak righteous truth when I say these things because the Lord has told me that I am never wrong!

There was one time when I *thought I* was wrong.

But I was wrong.

But some of the members of my congregation say, "Dr. Jerry-Jim, what about the black folks?"

Why, I love the black folks. I also have a deep fondness in my heart for Negroes.

And a special liking for colored people.

In fact, it warms the cockles of my heart when I see these three separate groups sitting down together to work out their differences.

But I say to my dearly beloved chocolate-skinned friends, I love you, I love all darkies everywhere.

And I love the music the black folks make. I love all the fine black composers—Duke Ellington, Fats Waller, Cole Porter.

I was . . . what? Cole Porter wasn't black?

Well, he's got the blackest name I ever heard.

Now, I have no doubt, dear friends, that I will be criticized for speaking truth as I do. I will be accused of bigotry, of prejudice.

But I say no-uh.

Now I have been recently to the capital of our great nation, to the home of Uncle Sam, of the federal bureaucrats, and I have asked questions about the war on poverty.

And I can tell you tonight, my friends, that the war on poverty is going just great. Last week alone they shot over 300 poor people.

War is war, my friends.

But I am strengthened by your support. I say to you, give me your support.

Give me your love.

And give me your money—and fast.

But we've got to return this nation to decency. We've got to stop all this dancing! Dancing is an abomination in the eyes of the Lord.

And three of the worst offenders of the century have been Fred Astaire, Gene Kelly, and the June Taylor Dancers, my friends!

And why is it that we have all these black football players dancing in the end zones?

I say to you, my friends, leave the dancing to the liberals. If you want to get some exercise, you go out and march. And don't bend your knees when you do!

(*Drummer plays in sync as Steve goosesteps.*)

Now a young man came to me one time and he said, "Dr. Jerry-Jim, I think I'm going to tear up my draft card."

And I said to him, "No, sir, don't you dare tear up your draft card. You tear up your *union* card. If the good Lord had wanted us to be members of unions, he would have said something about it."

But wait. There are some good unions. I refer to the unions in Poland, of course.

But I don't find any references to unions in the Book.

In fact I find a lot about slavery in the Book.

We may have been too hasty, my friends, in getting rid of slavery.

Oh, sure, I know there were abuses, but you don't throw the baby out with the bathwater!

And be careful where you throw the bathwater anyway.

Don't water the trees with it. That would only encourage them to further pollute our great nation.

But be not of faint heart, my friends. Don't worry about the environmentalists, and the bureaucrats, and the civil libertarians.

Never mind them. Think of the men who built this great country of ours: Daniel Boone, John Wayne. Now in the movies you never saw John Wayne *arguing* with his adversaries!

No, sir! He knocked them down!

(*The drummer catches the punching and kicking movements.*)

He shot them. He kicked the hell out of them!

And it did my heart good to see him do it.

I say it's time we cleaned house.

And the black folks will help us do *that!*

For too long, my friends, we have put up with the liberals and the com-symps.

And the sitcoms.

Although personally I always thought Archie Bunker made a lot of sense.

But we've got to return to the old-fashioned ways, my friends. I ask you tonight: What's so bad about sitting in the back of the bus?

(*Two men in white jackets throw a large net over Steve and carry him away. The playoff music is heard: "The Miracle of America."*)

Group Names

It's no longer news that, compared to the old days, vocal groups, not only rock people but also jazz *groups, now deliberately give themselves strange-sounding names.*

If that were the only factor that were changed it wouldn't be too hard to understand what some disc jockeys, particularly on FM stations, are saying. But at the same time, the names of songs— *particularly* instrumentals—*have also gotten pretty Twilight Zone-y. Sometimes when I listen to radio stations, I have a lot of trouble figuring out what the hell the people are saying.*

"And that was *Eggs Over Easy* doing *'Intensive Care,'* followed by *Indecent Exposure* doing *'Plenary Indulgence,'* the big track from their new album titled *Illegal Immigration*.

"During the next hour you're going to be hearing *Sodom and Gomorrah* with a little ditty titled *'Croutons and Garni'* from their recent CD, *Habeas Corpus*.

"And now, rolling right along, today we introduce *'The Square Root of Your Sister'* as done by *Scandinavian Lube Job*, as originally recorded by *Sistine Chapel* and their great lead singer, *Gastro Enteritis*.

"By the way, got some nice mail from you folks out there, for our special show last night featuring *Swash Buckler* doing his wonderful *'One, Two—Buckle My Swash,'* the title theme from the motion picture *Jurassic Acid.*"

"Tomorrow we'll be featuring *Osteoporosis* doing *'Trebecular Meshwork'* from the new album *'The Graf-Wellahusen Hypothesis,'* on the *Tourette Syndrome* label.

Talk Show Monologue

Just because I invented the television talk show in the first place, people think that I love to watch all the versions that are on the air now.

Actually I don't.

And the kinds of shows that I'm not enjoying much at all anymore are the—what we call in the business—*theme shows.*

You know. "Lesbian nuns! Should they be permitted to have abortions? Today on *Geraldo!*"

"Tomorrow on *The Maury Povich Show*—Four old priests who were sexually abused by altar boys!"

"I'm an arsonist today because I just learned from Shirley MacLaine that in a pervious life I burned people at the stake during The Inquisition."

"When my wife told me that she was a *hooker,* I thought she meant that was her father's last name."

"*Orthodontists* who have been arrested for posing as Orthodox *Rabbis.*"

But shows of that sort have taught us something that even the ancient prophets didn't know. All theologians have agreed that man is innately depraved.

But tell the truth—didn't you always think they were *exaggerating* a little bit?

I mean, you knew about Jack the Ripper and Al Capone and John Dillinger and Hitler and a lot of other terrible people, sure. But you thought that *most* folks were pretty straight, right?

Well, I did—until Phil Donahue and Jerry Springer and Sally Jesse Raphael.

It's gotten so bad that I haven't seen a normal person on any of those shows for about ten years now.

Wouldn't it be wild if you tuned in to *Jerry Springer* tomorrow and the theme of the show was "Four perfectly normal people with nothing much to complain about"!

Wouldn't that be something? It would go something like this:

"Mr. Johnson, it's nice to have you with us on our guest panel today. Now, as I understand it, you have basically no serious problems at all, is that right?"

"That's right, Jerry. Oh, you know, now and then little things, like maybe a flat tire, a paper cut. An airline lost one of my suitcases once, but that was about six years ago. No, actually, I'm a pretty lucky guy."

"And your wife?"

"She's a doll."

"What kind of parents did you have?"

"Nothing but the greatest. It's been *Father Knows Best* and Donna Reed all the way."

Just for once I'd like to see Jerry Springer do *that* kind of a show.

I was watching a baseball game on TV the other day and noticed a peculiar thing. Years ago about all an announcer did was give you a play-by-play description of the game, but nowadays every time a player comes up to bat the announcer suddenly comes on like an encyclopedia and gives you a barrelful of statistics and folksy gossip. For example:

All right, fans, Delmonico was the last man up for Los Angeles. He has now hit safely in seventeen straight games, his batting average is .321 and he took a good healthy swing at the ball, too, as he stood there wearing his six-and-seven-eighths baseball cap. Jimmy, as most of you fans probably know, is one of the nine players on the L.A. team who wear their socks inside out, and, of course, it's all part of the game.

Klavenborn is the next man at bat. He's from East Birdbath, Mississippi, a town that gave us several other great players, and he has now sprained his ankle in fourteen straight games, quite an impressive record.

Marty was injured early in the season. He had a slight spike wound running from his left hip to his right kneecap, but he's been playing a whale of a game lately, and up to this afternoon he was one of the fourteen players in the major leagues who regularly refused to take a shower after the game. He's coming out of the dugout and the crowd recognizes him by that peculiar little habit he has: chewing on the rosin bag. And now, while Marty gets ready for the first pitch, I just want to say a word to you men.

Men, you owe it to your face to try the new Zip-master special razor. Notice how easily it works. *Zip,* it's open, *click* it's loaded. *Mop,* it's empty. *Zam,* it's full. *Squish,* it's moistened. *Clang,* it's broken. Wow, it's fixed. *Bong,* it's sharpened. *Push,* it's tightened.

Pull, it's loosened. *Plunk,* it's twisted. Crack, it's straightened. *Swunk,* it's dirty. *Swish,* it's cleaned. *Zoom,* it's shaving. *Scrape,* you're bleeding. It's as simple as that!

All right, Clyde is pitching for St. Louis and he's ready to go now. Harry is four for three today. He was on an island in the Pacific during the war for four years. I think it was Alcatraz. He's a big six-foot-four right-hander from Watch-It, South Carolina, who has a lot of stuff on the ball, although I see that right now the umpire is making him scrape it off. He has three children, and he's out there today, of course, with the usual number of fingers on his glove. Six. And now I see that the catcher is giving him the sign, which he always takes with his left eye. He has 20-47 vision, as most of you fans know, and he buys his socks at Abercrombie & Fitch. Last time he was up, two men died on base. The funeral is Friday at twelve o'clock.

Next . . . an open letter to John Rocker. *(Struggles with envelope):* Sorry, I can't seem to get the letter open.

And now it's time to play ball!

School for Fight Announcers

All the great sports announcers of the 1940s were pretty much alike in their style of speaking and it's come to that in television, too. But in the early 1950s some of the guys—perhaps because they were former journalists—seemed to want to make every sentence as colorful as possible. To me they sounded like this:

"All right, class. Welcome to the school for prize-fight announcers. You men will go through a twelve-week course here, after which we'll get you jobs at out-of-the-way TV stations. Eventually you may work your way up to the big time. Riley, we'll start with you. Pretend we're on the air. Just make it up as you go along. Describe a fight for us."

"Okay. There's the bell for the first round and Clay lashes out with a right-hand punch that—"

"Wait a minute! What kind of talk is that? 'Lashes out'? Thank you, David Brinkley. What did you say Clay threw?"

"A right-hand punch?"

"Not a right-hand punch. Just a *right*. Did it land?"

"No."

"All right. Clay misses with a right! Class! Repeat: Clay misses with a right!"

"Okay, go on."

"Liston lands a left. Clay engages his arms to stop him punching in—"

"Hold it! 'Clay engages his arms'?"

"Well, I meant that he—"

"I know what you meant. You meant he went into a *clinch*. So, say 'Clay ties him up!' class."

"Clay ties him up."

"Fine. Continue."

"Both men are really fighting hard now. They're punching vigorously in the—"

"Cut! They're *not* fighting hard or punching vigorously."

"They're not? What *are* they doing?"

"They're throwing plenty of leather. Got it?"

"I think so. Both boys are throwing plenty of leather in the ring now—"

"Not 'in the ring'! Never mind 'in the ring.' Just make it 'in there. Both boys are throwing plenty of leather in there.' They're sparring around in there. They're mixing it up in there. It's *all in there*. Got it?"

"I see. Both boys are throwing plenty of leather in there and now there's a cut over Clay's right eye and the blood is falling on the—"

"Now, stop! What is that with the 'blood-is-falling' business? Blood isn't falling!"

"It isn't?"

"No. The claret is beginning to flow. Class!"

"The claret is beginning to flow!"

"Okay. The claret is beginning to flow . . . in there . . . and Clay is retreating a little—"

"He is *not!* He is *giving ground!* He's bicycling. He's back-pedaling. He is not retreating."

"Sorry. Clay is back-pedaling . . . *in there*. But he's very brave and it looks—"

"That's all. Boy, what an idiot! He's 'very brave.' Clay is *not* very brave!"

"All right. Clay is chicken in there—"

"Don't try to be funny! I meant you're supposed to say dead game, not 'very brave.'"

"All right. Clay is dead game . . . in there . . . where the claret is . . . and it's turning into an exciting match."

"No. Try pier-six brawl."

"Okay. It's turning into a real pier-six brawl—"

"Now you're getting the idea! Men, remember this rule: at no time are you to be original. If these lines were good enough for Graham MacNamee fifty years ago they're good enough for you today. Class dismissed."

Alice Kupperman

HOST: We're very honored to be interviewing one of the great rock stars of all time, Alice Kupperman. It's nice to talk to you, Alice.

ALICE: Thank you, man.

HOST: Perhaps for middle-aged people who might be listening we should explain that Alice Kupperman is really a man.

ALICE: Yeah, man. It wouldn't hurt if you'd explain it to *me* either.

HOST: Alice—it *is* all right if I call you Alice, isn't it?

ALICE: Yeah, it's cool, man. It's better than calling me *Miss Kupperman,* you know?

HOST: Well, now. You're noted for flamboyant theatricality and your really wild wardrobe. For example, at the moment you're wearing gold-sequined platform shoes. Would you mind telling me how thick those soles are?

ALICE: They're three-feet thick, man. Would somebody please help me down off my shoes? Well, never mind. I'll just hang around up here. It's a cheap high.

HOST: Are there any medical problems that those shoes present? For example, I've heard that recently doctors have been warning people about the dangers of such thick soles.

ALICE: Oh, no, man. There's no medical problems. I get a little nosebleed once in awhile. But you know . . .

HOST: Do you mind if I ask . . . Is Alice Kupperman your *real* name?

ALICE: Yeah, I do mind. No, it's not my real name.

HOST: What *is* your real name?

ALICE: Irving Chutspa.

HOST: Tell me, Alice, what songs are you recording at present?

ALICE: Well, like I just did an album last week called *Alice Kupperman with Strings.*

HOST: Oh, you used violins?

ALICE: No, man, strings. You know, like *twine, thread,* stuff like that. You can get groovy sounds out of those little mothers if you pluck them just right, you dig?

HOST: I see. Alice, you're noted for the fanaticism of your followers. Your fans are perhaps the wildest in the business. What would you say to young people who might want to follow in your footsteps?

ALICE: If they see anything I dropped, I hope they'll bring it to me before the fuzz finds it.

Alligator Farm

HOST: As you know, we bring you, from time to time on our program, unusual people who do unusual things. If you've ever been fortunate enough to visit Florida, you've undoubtedly been taken to one of their famous alligator farms.

But statistically, I suppose, comparatively few people do have the pleasure of visiting the great state of Florida, and so today we have in the studio a gentleman who probably knows more about alligator farms than anyone in the world.

I'd like you to meet Mr. Bob "Gator" Klaveman.

Good morning, Mr. Klaveman.

KLAVEMAN: Good morning.

HOST: First off, Mr. Klaveman, can you explain just what is an alligator farm?

KLAVEMAN: It's very simple. An alligator farm is a farm with alligators.

HOST: Well, yes, that does seem simple enough, but could you describe what goes on at an alligator farm?

KLAVEMAN: Well, I can tell you what goes on at Gator City.

HOST: That's what your farm is called?

KLAVEMAN: Yes.

HOST: All right, what does go on at Gator City?

KLAVEMAN: Well, on our alligator farm we've got about forty-five alligators, give or take an alligator or two.

As a matter of fact, we were given one last week, but then somebody took two of 'em, so I'm not sure what the number is.

Anyway, what these alligators can do is really remarkable. Some of them are raising corn. Some of them are growing tomatoes, and—

HOST: Wait a minute. Alligators are growing tomatoes?

KLAVEMAN: Listen, it's an alligator farm, ain't it? But it's remarkable what those little sons-of-guns—or *big* sons-of-guns—can do. It's really wonderful to see them out there in the morning with their rakes and hoes and their little straw hats.

HOST: Alligators with straw hats?

KLAVEMAN: Yes. And it's not easy to get an alligator into a straw hat, believe me.

HOST: I believe you.

KLAVEMAN: Some of the alligators down on the farm have about ten acres in wheat and barley. As a matter of fact, I have to be running along now.

HOST: Why is that?

KLAVEMAN: Well, it's the threshing season. I have to go down and get things organized.

HOST: I see.

KLAVEMAN: We don't want any trouble with Caesar Chavez, you know.

HOST: Certainly not. Thank you very much, Gator Klaveman . . . and now back to New York.

ESSAYS

The essay form has for centuries been a useful one for humorists. Most of our famous literary wits, in fact, specialized in the form; your neighborhood library or bookstore can provide you with glorious examples from the pen of Robert Benchley, S. J. Perelman, Ring Lardner, Dave Barry, Woody Allen, and others.

The following are a few examples of my own creation.

Cowboy Sidekick Language

As an inveterate word freak, I from time to time conduct research into obscure corners of our language and subsequently share my findings with others either less blessed or similarly afflicted, as the case may be. Recently I've been interested in that branch of our national tongue that I call Cowboy Sidekick Talk. This is a special language that, so far as diligent study has been able to establish, has been spoken by no more than half a dozen men in our century, or even—for that matter—through all recorded history of the English-speaking peoples.

Gabby Hayes, Walter Brennan, Pat Buttram, and a few other old-timers, who spoke their rare lingo in films starring Gene Autry, Roy Rogers, John Wayne, Gary Cooper, and others of their heroic ilk, are the only human beings known to have actually spoken Cowboy Sidekickese. I would, of course, be grateful to any reader who could identify others who actually employed such a form of communication.

The range of messages conveyed by such a language was surprisingly narrow. Chiefly it was employed to indicate that the speaker was angry. There were other clues to his emotional condition, of course. He might attempt to gnash his teeth, except that he usually had none. Let us say then that gum-gnashing was a concomitant of the Cowboy Sidekick language.

And exaggerated protrusion of the chin was also part of it.

When particularly irate, the old sidekick might shout, "Dad burn it!" It was commonly supposed that the phrase was a euphemism for the more familiar request that the Deity consign someone—or something—to the flames of hell for all eternity. Like many popular beliefs, however, this one is erroneous. The original speaker actually wanted his dad to burn something, which might be the offender's house, his cowboy hat, his chuckwagon, or whatever.

Another common expression in this rare language was "Dad gum it!" Again, this was no euphemism for the more common curse but rather a fervent expression of the wish that one's father—dad—would gum something. It will readily be seen that since the average cowboy sidekick was well into his sixties, his dad would figure to be in his eighties, and hence no longer able to bite anything, although still apparently capable of gumming.

A more troublesome instance involves the phrase "Dag nab it!" The last two words present no problem, since we all know what it is to nab something. But what about the word *dag*? Many are aware that it is a common Scandinavian name—remember Dag Hammarskjold? The first cowboy sidekick to introduce this phrase to the American West had, as a boy, emigrated from Sweden.

"Dad blast it!" naturally presents no difficulty, since the use of dynamite by miners, prospectors, or tree-stump removers was common in the Old West.

The phrase "ornery critter" is also unique to the Cowboy Sidekick language. A recent poll taken by the Recent Poll Company revealed that 47 percent of those questioned had no idea at all what a critter was. Thirty-seven percent held the view that the word was a mispronunciation of *creature*. The remainder took the poll-taker's question as a personal insult and hit him right in the mouth.

As for the word *critter,* the suffix *-er* reveals that it is related to a verb form, in the sense that *sitter* is related to the verb *sit, runner* is related to the verb *run,* etc. Therefore, if a leaper is one who leaps, it follows that a critter is one who crits. Unfortunately, I have not been able to find anything on the verb *to crit,* but I will share this information with you in a subsequent column if my luck holds out.

In the early 1950s, in addition to my daily television work, I was also writing a regular humor column for Downbeat *magazine, which covered the Big Band and jazz business. One day the guitar player on our show came to my apartment in New York for a brief rehearsal and happened to tell me about something amusing his six-year-old son had said a day earlier. "I asked him a typical parents' question, 'What did they teach you at school today?' And he said, 'Oh, they taught us about some cat named George Washington.'"*

Obviously the child had picked up the jazz musician's lingo from his father, but this little story gave me the idea of telling the old, traditional Mother Goose tales, the Hans Christian Andersen material, and anything of that sort, not in the regular way, but as if related by a jazz musician. Here are two examples:

Crazy Red Riding Hood

Once upon a time, many years ago, in the Land of Oobopshebam, there lived a lovely little girl named Red Riding Hood.

To give you an idea of what a sweet thing she was, children, I'll just say that she was not only a lovely little girl; she was a fine chick.

One day Red Riding Hood's mother called her into the kitchen and said, "Baby, I just got word that your grandma is feeling the least."

"What a drag," said Little Red Riding Hood. "What's the bit?"

"Hangoversville, for all I know," said her mother. "At any rate, I've fixed up a real wild basket of ribs and a bottle of juice. I'd like you to fall by Grandma's joint this afternoon and lay the stuff on her."

"Crazy," said Red, and picking up the basket, she took off for her grandmother's cottage, going by way of the deep woods.

Little did Red Riding Hood know that a big bad wolf lurked in the heart of the forest.

She had traveled but a short distance when the wolf leaped out from behind a bush and confronted her.

"Baby," he said, grinning affably, "gimme five."

"Sorry, Daddy-o," said Red. "Some other time. Right now I have to make it over to my grandmother's place."

"Square-time," said the wolf. "Why don't you blow your grandmother and we'll have some laughs."

"Man," said Red, "Cootie left the Duke and I'm leavin' you. For the time being we've had it."

"Mama, I'm hip," said the wolf. "Dig you later."

So saying, the wolf bounded off through the forest and was soon lost to sight. But his evil mind was at work. Unbeknownst to Red Riding Hood, he took a shortcut through the trees and in a few minutes stood panting before the helpless grandmother's cottage.

Quietly he knocked on the door.

"That's a familiar beat," said Red Riding Hood's grandmother. "Who's out there?"

"Western Union," lied the wolf. "I have a special invitation to Dizzy's opening at Birdland."

"Wild," said the grandmother, hobbling across the room.

Imagine her horror when, upon opening the door, she perceived the wolf. In an instant he had leaped into the house, gobbled her up, and disguised himself in her night-clothes.

Hearing Red Riding Hood's footsteps on the stones of the garden path, he leaped into the poor old lady's bed, pulled the covers up to his chin, and smiled toward the door in a grandmotherly way.

When Little Red Riding Hood knocked, he said, "Hit me again. Who goes?"

"It's me, Gram," said Red Riding Hood. "Mother heard you were feeling pretty beat. She thought you might want to pick up on some ribs."

"Nutty," said the wolf. "Fall in."

Red Riding Hood opened the door, stepped inside, and looked around the room. "Wowie," she said. "What a crazy pad!"

"Sorry I didn't have time to straighten up," said the wolf. "What's in the basket?"

"Same old jazz," said Red.

"Baby," said the wolf, "don't put it down."

"I have to," said Red. "It's gettin' heavy."

"I didn't come here to play straight," said the wolf. "Let's open the basket. I got eyes."

"I'm hip," said Red, "not to mention the fact that you can say that again. Grandma, what coo-coo eyes you have."

"The better to dig you with, my dear," said the wolf.

"And, Grandma," said Red, "I don't want to sound rude, but what a long nose you have."

"Yeah," said the wolf, "it's a gasser."

"And, Grandma," said Red, "your ears are the most, to say the least."

"What is this," snapped the wolf, "face inspection? I know my ears aren't the greatest, but whadda ya gonna do? Let's just say somebody goofed!"

"You know something?" little Red Riding Hood said, squinting suspiciously at the furry head on the pillow. "I don't want to sound like square or anything, but you don't look like my grandmother at all. You look like some other cat."

"Baby," said the wolf, "you're flippin'!"

"No, man," insisted Red. "I just dug your nose again, and it's too much. I don't want to come right out and ask to see your card, but like, where's my grandma?"

The wolf stared at Red Riding Hood for a long, terrible moment. "Your grandma," he said, "is gone."

"I'm hip," said Red. "She swings like a pendulum do, but where is she?"

"She split," said the wolf.

"Don't give me that jive," said Red, whereupon the wolf, being at the end of his patience, leaped out of bed and began to chase poor Red Riding Hood around the room.

Little did he know that the wolf season had opened that very day and that a passing hunter could hear Little Red Riding Hood's frantic cry for help.

Rushing into the cottage, the brave woodsman dispatched the wolf with one bullet.

"Buster," said Red gratefully, "your timing was like the end, you know?"

And so it was.

To my surprise the line about something being "the most, to say the least" was promptly picked up by assorted disc jockeys and comics and entered the national language.

The Three Little Pigs

Once upon a time, in the land of Nitty Gritty, there lived three little pigs. One of the little pigs was very cool, another was more on the commercial side, and the third was, beyond the shadow of a doubt, as square as they come.

One day as the three pigs were taking five, one of them chanced to pick up a copy of *Downbeat*.

"Say, boys," he said, "I see here where the Big Bad Wolf is playing a one-nighter in this area next week."

"Oh-oh," said the second little pig. "That wolf is baa-a—ad for sure. That means it's panic time in Porky Park."

"This," said the square little pig, "is the most depressing news since Ronnie Reagan got out of show-business."

"Right," said the hip little pig. "We'd better boogie."

Since the approach of the Big Bad Wolf indeed signaled danger, the three little pigs immediately set about the business of constructing suitable shelter.

The square little pig arranged a quick GI loan and in no time erected a sturdy Orange County modern bungalow, complete with wall-to-wall floors and a TV antenna.

The commercial little pig moved right into a foreclosed condominium, but at the last possible moment the cool little pig built himself a small A-frame temple out of clarinet reeds and Scotch tape.

The Big Bad Wolf eventually arrived in town and the first place he went was the home of the square little pig. Applying his hairy knuckles to the door, he laid down a crisp paradiddle and said, "Man, it's a raid!"

"Pops," whispered the pig from behind the locked door, "it's after closing."

"Don't hand me that jive," said the wolf impatiently. "Open up!"

"Sorry, Irv," said the pig. "You gotta make reservations. Besides, you shouldn't even be out this late. Ain't you hip to the curfew?"

"The what?" said the wolf.

"Curfew," said the pig.

"Gesundheit," said the wolf, hoping to pass as a television comedian.

"Fun-nee," said the pig. "I'll catch you next week, same time, same channel."

"Charlie," said the wolf, with ill-concealed displeasure, "if you don't open that door right now, I'll huff and I'll puff and I'll blow your house down."

"Tell me one thing," said the little pig. "What condition is your lip in?"

Enraged at this impertinence, the wolf came on like Joshua, the walls came tumbling down, and in no time at all the poor little pig was really gone.

The following day the Big Bad Wolf traveled across town and knocked at the door of the second little pig's condominium.

"Who dat?" said the pig, trying to sound hip.

"Never mind," snapped the wolf, anxious for destiny to resume its inexorable march, "open that door and gimme some skin, pig. Or gimme some pigskin, as the case may be."

"I'll handle the jokes," said the pig. "Did you have an appointment?"

"Don't bug me, Buster," said the wolf. "When I'm in town I always stop at the Pork Club. Now open up!"

"No, man," said the pig. "In fact, not by the hair on my chinny-chin-chin."

"Well, what do you know about that," said the wolf. "That must be Dizzy in there!"

"Never mind the whisker jokes," said the pig. "I ain't gonna open up, no how."

"Tell you what, baby," said the wolf with wily warmth. "I'll just peek through your keyhole."

"In a pig's eye you will," said the little pig, which angered the wolf so terribly that he huffed and he puffed and he blew the house down.

In a very short time the second little pig met the fate that had befallen his unlucky friend.

The next day the Big Bad Wolf went to the home of the cool little pig and knocked on the door.

"Have no fear," he said, "Wolfman Jack is here."

"I don't care if it's Reverend Ike," said the little pig. "Hang tough."

"Hey, Ace, wait a minute," said the wolf, pretending not to have heard the rebuff. "I understand there's a session going on here today."

"Cut out, brother," said the pig. "We are not televising the hearings."

"But I heard I could get my kicks here," said the wolf. "I'd like to sit in."

"I'm hip," said the little pig, getting an idea. "And if you'll just slide down the chimney, I'll really give you something to sit in."

"You're not putting me on, are you, brother?" asked the wolf.

"Well, yes and no," said the pig.

"Hey, LeRoy," the wolf said, sniffing at a wisp of smoke, "you wouldn't be lighting up in there, would you?"

"Can you dig it?" said the pig.

Losing his patience at last, the wolf leaped to the roof, and in so doing dislodged a brick, which fell down the chimney and clanged loudly against the great iron pot in the fireplace.

"What was that?" the wolf shouted.

"E-flat," said the pig. "Daddy, fall in."

And fall in the wolf did—down the chimney and right into the pot. Nimbly the little pig clapped a cover on the top, and the wolf was trapped.

"Let me out!" he howled. But the little pig was merciless. "Burn, baby, burn," he replied.

After allowing the water to simmer for forty-eight hours over a low flame, the little pig lifted the cover and peered down into the pot, sniffing tentatively.

"Ah," he said, with a broad smile, "my favorite soup. Cream of Nowhere."

Argument

Whether formal or informal, argument is always a somewhat tedious process. Questions of fact are difficult enough; differences and nuances of opinion are even more troublesome. Part of the difficulty of the endless dialogue on religious questions grows out of the fact that to at least one sort of religious mind, there is generally no proposition too preposterous to "prove," at least to the satisfaction of the proposer.

To be specific, I will here introduce a deliberately nonsensical assertion and then proceed to "prove" it. The proof will not, of course, be of the scientific sort, but it will be consistent with a certain kind of theological argumentation that has persisted down through the centuries.

Let our true believer assert, for example, something patently absurd: that God is a hockey puck. Now the reader and I are both perfectly aware that God is nothing of the sort. But let us see how we fare in a debate on this simple point.

BELIEVER: God is a hockey puck.

SKEPTIC: That is the worst nonsense I've ever heard.

BELIEVER: I doubt that very much. We do, after all, live in a day when we are constantly exposed to nonsense of all sorts.

SKEPTIC: Well, we can agree on that much at least. But I don't see how you can possibly say that God is a hockey puck.

BELIEVER: My dear fellow, I have just said it, and with the greatest of ease.

SKEPTIC: Oh, the saying of it is easy enough, but I don't see how you can prove it.

BELIEVER: Of course you don't, with your limited human intelligence.

SKEPTIC: Are you suggesting that your own intelligence is superhuman?

BELIEVER: If unaided, no. But I have been granted, by the grace of God, the honor of personal communion with the Lord, and he has assured me that what I say is true.

But let us stop arguing about arguing, my friend, and get to the heart of the matter. I shall now demonstrate to you, with no great difficulty, that God in several senses is precisely a hockey puck.

SKEPTIC: Name one.

BELIEVER: I shall do far more than that. First of all, let us consider the properties of a hockey puck. The most evident is its blackness. Now what we, with our limited powers of perception and analysis, call black is really something that absorbs all light. That is certainly one quality of God. He not only creates all things but also possesses them all, takes them all unto himself, draws them back to the point of origin, as it were.

And is there not always mystery associated with blackness? And what can be said to be more mysterious than both the idea and the reality of God? Of course, it is in the very blackness of the puck that it is distinguished from its surroundings. The manufacturers of hockey pucks did not make an idle or random choice. No other color would stand out so clearly from the whiteness of the ice it moves across. And is not God the Ultimate Other when compared to all things natural, including the human? Does not God stand in stark contrast to the things of this world as the black puck stands in contrast to its frigid and pristine context?

SKEPTIC: But it is absurd to—

BELIEVER: Please, permit me to continue setting out my arguments. Consider now the relationship of the hockey players—individual men, representing all mankind—to the puck. What do they do ceaselessly? Ignore it? Pretend to be oblivious to it? Disdain it? No, they pursue it with the utmost abandon, sometimes to the point of seeming madness. They are drawn to it as fragments of iron are drawn to a magnet. They literally have no purpose on the ice except to pursue that puck. As for the thousands of observers and the millions more now capable of witnessing such spectacles through the medium of television, their eyes, too, follow the puck. It is the center of attention, the only true object of interest. The men, despite their individual strength, speed, or finesse, are not rewarded for the ease with which they skate or the handsomeness of the figure they cut in their uniforms. They are judged only for the effectiveness of their relationship to the hockey puck.

Consider next the material of which the puck is made. It is on the one hand quite hard but yet is made of rubber, which is the epitome of softness and resiliency. Are not these extremes also divine attributes? Is not God firm and unyielding and yet able to manifest a certain resilience of mercy and compassionate intervention in human affairs?

SKEPTIC: That's creative, my friend, but I still cannot accept it because—

BELIEVER: I'm not surprised that you can't. How could you, conditioned as you are to see things only in rational or coldly scientific terms?

SKEPTIC: But it doesn't take a scientist or a rationalist to see that a hockey puck is nothing but a little, round—

BELIEVER: Ah, roundness. Circularity. And what could be a better illustration of the essence of God? One never hears of the perfect square, or the perfect triangle, only the perfect circle. The circle is the only line form that endlessly returns to its point of origin. We gradually perceive that life has neither beginning nor end but only existence, only is-ness. Of, what else can this be said but the Almighty God?

SKEPTIC: But this is madness, to believe that one little thing—

BELIEVER: A thing? A thing indeed. And does not the very definition of divinity instruct us that all things must have a cause? And what can be their ultimate cause except God?

If you, my friend, were to make a watch, would not the artifact somehow represent you in a way that it could be said to represent no other individual, simply because you conceived, fashioned, and created it in all its parts?

Well, given that God made all things, and that a hockey puck is a thing, it follows that God made the hockey puck out of his boundless creativity, which is to say, out of himself. So it is inescapable that the hockey puck is God and God is the hockey puck.

And so goes the bizarre method of argumentation, which would not be considered convincing if applied to any other area of human activity but the religious or mystical.

Danger in the RCA Building

I had barely left my office and turned down the hall toward the water cooler when I saw him, closing in fast, head down, a sheaf of papers in his hand.

For a split second I froze. Then, walking backward in three quick steps, I slipped into the office and closed the door. I stood with my back pressed to the wall until he had walked past.

Deciding against a drink of water, I returned to my desk and had my secretary order some cold orange juice from the drugstore. After all, I had already passed Harbach in the corridor three times that morning. A fourth encounter would have been beyond both of us.

I mean, what are you supposed to say to people you keep passing in the halls all day?

If you work in your own shop or drive a truck, you probably meet the same people every day, but you meet them only once. You say, "Hi ya, Mabel" or "How are you, Gus?" and that's the end of it. But in a large office building things are a bit different.

Oh, it doesn't look like much of a problem early in the morning. You meet a fellow as you get on the elevator and you say, "Morn-

378

ing, George," and he returns your salutation and that's that. The first meeting is only a primary barrier in the obstacle course that your day has, in the instant, become. It's a low hurdle, automatically cleared. But sometime within the next hour or so, since people who work in office buildings rarely stay at their desks but are given to a great deal of walking purposefully down corridors, it is inevitable that you will meet George again.

It would be fortunate, in that event, if one of you should be doing something besides just walking. For example, if you are bending over to tie a shoelace or George is getting a drink of water, there is at once established a subject for conversation.

"Drinking some water, eh, George?" you say.

"Keeping those shoelaces tied, huh, boy?" he can respond.

But if neither of you is doing anything but walking, the problem assumes unnerving proportions.

Obviously you can't say, "Walking down the hall, eh, George?" I don't know quite what you can say, I only know you can't say that.

Research reveals that a second encounter almost invariably differs little from the first, except that "Good morning" is changed to "Hi" and the cheerful tone has given way to a certain wary lack of expression.

With the third encounter, you have but two alternatives. You can either exchange a mutual chuckle, or one of you can say, "Getting to be a habit." Up to a few years ago you might have said, "We've got to stop meeting like this," but the line quickly became a cliché and therefore decidedly un-hip.

The fourth meeting is somehow the worst. You can laugh at the third and marvel at the fifth, but the fourth will certainly defeat you unless you enjoy a stroke of luck. As George approaches, you eye each other desperately, minds racing. If fortune smiles, he might have papers in his hand. This entitles you to try something even as inept as, "Working overtime, eh?" But since George is your only audience and you have relieved him of the responsibility of filling the breach, his gratitude will render his critical powers inactive and he will respond gratefully, "You know me!"

The fifth time it is de rigueur to chuckle again. Keep the order in mind. Chuckles are appropriate the third and the fifth time. The sixth time one must be on guard against a surly note that is wont to introduce itself. You nod and George winks. The seventh time you wink and George nods. By the eighth time you have exhausted your creative capacities, but it is obvious that you cannot pass George and pretend not to see him.

So you stay at your desk, if you are smart, or venture from it only after careful scouting of the terrain. If egress is vital, approach closed doors warily and beware of corners.

Good luck.

Explaining Latvia

The following essay is a gentle enough spoof on the type of writing commonly encountered in encyclopedias. It was written, oddly enough, for an audience of one, my friend, humorist, playwright, film-scripter Larry Gelbart. In response to some now-forgotten joke that I had written in a letter he sent back the brief note, "What do you have on Latvia?"

The following essay was the result:

The word *Latvia* comes from the same route as *Latin* (see Xavier Cugat), just as the word *Romany* comes from the word *Roman* (see Polanski).

Location. In the north, Latvia borders on Estonia, in the east on Russia, and on the south it borders on the ridiculous.

As for its landscape, Latvia is essentially an undulating plain, which causes great havoc when, as sometimes happens, the undulations become violent.

While much of the topography is that of flat lowlands, the eastern part of the nation is somewhat more elevated, the most prominent feature being the ears on certain rural tribesmen of the area.

The capital city is Riga, which is situated 74 kilometers, or 487 miles, from Diga. The distance can easily be covered in two days, however, by traveling via the Riga-Diga Railroad, sometimes incorrectly rendered as Ringa-Dinga by certain popular American vocalists.

Residents of the two cities carry on a not always good-natured rivalry, rather like that of the confrontations between Houstonians and Dallasites in Texas, or Beverly Hills and The Valley in the greater Los Angeles area.

History. In prehistoric times the Baltic lands were inhabited by many different tribes; but then, in prehistoric times all the lands of the earth were inhabited by many different tribes, so that's not such a big deal. The Estonians and Livs occupied the northern and western areas, bordering the Baltic, the Latvians and Lithuanians the southern portions. The original dominant tribes were the Lats or Lets. In the fifth-century B.C. they absorbed such neighboring tribes as the Crustaceans and the Stalactites, with dimly anthropomorphic figures representing the sun, moon, lightning, and the men's room.

The ancestors of one branch of the present-day Latvians were thought to have been the Kurds of Kurdistan and, to some extent, Fluoristan, chiefly noted for its toothpaste mines.

In addition to the Liths, the Latvians were also related to the Laths, who bequeathed to the world the art of drywall home construction.

As of this early period, writing had not been developed in the area. Consequently, the few Latvians who claimed to be able to read were met with a puzzled skepticism.

In the twelfth century Pope Innocent III (see Comedy Names) organized a crusade against the Livs and the Lats, and it was from this historic confrontation that the expression "Liv and Lat Liv" came. Although Innocent failed in his grand scheme to convert the region's tribes, he did slaughter many thousands for Christ, or so it is assumed from the incident in which, when a perplexed officer inquired as to what should be done with some 7,000 captured Latvians, the reply was given, "Kill them for Christ's sake."

The next several centuries were a nightmare of invasion, rapine, and pillage, rapine proving to be more popular among the invaders than pillage. In the fourteenth century the dominant invaders were the Boyars, under the leadership of the fierce Chef Boyardee.

The Boyars were, in turn, overthrown by both the Tartars and the Tatars, who were denied what seemed an inevitable victory by going to war between themselves over the question as to who was responsible for losing the *r* in the word *Tatar.*

The next period of Latvian history is that dominated by the Teutonic Orders. Among the more memorable orders are, "Hey, you, get out of my way" and "All Jews will report at once to the village square." This last Teutonic order, parenthetically, was not as alarming as one might think since the village square turned out to be a generally affable fellow. And when the Teutons' backs were turned he gave their orders short shrift (see Long Schrifft).

Russian dominance became manifest in the sixteenth century as tribes from Novgorod and Notsogood moved into the area. During the next two centuries the Latvians suffered tragically under Ivan the Terrible, Alfonse the Awful, and Seymour the Silly. The Poles, too, contended for the area to the extent that by the nineteenth century a good part of Latvia was little more than a Polish fief.

Latvia became an independent republic in 1920 and at once conducted a vigorous program of democratic reform. The program, unfortunately, was canceled by the programming department of the Soviet Union in 1940, since which time the once-vaunted independence of Latvia is much analogous to the independence of Cleveland in the United States.

The People. In physical appearance Latvians and Latts—originally Letts—are indistinguishable from Estonians, with whom there has, for several centuries, been a great deal of commingling, not to mention wilding it up. Close inspection of any random group of Latvians and Estonians, however, will usually divulge that the Latvians are of sober mein while the Estonians are estoned.

The Latvians have frequently been confused—well, about a good many things, come to think of it—but most specifically they have been confused with the Lithuanians (see Lithium).

Religion. Sixty percent of Latvians are Lutheran, whereas among the Lithuanians the same percentage is Litheran. Nine percent are Roman Catholics, although the Catholic population consists entirely of priests and nuns. Exorcists are surprisingly common, though they do little more than go out on Saturday night and raise hell.

Form of Government. The governing body of Latvia, in addition to any passing Russian who wants to shoot off his mouth—or anybody else's mouth if he is crossed—is the Latvian Diet, which is not only elected for a term of four years but is also very fattening.

Much of what we know about its inner workings has been learned from Josep Kolslaw, the only living legislator who has served in both the Latvian Diet and the Scarsdale Diet. The Latvian Diet, or Congress, is a bi-cameral house, although individual members have the option not to buy a camera if they so choose.

Rather than establishing one speaker, as is the custom in Western legislatures, Latvians set up two speakers, which makes for a nice stereo effect.

Since the Latvians were the originators of the secret ballot, one should perhaps not be surprised that their balloting process continues to be the most secret in the world, inasmuch as the ballots are not only cast sub-rosa, but are, in fact, at once destroyed without being counted at all, an act which some see as a gesture of defiance of the Russian invaders.

As of 1975, there were 1,389,000 head of cattle, 1,195,000 pigs, and 7,684,000 poultry. Such animals, which enjoy scant social stature in the more industrialized Western nations, are granted a significant measure of respect in Latvia, with the result that in the 1983 Latvian Congress three seats were held by cows and at least two committee chairmen were known pigs. Although there are more chickens than either cattle or humans in Latvia, they nevertheless enjoy few privileges, being perhaps content with the fact that the major crops of Latvian farms are chicken-feed, which costs peanuts, as we say, and peanuts, which cost chicken-feed.

Weather. Skies are cloudy and gray, but they're only gray for a day, so wrap your troubles in dreams and dream your troubles away. Humidity is high and so, usually, are the villagers. Precipitation is incessant, although there is, fortunately, little rain. The frost-free season lasts from 125 to 12 days, during which time inhabitants of the area can have all the frost they want, absolutely free.

Summers are cool, though rarely hip. The mean air temperature is 63 degrees but is known to become even meaner when irritated.

Forests, which account chiefly for trees, are dense and dark and are often the scenes of gay musical festivals during which the natives raise their voices in singing, "Densing in the Dark," an old Latvian lay concerning which it would be folly to comment.

As for vegetation, it is valued chiefly in the form of roughage. Contrary to its rural, backward image, Latvia is a thriving industrial republic, the chief products of which are sawdust, pig iron, lint, birdseed, garter belts, portable washing machines, rolling stock, laughing stock, dowsing rods, and jokes. A good Latvian joke is said to amuse even blasé Poles.

Flora and Fauna. These are the names of the two daughters of the founder of Latvia, Lech Latsfogel, who emigrated to the area in the fourth century from parts unknown.

Arts. The dramatic arts have always held a particular fascination for Latvians. Some linguists maintain that the common theatrical salutation, "Good evening, ladies and gentlemen," is a bastardization of the old Lett, "Gooden even, Latvians and Germans."

The national hero of Latvia is the sixteenth-century figure, Dimitri Tatashore, a carnival weight-lifter who, upon learning that an ant can lift 157 times its own weight, injected himself with a quart of ant-fluid and the next day actually bench-pressed 1,795 pounds. Tatashore, sad to say, was stepped on at a picnic the following day and killed. A life-size statue of him still stands in the center of Drek, a provincial capital.

The towering literary figure of Latvia's cultural history is Anton Macrame, whose epic poems include *Tutzi,* the story of a female impersonator; *This Lamb Is Mine,* the tragic story of a showdown in a meat market; and *Some Day My Prints Will Come,* a remarkable prophecy of the development of home photography. Among the Latvian lower classes Macrame is beloved as the author of the simple story of villagers taken in by an itinerant jeweler, called *How Green Was My Wedding Ring.*

The song festivals that have been held in Latvia since 1873 are still popular, so much so, in fact, that every five years the local districts and towns hold their own festivals and send their best choirs, orchestras, and dance companies to the national festival in Riga, on the condition that all participants promise never to return home.

Noted Latvian composers include Janos Prohoska, Euripides Pantz, and bandleader Tomas Doornob, known as "the Sentimental Gentleman of Schlong." We should not be surprised by the existence of Latvian composers of note since, for one thing, all composers use notes, but more importantly because of the Latts' long historic tradition of welcoming itinerant musical groups, the first of which was Richard the Lionhearted and the Crusaders.

Among the popular modern Latvian folk dances are the Hucklebuck, the Boomps-a-Daisy, the Curly Shuffle, and the Gaza Strip. Some scholars believe that the Latvians are also the original creators of break dancing, which is said to have originated in a Latvian leper colony.

Latvia is noted among world travelers for its Baltic Sea beaches, for it was here, in 098, that the Latts first invented sand, which they created by melting down broken glass.

Passengers aboard steamships of the Latvian Lines often enjoy the celebration of its Latvian Night, because, when the carefree peoples of Latvia celebrate, anything can happen, though it rarely does. But precisely at 9:00 P.M., those who had dined at the first sitting are treated to a lively and colorful display of folk dances performed, albeit with some reluctance, by the ship's staff and crew.

Members of the troupe don—and at other times doff—their intricate, handmade costumes, called *strangeklothes,* and engage in a bewildering variety of dances of different ages and origins, which is perhaps only fitting, considering the different ages and origins of the singers and dancers themselves. The oldest of the dances is called the Best Dance, while the best of the dances is called the Old Dance.

Following both, or either, passengers are regaled by the Song Dance, which originated in 1206. It was, in fact, vigorously practiced in 1206 for several years, after which the dancers and other drunken revelers moved across the hall to 1207, where they continued their celebrations until arrested and strip-searched by a contingent of Russian dragoons, which explains the origin of the term *drag strip*. The Song Dance officially reached Latvia in 1412, coming from France via Austria and Poland, along with a variety of venereal infections.

In Southern Latvia, musicians join the dancers in the Song Dance, whereas in the north the musicians stand idly by and sulk until the dancers tire, and retire. The main melody line of the songs is carried by long, wooden, birch-bark horns, which are called Long Wooden Birch-Bark Horns. The term is sometimes abbreviated, however, as Long Horn, which will not come as a surprise to those familiar with the many early Latvian settlements in the Texas Panhandle (see Latvian *Pannhondel*).

Every Song Dance or Dance Song, whichever comes first, starts with a man and a woman facing each other, each attired in the other's garments.

Cultural preservation remains of vital importance in Latvia and is still vigorously promoted by various Riga-based talent agencies. The very young and very old frequently come together in folk dance clubs throughout the country dressed in *latgarben, gedentebrust,* and *shashlik,* and stare sullenly at each other across a crowded room. One minute before midnight the two groups approach each other, however warily, and stamp their feet vigorously to the musical accompaniment of assorted fiddler crabs, glass-blowers, escargot stompers, mandolin strummers, chicken pluck-ers, and cotton pickers.

The costumes worn by the evening's performers are products of tradition, heritage, and Macy's. Colorful flowers embroidered in richly hued patterns are standard in Latvian costumes. Birds and abstract designs are $3.00 extra. The methods of weaving and em-broidering derive from the Renaissance, a small cocktail lounge on the outskirts of Paramus, New Jersey.

At one time, Lat women had two separate costumes—one for everyday wear and one for more festive, public occasions. At pres-ent the everyday costume is virtually extinct, while most Latvians no longer own the special dress. For at least two centuries this led to a great deal of nakedness, which in turn led to lewdness, culmi-nating in the modern-age reputation of Latvian airline stew-ardesses. In less-populated mountain areas, however, women still wear the special dress at weddings, the christening of children, and the signing of record contracts.

Because of the natural topographical barriers, which in turn led to a lack of communication among various districts, there is a great variety of Latvian costumes. This accounts for the hysterical laughter with which individuals from various parts of the country sometimes greet each other.

A variety of tasty Latvian delicacies and appetizers particularly charm tourists, who often have special interest in the open-faced sandwiches, the close-faced salads, the two-faced soup, and the about-faced desserts.

Contrary to what is commonly assumed, the open-faced sand-wich is not so called because one piece of bread is missing but be-cause you have to open your face to eat it. But there is some disagreement about this along Latvian-Hungarian lines, separated, as the two groups are, by a hyphen.

Since World War II, most Latvians wear standard Western attire, a custom that helps support a thriving cloak-and-suit industry. The industry in turn is noted for being the only one of its kind on earth that actually still makes cloaks.

Health and Welfare. Latvia has developed a novel approach as regards the question of health and welfare. Upon reaching the age of twenty-one all Latvian citizens are permitted to choose either one or the other.

Teaching in the country schools is in Latvian or Russian. In Latvian language schools, the study of Russian is compulsory. In fact, in all the republics of the Soviet Union everything is compulsory.

Latvia's modern hopes for freedom from the Russian yoke are premised on the Sino-Soviet confrontation of recent years. Consequently, Latvian scholars miss no opportunity to visit the Soviet Union, though few of them have been to Sino.

From the Gooniest Book of World Records

Although I've had, to date, fifty-four books published, there are also a few manuscripts that have been started but not yet completed, including a satire on the Guinness Book of Records. I might have been accused of biting the hand that feeds me had I persisted with that particular manuscript, since the Guinness people have been kind enough to refer to me in their Most Prolific Composer category.

In any event, the following are entries from the original satirical manuscript:

Adhesives. The most powerful adhesive known is Rox-Epoxy resin, which—after being supercooled to -450°—can withstand a pull of 8,000 pounds per square inch. Roxy-Epoxy resin was invented by Professor J. P. Klum, who reached for a handful of it on his laboratory table in January of 1947, and has been standing there ever since.

Airplanes, paper. An 11-year-old boy, Greg Residue of San Clemente, California, is reported to have flown a paper plane 17,000 yards on May 7, 1972. Authorities strongly question, however, whether the plane actually took off on schedule.

Births, multiple. Regarding multiple births, the editors report with regret that exaggeration is the rule rather than the exception. Since 1906 two cases of nonuplets, seven cases of octuplets, fourteen cases of septuplets, three cases of Scotch, and five cases of Dr. Pepper have been reported.

Mrs. Pitney Bowes (whose husband is a member of the famous rock group The Stampers) gave birth to seven boys in Capetown, South Dakota, on June 4, 1971. Although two of them were stillborn, the others made a great deal of noise indeed. The two still ones are, fortunately for all concerned, today as noisy as the rest.

Archbishop Eustachios Eustachian of Crete once alluded to a woman in the New Hebrides who produced nine surviving nonuplets. The woman, understandably enough, took bitter exception to the allusion.

The world famous Siamese twins Yin and Yang (who incidentally were world famous everywhere but in Siam, where, for understandable reasons, they preferred to lay low) married sisters at age 32 and fathered ten and twelve children respectively, if not respectably.

Since their mates were Siamese twins, too, it was naturally quite difficult to engage in any reproductive behavior whatever without offending not only the Judeo-Christian moral code, but also the Puritan, the Victorian, the Muslim, and the Santa Fe. Each time, in fact, it was even suspected by neighbors that either Yin or Yang or Lisa or Louza were "at it again," as the local sheriff used to put it, complaints were lodged and the twins' living quarters were raided.

After a number of formal charges had been brought over a period of several years, it was eventually determined that Yang was the troublemaker. He was thereupon arrested for encouraging orgiastic behavior, but never served a day in jail since Yin was deemed totally innocent and the Bill of Rights prevented his incarceration.

Bones. Hard things that keep people and animals from just lying in a heap of skin and stuff.

The stapes, or stirrup bone, one of the three auditory ossicles in the middle ear, or vesicle, is the smallest human bone, the precise measurements of which are so minute as to be of no interest whatever.

The stapes of the apes is even smaller than that of humans. The stapes of apes are, of course, connected to their irrup bone, which is in turn connected to the head bone. The head bone connected to the neck bone, the neck bone connected to the shoulder bone, the shoulder bone connected to the chest bone, the chest bone connected to the hip bone, Ezekial saw de Lawd.

The thigh bone, or *femur* (see South American femur, merely because it is much more interesting than this entry), is the longest of the 206 bones in the average human body. Because of its great size and strength it is, understandably enough, the bone most likely to be found thousands of years after one has died, or long after it has ceased to be useful in the slightest to the owner.

The longest recorded bone—made famous just last year at the Fifty-Seventh Annual Bone Recorders Conference in Brussels—was the femur of the German giant Lout Von Schmuck, who died on his forty-third birthday in Mons Veneris, Belgium, in 1902, at the age of 37. Actually there was no good reason for Von Schmuck to die at that time, had his family physician not been hard of hearing. The doctor thought he said, "I've got a terrible fever," whereas what he was actually attempting to communicate was, "I've got a terrible *femur.*" The doctor, on the basis of his faulty diagnosis, dosed Von Schmuck with the wrong medicines, causing his death.

Garbage Rock

I have never publicly argued that all participants in the field of rock music should be subjected to legal discipline. I do insist that, with extremely rare exceptions, the average rock song is simply inferior to the kind of Golden Age music provided by George Gershwin, Duke Ellington, Hoagy Carmichael, Richard Rodgers, Cole Porter, and the other giants of the earlier age. If the reader does not take my word for this then I recommend that he consult the brightest young students at any local music school. There you will find a good supply of eighteen-, nineteen-, and twenty-year olds who are perfectly aware that today's songwriters—particularly of the rock genre—are simply not as talented as Irving Berlin, Harold Arlen, Vernon Duke, and the other early masters.

But I have charitable feelings toward the modestly talented people who are turning out today's fare. I wish I could say the same for the critics who praise their work, particularly when the vocalists and groups involved are deliberately attempting to disgust, antagonize, or otherwise provoke their audiences. The following essay is a satire on some rock criticism I have read. It is not, though the reader may find it hard to believe, much exaggerated.

This critic has the distinction of having been the first to detect the garbage rock movement. It is easy enough to assert, after the fact, that anyone might have realized the inevitability of the trend, given the success of punk rock. The fact remains that others did not. The shifting of the ground under all our feet was, in any event, over very quickly. Within less than a month the entire field of serious rock criticism had come to take garbage rock seriously, in large part because of my discovery that there are important clues to garbage rock music in the actual garbage produced by its more creative practitioners.

The historic breakthrough came when this writer, upon leaving the Bel-Air pad of Stanley Sickening, happened casually to glance at the contents of the four garbage cans (not to be confused with the group of the same name) that stood in the driveway awaiting pickup. A broken pair of "sunglasses" (the quotation marks because he steadfastly refused to wear them except at night or while performing), lying atop (athwart?) the rind of half a grapefruit, first caught my eye.

It was only the certainty, having just left the premises, that Stanley himself was passed out cold, along with his business manager and tax attorney, on the kitchen floor, that gave me the courage to lift one of the cans into the back of my underslung '74 Chevy pickup. One could hardly, after all, pore through the gold mine of decaying artifacts in broad daylight.

Once home, I lugged the container, somewhat weightier than I had first thought, into my kitchen, got out a yellow legal pad and

Gucci writing instrument, and set about the task of classification and analysis. One of the first clues fell easily enough from the tree, perhaps because I had been the first to note the superiority of Sickening's "Stab Me with Your Love" to the tiresome MOR harmonics of Jerome Kern's "All the Things You Are."

Can it really surprise the reader that I next noted a toy rubber dagger, encrusted with—gravy? chopped liver? Not the sort of thing, certainly, one ordinarily sees in a garbage can and yet very reasonably discarded. It was, after all, broken. Perhaps Stanley, tired of terrorizing stagehands and groupies with real knives (never mind the Cleveland incident and the three deaths), had resorted to the blatantly show-biz fakery of a rubber approximation of the sadistic hardware which, even more than his inventive three-chord harmonies, initially brought him to public attention.

And what were the assorted broken eggshells? Clear but excruciatingly obvious representations of Sickening's own psychosexual emphasis on germination, birth, rebirth—the salacious appeal of apocalyptic destruction.

The three Campbell's tomato soup cans seemed almost to cry out loud, "Andy Warhol, Andy Warhol!" as I set them to one side of the kitchen table. The connection between Sickening and Warhol was evident enough. They both wore size ten-and-a-half shoes, were totally unknown in that insignificant area of the country between Pennsylvania and Wyoming, and—the clincher—had, during their teenage years, never learned the bridge to "Heart and Soul," but merely the first sixteen bars.

Perhaps only William Blake could have known the spiritual ecstasy with which, fingers trembling, I lifted three compartmentalized aluminum frozen TV dinner containers from the odiferous mélange. Here it was again, the constant, even dominant, Stanley Sickening motif—the emphasis on the quick, the least troublesome, the slick, the prepackaged. And leave it to Sickening, with his incredible cat's sixth sense of where it's at, not to have scraped the last now-dried dollops of gelatinous pink gravy from the tins, as if to say, "Up yours, world! I'll take some of what you're dishing out, but I won't take all of it!"

Is it any wonder that many groupie Lolitas have publicly pleaded with Sickening and the other garbage rockers *not* to have sex with them—not even to do what he so gloriously celebrated in his early classic, "I'm Gonna Cop a Feel," but rather to punch them repeatedly about the abdomen?

Letters to the Editor

The following essay, though titled "Letters to the Editor," is not *the routine I've had so much fun with on television over the years. That involved my reading actual letters—usually from the New York* Daily News—*but doing so in the emotional tone appropriate to the writer's message. Something about the contrast between the seriousness of the issue and the hysterical tone of the wording and the performance always induced laughter.*

Have you ever had the experience of getting in an elevator on, say, the nineteenth floor and finding yourself in the middle of some conversation that, because of its truncated nature, sounded almost meaningless?

". . . and as soon as he did that, they sent in the green one."

"No kidding? I would have thought Charlie would have put the grilled cheese in the cockpit by himself."

"No chance. As soon as you get up beyond the $50,000 range, you've got as much chance of getting all that cinnamon to Singapore as I have of making it with Dolly Parton."

"Well, no matter what you say, I still think that if Irene had married the midget in the first place, it wouldn't have turned out so bad."

Almost all conversations on elevators sound like that to me. I have a somewhat similar reaction to the experience of opening one intellectual journal or another and reading exchanges of letters referring to stories published in earlier issues. No doubt subscribers who read the original material later being commented on would have no such difficulty, but since no one can keep up with all the worthwhile periodicals, I often encounter bitter exchanges of correspondence that sound rather like the following:

In his July story on the dwindling influence of the Catholic church on international conglomerates, Morton Feinman referred to Gabby Hayes, the well-known cowboy sidekick, as having given Dr. Mengele the original inspiration for the medical experiments that have quite rightly forever blackened the name, of not only Dachau, but also Cleveland.

While I agree with the initial thrust of Feinman's thesis, I must take exception to his reference to me as Annette Funicello's hairdresser. Feinman would appear to be unaware that novelist Theodore Dreiser and Paul Dresser, the songwriter, were brothers. Dreiser, because of his ambivalence on the subject of his German-ness, took great pains never to be addressed as Herr Dresser. Perhaps it is the confusion of this term with *hairdresser* that led Feinman into the morass of CIA and fundamentalist Christian clichés, which marred an otherwise insightful analysis.

Oh, and one more thing: Comedian Don Rickles most assuredly did not coin the term *hockey puck.* Shakespeare, in his third draft of *A Midsummer Night's Waste of Time* says, "Harken, Puck, to that most limpid wrist of eventide . . ." It is not difficult to see that the Elizabethan *harken, Puck* led to the nineteenth-century *hockey puck,* which became common in southern Canada after the defeat of the English in the French-Canadian War. I must confess my indebtedness, in this connection, to Wolfgang Wolfe, great-grandson of General Thomas Wolfe, victor at the Battle of Quebec. When the English monarch was told that Wolfe was mad, he remarked, "I wish he would bite my other generals."

Feinman would seem to have been aware that Wolfe did engage in general-biting but, unfortunately, erroneously attributes this to Wolfe's sexual proclivities, about which the less said the better.

Salmon P. Chazenheimer
Vice President
Bechtel Power Corporation
San Francisco, Indiana

Morton Feinman hits the nail on the head in his insightful piece "How to Hit a Nail on the Head." There being no perfection in human experience, however, I must point out two minor errors in Dr. Feinman's otherwise well-developed argument. First of all, he depended, for some of his documentation, on the Sauerkraut section of *Frankfurter Allgemeine,* the notorious journal of the lower-German meat-packing industry.

This leads, no doubt inevitably, to Feinman's pathetic misinterpretation of the phenomenon of strange attractors, whereas it has by now been well established that in refusing to address the apparent existence of order in chaos, the hypothesis that calls into question not only Newtonian but also Einsteinian physics, Feinman never for a moment considered the implications of the resurgence of the Chicago Cubs in the late summer of 1984, a possibility which would have seemed preposterous even to Alvin Toffler.

Sincerely,

Zymole Trochee

South Bend, Mississippi

Feinman replies:

With all due respect to the conscious intentions of Messrs. Chazenheimer and Trochee, I suggest that interested readers re-study my original article in the light of a pharmacology suggested by Revelations 6:19 before making up their minds as to whether my interpretation of Ronald Reagan's pathetic dependence on Grecian Formula, cue cards, and Tele-PrompTers is more reliable than that of my critics.

I am certainly not remiss in asserting that readers have the right to know that Chazenheimer's argument stems more from his status as a leader of the neo-synephrine movement than out of any inherent weakness in my own formulations.

One does not have to turn to Liebnitz—though there's nothing terribly wrong with that—to perceive that Mortimer Adler, to whom Chazenheimer often slavishly appeals, is on the shakiest possible philosophical ground when he argues that if the driver of the Chrysler is not in the car but leaves his key in the ignition so that the voice-reminder computer tapes are activated, there is actually no sound within the car's interior because there are no human ears to perform the act of perception. Does Feinman actually think that in resorting to the tiresome if-a-tree-falls-in-the-forest argument (see *Weyerhauser* v. *the State of Oregon*) he is really saying something new and insightful about punk rock? If so, I refer him to the comparative statistics on Too Tall Jones, Too Short Johnson, Too Weird Wennerholm, and Too Dumb Davis. Nuf—as we say—sed.

But, all seriousness aside, the airy assumption that the zoot suit of 1940s' Los Angeles was named after Zoot Sims is surely something that would make even Nat Hentoff gag, were it not for his recent application to study for the Jesuit priesthood.

Perhaps the recent collapse of the Newt Gingrich chain of charm schools, which Feinman had assumed was unlikely, unnerved the scholar whom I have elsewhere conceded does not wear a hairpiece. Moreover, I have not only withdrawn the original aspersion but have discovered that it came from careless listening to a conversation in which the party of the first part said, "I do have herpes." Whether my digressions are irrelevant, or my irrelevancies are digressive, is, I submit, totally beside the point. Certainly it is sheer McCarthyism to suggest that a mere three or four convictions for child molestation ill-befit a candidate for high office in the John Birch Society. To me, the fact that the gentleman molested only left-wing children speaks volumes.

Lester Feinman
Justice Department
Washington D.C.

Gutsy Jimmy Slattery

The following entry is another satire, this time on a sort of hardboiled sort of sports reporting.

"I'll tell you a really inspiring story," Harry said. "Did you ever hear of a guy named Jimmy Slattery? No? Well, let me tell you about him. He was a prizefighter, a middle weight, and one of the best. Maybe you never heard of him 'cause he never got to the big time. But the reason he didn't is that, at an early point of his career, he suffered a really rotten break. He was one of the best fighters in the South. Whipped everybody in Macon, Birmingham, New Orleans, Jacksonville. There were damned few in that part of the country who could stay in the ring with him for more than five rounds.

"Well, by God, one day he was out at his father's farm helping him run his tractor. The thing hit a ditch, rolled over on Jimmy, and the poor bastard lost his right leg. Now you and I, we'd just cash in our chips after a thing like that, wouldn't we? But not Jimmy, by Christ. No, sir. You may find it hard to believe but within six months that scrappy bastard was back in the gym, hopping around *on his one leg,* sparring, punchin' the bejesus out of the bag, the big bag, doin' pushups, knee-bends—or at least one knee-bend.

"After two years of this, scrappy Jimmy Slattery said to his manager, 'Listen, get me another fight.'

"'Are you crazy?' his manager said.

"'I'm serious,' Slattery said.

"'You poor, dumb sonofabitch, have you lost your mind? I didn't say anything when you came around the gym here and worked out. I figured it's not a bad idea if you keep in shape. Everybody should keep in shape. But Christ, you couldn't get into the ring with an old lady.'

"Well, sir, Jimmy Slattery just looked him in the eye, 'cause Jimmy had more guts than anybody I ever heard of. He fired his manager on the spot and handled himself for a while. Finally, just to do him a favor, somebody got him a fight at an American Legion Hall down in Birmingham one night. No publicity, no attention.

They just introduced a guy with more guts, more courage than anybody in the history of the world.

"Jimmy's regular weight was about 155. Now, with the leg gone, he weighs about 20 pounds less, so he's in the ring with a lightweight. Nobody good, you understand. Naturally they set him up against a real dummy. Well, sir, the crowd went wild when Jimmy Slattery hopped into the ring and they suddenly realized what was happening. There he stood, the crazy bastard, hopping up and down on his one leg in the corner, rarin' to go!

"And then came the bell for the first round. Jimmy hopped out there to the center of the ring and within two minutes the other guy had kicked the ——— out of him!"

What Is a Clyde?

For reasons that have always eluded me, since childhood I have had the habit of making up words and sprinkling even my most serious conversations with occasional double-talk terms. The following TV monologue, written in the 1950s, is a satire on some serious readings, which were at the time enormously popular. The first was "What Is a Boy?" Its success made inevitable the release of "What Is a Girl?," "What Is a Husband?" and "What Is a Wife?" At that point I honestly lost track.

In creating the following routine I adhered strictly to the formula that all the earlier versions had used. They all had touched upon where boys—or girls, husbands, wives—might be found, then what they would like, or hate.

Perhaps I should explain that comedians never dealt with such material. The readers were always people like Arthur Godfrey, Art Linkletter, or unknown announcers with deep, throaty voices.

To the accompaniment of emotional organ music:

What is a Clyde?

Well, Clydes are found in the strangest places. In your crile, on the phone, from the weirdos of Greenwich Village to the Straits of Magellan, in cesspools, in fingertips, near your bird, and playing on your heartstrings.

A Clyde likes: ferns, shtick, little black things, unmitigated gall, chicken wire, salami, Goo-Goo dolls, birdseed pudding and . . . *other* Clydes.

A Clyde hates: clarinet reeds, fricassee of beaks and claws, turkey wattles, protozoa, anthracite, income taxes, or pain of headache, neuritis, neuralgia.

Nothing else can come home so frail, grove up the dell of a good Bertrand so often, or lose so many file saws.

A Clyde is dignity with a stall in its fame, bronchitis with a frog in its throat, and stupidity with a bone in its mouth.

What is a Clyde made of? Well, it takes the strength of a lion, the wool of a lamb, the back of your hand, the night of the hunter, the Top of the Mark, the last of the Mohicans, and a hair of the dog.

There are several ways to *get* a Clyde. Advertise in the paper, jump in the lake, blues in the night, or punch in the mouth.

Mothers-in-law don't particularly krelm for Clydes, traffic cops grab them, little boys eat them, and Don Rickles has dinner with them.

But, you know, when you get home in the afternoon, after a long tiring day's work, when you're tired and weary and worn and sick and miserable and dirty and crummy and shaking and nervous and frightened and panicky, and drunk and raggedy and rotten and staggering and reeling and rolling in the gutter . . .

Ah, when you come home and sit down in your easy chair and that little Clyde jumps up on the bridge of your nose and sits there and stares at you, why I tell you, friends, it just kind of makes life worthwhile to hear those three little words, "You're under arrest!"

And when the sun goes down, and the tide comes in, there is nothing finer than to breakfast in the diner. And if you can keep your Clyde, when all about you are losing theirs and blaming it on you; if you can ask yourself, "What kind of day has it been?" then you'll know that a boom is only a ding-dong, but a good cigar is a Clyde!

Speaking in Numbers

The following entry was submitted to Paul Krassner, editor of the hard-hitting satirical magazine The Realist. *It embodies a criticism of an aspect of organized religion that—if I may speak honestly—has always seemed to me not only one of the least appealing, but one of the dumber manifestations of religious emotion. I refer to the peculiar practice invariably referred to as "speaking in tongues."*

If we leave uncontested the assertion that there is a God and that He is perfect I do not see what earthly—or, for that matter, heavenly—good the Deity can hope to accomplish by occasionally having some of his admirers babble so incoherently that no one in their presence has ever claimed to understand a word they say.

Knowing the many forms of weakness of which humans are capable and upon which—alas—they almost daily act, we would not be surprised by such a phenomenon. But that is invariably claimed to be inspired by the Almighty Himself—well, need I say more? In any event, the following, another example of satire was written out of my bias on the question.

On March 24, 1989, in a basement meeting room of St. Malachy's parish, on Chicago's northwest side, there occurred the first known manifestation of a spiritual phenomenon that by December seemed likely to sweep at least the American branch of the evangelical and fundamentalist wing of Christendom. According to reports of witnesses there had already been three instances, earlier during the scheduled prayer meeting, of glossolalia or "speaking in tongues."

For those unfamiliar with the practice, it involves what to a disinterested observer would appear to be totally meaningless babbling. Far from being frowned upon by modern Christians, it is considered a rarely valuable experience, the precise cause of which is a personal visitation by the Holy Spirit. On the occasion in question, however, a parishioner named Matthew Donohue, a 47-year-old certified public accountant, suddenly stood and began part mumbling, part shouting a series of numbers.

"My memory of the incident," parishioner Joseph DeMaris recalled, "Was that Donohue started speaking in tongues, at least for the first few seconds, but suddenly converted to numbers." Asked by an investigative journalist if he could act out Donohue's spoken words, DeMaris cooperatively said, "Sure. It sounded like this. Bahaba, lama, ma-ma-ma-do, maga 7.7, 47, 9, 3, 6, 0—oh God— 49, 56, 56!"

"He repeated some numbers, did he?"

"Yes," DeMaris said, "sometimes he would say a number and then repeat it four or five times, but mostly it was just a bunch of numbers that were disconnected."

According to other participants in the ceremony, Donohue appeared to become increasingly excited as he stood, eyes closed, knees slightly bent, swaying back and forth and half speaking, half singing the lengthy sequence of numbers to which he was giving voice. He seemed to emphasize some arithmetical information but the meaning of this, if there was any, eluded those who were present.

Asked if he thought that Donohue's outburst was a legitimate manifestation of inspiration by the Holy Spirit, Father Leo Tierney, pastor of St. Malachy's, said, "We cannot be absolutely certain about such things but I personally believe that Donohue's experience was just as legitimate as that of the others who spoke in tongues that night. To those who don't know anything about glossolalia there may be a problem as regards what seems the total lack of meaning of whatever is spoken out, but people seem to feel so much better after they have this experience that I personally must respect their sincerity and the obvious benefits the experience confers on them."

Whatever the authenticity of Donohue's personal drama, the phenomenon is presently "spreading like wildfire," as one nun, a teacher at St. Malachy's parish school, put it.

"Perhaps," she said, "God is trying to teach us something by enabling us to communicate in what might seem, to others—or to skeptics—a meaningless manner. Perhaps He is saying that many of today's terrible problems—divorce and sexual promiscuity, drugs, alcoholism, terrorism—all of that—came about because of modern man's over-emphasis on reason."

Father Tierney differed on this one point. "It's difficult to say," he conceded, "how you can blame intellectual rationality for political terrorism, sexual license, pornography, drug-taking, and all that, but even so there might be a degree of truth in what the Sister has said. Perhaps there has been too much emphasis on reason and science during the last hundred years or so. The Holy Spirit may not be telling us to return to emotion, which is certainly as God-given as the reasoning faculty. Perhaps He is telling us to become like children, willing to express our feelings by babbling innocently rather than the usually rationally coded messages."

Asked what connection there was between the apparently nonsensical syllables of a typical speaking-in-tongues experience and the new speaking-in-numbers, Father Tierney said, "I personally don't know. But I have now witnessed this sort of thing in over a dozen instances and what impresses me most are the clear-cut emotional and psychological benefits that the people enjoy as they stand up and begin shouting numbers.

"Of course since I'm personally, by nature, a somewhat reticent type, there's part of me that still wants to 'make sense' of these numbers. For that reason I've taken to tape-recording them and having the sequences typed up. I have some of my friends who are experienced in mathematics and the use of computers checking to see if there are any noticeable patterns in the numbers or whether they are indeed, as they seem, totally random.

"It may sound superstitious but one of the women in our parish said she knew a numerologist—a kind of fortune-teller who reads numbers in the way that other people might read tarot cards or tea leaves—I'm hoping I'm not doing anything here that'll get me in trouble with my theological superiors," Tierney smiled, "but—who knows? Perhaps certain members do have the ability to carry coded messages. We're all familiar, for example, with the references, in the new Testament, to the number 666 as somehow representing the antichrist.

"And numbers, of course, have been very important, even long before Christianity, in the history of religion. There are frequent references, particularly in the old scripture, to 40 days of this or that, things that come in tens—like the Commandments—and the number seven is very frequently referred to, so I argue that we should at least keep our minds open about this new manifestation of the Holy Spirit."

Reports that have come in, during recent months, from generally similar events in New York, Denver, New Orleans, Seattle, and other metropolitan areas, are generally consistent with the original instance reported.

An interesting aspect of the mysterious phenomenon has emerged in that speaking in numbers has now spread to the Spanish-speaking Christian community in both Catholic and Protestant groups. The numbers are, of course, being stated in Spanish. Because of the more mellifluous character of the Spanish language a number of students of the phenomenon have pointed out that in that language the numbers sound much more like traditional glossolalia than they do as communicated in English.

Robert S. Cartwright, S.J., theologian and professor of philosophy at Fordham University, observed, in a recent commentary published in *Theological Review,* "At first there seems to have been a generally negative reaction to reports of the Speaking-in-numbers phenomenon, but during the last few months this trend has been sharply reversed on the grounds that while the more traditional glossolalia appears to consist of speaking truly meaningless syllables, the same certainly cannot be said as regards numbers, for such words as seven, twelve, nineteen, etc., obviously have sharply precise meanings.

"It remains to be seen, of course, whether there is any to-the-present hidden meaning in the combination of numbers, themselves. It's theoretically possible—because the Vatican has yet to take a position on the new practice, so far as I'm aware—that the phenomenon will eventually be attributed to nothing more than well-intentioned religious hysteria.

"But we must recall that, for Christians—the debate on glossolalia itself has been long settled. It has, from the earliest days, been generally regarded by perfectly responsible Christian authorities, as an actual, validated manifestation of a visitation by the Holy Spirit. Because of that background, we should therefore sympathetically reserve judgment as regards speaking in numbers."

Limitation of space precludes further exploration of this phenomenon in the present study. I intend, however, to have more to say about it at a future time.

Perspectives on the Presidential Election:
Give This Guy More Air Time

When the Los Angeles Times *asked me to report back from the 2000 Republican National Convention in Philadelphia, I brought along my tape machine so I could record some interviews. The big names were already committed—and some of them should have been—so I chatted with minor players, the kind who ordinarily don't get much airtime. By far the most interesting was an old friend, Senator Phillip Buster, who used to make appearances on my TV comedy shows.*

I introduce into evidence the transcript of our exchange:

STEVE ALLEN: Senator, I understand that you're here as a delegate-at-large.
SENATOR: That's right. How much longer I'll be able to remain at large we'll soon see.
S.A.: What do you think of George W. Bush's "compassionate conservatism"?

SENATOR: I think it's only fitting that we show our conservative friends a little more compassion.

S.A.: But do you agree with them, say, in their opposition to gun control?

SENATOR: Personally, I have three words for you on the subject of guns.

S.A. And what are those words?

SENATOR: Stick 'em up!

S.A.: But how do you feel about world trade?

SENATOR: It's absurd. Poems are made by fools like me, but only God can trade a world.

S.A.: How do you feel about separation of church and state?

SENATOR: A dirty communist idea, if I ever heard one.

S.A.: But Senator, it's in our Constitution. It was proposed by the Founding Fathers.

SENATOR: What I'd like to know—and I say this as a firm supporter of women's lib—how come we never hear about the founding mothers?

S.A.: Senator, even though the American economy is stronger than it has ever been, the happy results have certainly not "trickled down" to millions of people. Do you therefore think that we should continue the War on Poverty?

SENATOR: Yes, I do. If fact the War on Poverty is going very well. Last week alone, we shot more than 200 poor people.

S.A.: Senator Buster, at one time we thought the problem of alcoholism was solved, but now it appears to be worse than ever. Do you have any idea how many drunks there are in our country?

SENATOR: The statistics are staggering.

S.A.: You know, I've heard talk on the convention floor that the Democrats may have distorted the statistics about low unemployment. Some say that unemployment is still a problem. Do you agree?

SENATOR: Absolutely not. I say that all this damnable talk about unemployment is nothing but a rumor.

S.A.: But who starts these rumors?

SENATOR: Oh, people who are out of work, I suppose.

S.A.: Frankly, I don't really envy you politicians. Yours is such a precarious profession.

SENATOR: I was just making that very point to my waiter at dinner this evening—Newt Gingrich.

S.A.: Third-party candidates are complaining about being squeezed out of the election process. Do you think that Pat Buchanan really has a chance of being elected president?

SENATOR: I'll say this for the man—if he ever gets elected to the White House, it would sure cure your hiccups.

S.A.: Senator, how is the War on Drugs going?

SENATOR: Frankly it's a colossal failure.

S.A.: Why do you say that?

SENATOR: Well, look at the names of some of the people on TV these days—Cokie Roberts, Stone Phillips . . .

S.A.: Despite the booming economy, there seems to be a surprising amount of labor unrest. How do you account for all the strikes?

SENATOR: Well, there are issues other than the truly financial. In Chicago the day before yesterday, I saw a group of workers striking for shorter hours. And I must say I agree with them.

S.A.: You do?

SENATOR: Yes, I always did think that 60 minutes was too long for an hour.

S.A.: Some workers and picketers are becoming physically aggressive. What do you think of striking workers?

SENATOR: I say if the shoe fits, wear it. I personally struck three workers as I was coming out of my hotel this morning.

S.A.: And what do you think of Dick Cheney?

SENATOR: We old-timers fondly remember his work in horror movies.

S.A.: No, no, I wasn't talking about Lon Chaney, I meant Dick. Well, Senator, I really want to thank you for coming down here to talk to us tonight.

SENATOR: Oh, it was nothing.

S.A.: That's true, but thank you anyway.

About the Author

Steve Allen was the creator and original host of *The Tonight Show*, and has been inducted into the Television Academy's Hall of Fame. In 1993, he succeeded Milton Berle as Abbot of the world-famous Friar's Club. Mr. Allen is married to actress-comedian Jayne Meadows and lives in Encino, California.

To learn more about Steve Allen or to contact him directly, visit his Web site at steveallen.com